Praise for *Blindfolds Off* and Joel Cohen

"*Blindfolds Off* takes a revealing and fascinating look at what judges bring to their cases and how they decide them. In no-holds-barred interviews—cross-examinations might be a better term—of federal judges about significant and highly controversial cases that came before them, the role of the judiciary is explored in an engaging and arresting manner."

Floyd Abrams
Cahill Gordon & Reindel LLP

* * *

"Joel Cohen's brilliant book *Blindfolds Off: Judges on How They Decide* is an essential guide to one of the best kept secrets of our legal system: namely that it is we the public, rather than the judges, who are wearing the blindfolds. Judges make their decisions in secret, and the processes they use to decide are also secret. This book, which exposes these secrets, is an essential tool of democracy, visibility and accountability."

Alan Dershowitz
Author of *Taking the Stand: My Life in the Law*

* * *

"Joel Cohen's in-depth conversations with 13 federal judges who sat in leading, often headline, cases illuminate for readers, and perhaps even for the judges themselves, the logical and intuitive paths that judges take in reaching their decisions. In its methodology and lessons, the book is unique."

Stephen Gillers
Elihu Root Professor of Law
New York University School of Law

* * *

"As a former district judge, reading Joel Cohen's insightful *Blindfolds Off* was eye opening. Cohen interviewed 13 of my former colleagues, each of whom spoke with unanticipated candor in the face of sometimes forceful questioning. Their responses led to considerable introspection about the subtle, and not-so-subtle, influences on how I, myself, decided cases."

Judge Richard J. Holwell (Ret., S.D.N.Y.)
Holwell, Shuster & Goldberg LLP

* * *

"For every lawyer, law student, and even judge who wonders what judges really think when deciding a case, this book will be a revelation. Cohen is a skillful and dogged interlocutor and his judges are surprisingly candid and realistic. *Blindfolds Off* gives you the opportunity to listen in on judicial thinking in one high-profile case after another."

Dahlia Lithwick
Senior Editor, *Slate*

* * *

"*Blindfolds Off* is a surprising, fascinating, and unusually candid examination of what judges think—told in their own words."

Jeffrey Toobin
The New Yorker

BLINDFOLDS OFF

OFF
JUDGES ON HOW THEY DECIDE

JOEL COHEN

BLINDFOLDS OFF

JUDGES ON HOW
THEY DECIDE

FOREWORD BY **HON. RICHARD POSNER**
7TH CIRCUIT COURT OF APPEALS

Printed in the United States of America.

ISBN: 978-1-62722-679-0

18 17 16 15 14   5 4 3 2

Library of Congress Cataloging-in-Publication data on file.

Discounts are available for books ordered in bulk. Special consideration is given to state bars, CLE programs, and other bar-related organizations. Inquire at Book Publishing, ABA Publishing, American Bar Association, 321 N. Clark Street, Chicago, Illinois 60654-7598.

www.ShopABA.org

Contents

About the Author

Joel Cohen is a highly respected white collar criminal defense lawyer in New York. He has practiced in that field as well as complex civil litigation at Stroock & Stroock & Lavan LLP for nearly thirty years, after having worked for ten years as a prosecutor with the New York State Special Prosecutor's Office and then with the U.S. Justice Department's Organized Crime & Racketeering Section in the Eastern District of New York. Joel writes regularly for the *New York Law Journal*, Law.com, and the *Huffington Post* on criminal law, legal ethics, and social policy. He frequently lectures lawyers, judges, and the public on varied issues, including ethics and religion. He teaches Professional Responsibility at Fordham Law School and has cocreated a new seminar based on this book to be given at Fordham Law. *Blindfolds Off* is Joel's first book of nonfiction—he has published several works of Biblical fiction, including *Moses: A Memoir, David and Bathsheba: Through Nathan's Eyes*, and *Moses and Jesus: A Conversation*. Finally, he has also authored *Truth Be Veiled, a Justin Steele Murder Case*, a novel that addresses the criminal lawyer's dilemma in dealing with truth.

Foreword

Judge Richard A. Posner[1]

Remarkably little is known to the general public, or even to the practicing legal profession, about judges—the way they decide cases, the system they use to allocate work between staff (mainly law clerks) and themselves, their work ethic, their psychology, the extralegal influences that play on them. Much less is known about them than about other government officials, both executive and legislative, and other professionals, such as the lawyers who litigate court cases and the members of the various branches of the medical and military professions.

One reason is that, whereas these other professions I've mentioned are also very old, the legal profession, including the judiciary, hasn't changed a great deal, at least from the outside, compared to the other professions. The continuity between Roman law and legal institutions of the third century A.D. and modern law in most of the world, including the United States, is striking. And over this long period of gradual change, judges have developed a strategy of maximizing their autonomy, job security, and power. The strategy has several struts: secretiveness, impartiality (what Aristotle called "corrective justice," often misunderstood by modern jurisprudes), a pretense of passivity ("the law made me do it"), mystification (jargon), and political sensitivity.

1. Judge Richard A. Posner has sat on the Court of Appeals for the Seventh Circuit in Chicago since 1981, serving as its Chief Judge from 1993 to 2000. A prolific writer, he has authored some forty books and innumerable articles on judging and the law. He is the recipient of numerous awards, including the Learned Hand Medal for Excellence in Federal Jurisprudence. His latest book, *Reflections on Judging*, was published in 2013.

These are survival strategies and shouldn't be disparaged unduly because courts are valuable institutions of governance, and to maintain their power they need the strategies I've listed, though they tend to overuse them.

The ones I want to stress are secretiveness and passivity. Judges are far more reluctant to reveal the inner workings of their institution than other government officials and far more prone to deny the discretionary authority that they wield. Blackstone described English judges as the "oracles of the law," meaning that the law spoke through the judges the way Apollo spoke through the oracle at Delphi, and judges continue to represent themselves—though not by invoking the oracle at Delphi, no longer a familiar figure to Americans—to be transmitters rather than originators.

By being secretive and appearing passive, judges get away with exercising a good deal of power—benign power for the most part, but still power—which is to say discretion to confer real benefits and impose real costs, whereas the judge who mechanically applies the law—who is the law's ventriloquist's dummy—is transmitting rather than exerting power. (Actually that judge will often be fooling himself because often the law is not clear enough to be applied mechanically to the case before him.) Judges find facts, take many cases away from juries and decide the cases themselves, have largely created constitutional law by treating the Constitution's vague phrases as authorization rather than direction, and have done the same with many statutes. But they hide behind a veil of modesty. And they get away with it in part because their staffs, mainly law clerks, are almost as secretive as the judges. Because law is adversarial, secretiveness comes naturally, to judges and their staffs and to lawyers engaged in litigation or negotiation, both being forms of struggle.

How is the veil of secrecy to be penetrated? One tactic is the confessional. Judges will on occasion acknowledge the personal element in judging. The author of this book quotes a famous confessional passage by Cardozo. Earlier, Holmes had made a similar, though somewhat more guarded, confession (well, it wasn't *really* a confession because he was not yet a judge, though when his statement was published he was only months away from becoming one) when he said on the first page of his classic work *The Common Law* (1881): "The life of the law has not been logic: it has been experience. The felt necessities of the time, the prevalent moral and political theories, intuitions of public policy, avowed or unconscious, even the prejudices which judges share with their fellow-men, have had a good deal more to do than the syllogism in determining the rules by which men should be governed."

Academic lawyers, notably in the eras of legal realism and critical legal studies, sought without success to strip the veil. Those movements faded, to be replaced by social scientific studies, in political science and later in economics and psychology as well, that sought, for example, by examining judicial behavior, often in statistical terms—correlating for example the political slant of federal judicial decisions with the party of the appointing president—to uncover the real springs of decision, masked by the rhetoric of judicial decision making and often outside the conscious awareness of the judge. This book uses a different technique, that of the interview. Mr. Cohen is a skillful and tenacious, though invariably courteous, interviewer. He has picked as the interviewees federal district judges who have presided in famous, publicity-attracting cases, cases most likely to challenge a judge's fidelity to a passive, formalistic—which is to say traditional—mode of judicial decision making, and he has focused the interviews on those cases.

We learn a good deal about these judges. And one thing we learn is that judges, even when in the hands as it were of a skillful and persistent and unawed interviewer, are very reluctant to acknowledge a personal element in judging even in the most atypical and challenging case. There have been plenty of cases involving the prosecution of con men; but Bernard Madoff was not a run-of-the-mine con man. There have been in the last half century more constitutional cases concerning sex than one can count; but the case in which one of Mr. Cohen's interviewees, Vaughan Walker (incidentally a former student of mine), ruled on the constitutionality of forbidding homosexual marriage was more novel and fraught than any since *Roe v. Wade*. And so with the other cases discussed in the book.

So the judges are guarded, and that is one limitation of the interview method of piercing the veil. But another is the problem of self-knowledge. There is no inconsistency in saying that Judge X is utterly sincere in disclaiming any personal element in his decisions yet some of his decisions cannot be explained in formalistic, but only in personal, terms. There is no inconsistency because few if any people have total self-awareness. Indeed, people are great self-deceivers. Judges' response to the occasional case in which the conventional guides to decision making don't yield a result is likely to be influenced or even determined by priors (prior beliefs, which is to say beliefs they bring to the case rather than derive from evidence or the other orthodox materials of judicial decision making pressed upon them in the litigation) of which they may be unaware and by basic psychological dispositions, such as attitudes toward authority. And these priors and dispositions may not emerge in an interview because they reside for the most part at the unconscious level of thought.

The reader will learn a great deal about trial judges from this book, but the aura of mystery will remain.

R.A.P.

Acknowledgments

This project, while conceived by me, could not have been accomplished without the gracious participation of the 13 current and former judges, nine of whom I hadn't previously known. The stature in the federal judiciary of both Judge Jed. S. Rakoff and Judge Jack B. Weinstein, combined with their willingness to sit for interviews, enabled me to encourage—perhaps even cajole—many of the others to also be interviewed. Indeed, despite the general perception that federal judges sit in an ivory tower circumscribed by an almost institutionalized aloofness, in truth, only one judge (and for good reason) respectfully declined to be interviewed given the particular case (and parties) about which I had wished to interview her. Their willingness to participate in unscripted interviews by a total stranger not only is a testament to these judges individually but also perhaps represents a new day for that branch of government that traditionally has been seen as shrouded in secrecy. I thank and commend each member of this austere group for stepping forward.

Aside of course from Timothy Brandhorst, Director of New Product Development at ABA Publishing, who has ably shepherded this volume through publication, I must thank five individuals for their critical efforts to make this a reality: Dale J. Degenshein for her tireless efforts to keep this project literate, hopefully imaginative, readable, and on the straight and narrow; my friend, colleague, and teaching partner James L. Bernard for telling me way too often what I needed to be told; my friend Ivan S. Fisher for his (ever) critical insights and insightfulness; my friend of friends Elaine "Ellie" Kelman Grosinger for her warm-hearted encouragement and constancy during the roller coaster that inheres in venturing the previously untried; and my assistant Daniel Burke for enthusiastically converting recorded conversations into meaningful dialogue.

Finally, I thank the leadership of Stroock—the fine national law firm where I have been privileged to work for nearly 30 years—for recognizing the importance of giving back to the legal community (and society in general) by allowing me to use the resources and skillsets we have amassed.

Preface

Almost 100 years ago, our great jurist Benjamin N. Cardozo declared the seemingly unthinkable—that jurists are people, limited, affected, and influenced just as others may be. As he wrote:

> There has been a certain lack of candor in much of the discussion of the theme, or rather perhaps in the refusal to discuss it, as if judges must lose respect and confidence by the reminder that they are subject to human limitations. I do not doubt the grandeur of the conception which lifts them into the realm of pure reason, above and beyond the sweep of perturbing and deflecting forces. None the less, if there is anything of reality in my analysis of the judicial process, they do not stand aloof on these chill and distant heights; and we shall not help the cause of truth by acting and speaking as if they do. *The great tides and currents which engulf the rest of men, do not turn aside in their course, and pass judges by.*[1]

Without saying it in so many words, Cardozo wondered what makes one judge different from another, what informs the thinking of one judge but not his colleague. Do judges concede, or even recognize, these influences? And, when they do, if they do, how does a judge rise above them? Are they compelled—ethically, if not legally—to disclose them? These are the overriding questions explored in this book through the prism of controversial, and difficult, decisions 13 jurists have made.

Cardozo understood and articulated better than anyone that judges are human beings, not gods, and that however lofty their pronouncements,

---

1. BENJAMIN N. CARDOZO, THE NATURE OF THE JUDICIAL PROCESS, at pp. 107–108 (emphasis added). An extended quote appears in the section of this book entitled "Excerpt from *The Nature of the Judicial Process*," at page 295.

however hard they strive for the objective and impersonal, they will invariably fail in that endeavor. The judges who make the hard decisions are men and women with personal worries and concerns, achievements and failures. And lawyers and litigants should embrace their humanity—we probably wouldn't want to appear before an Ivy League magna who only knows about life through what she reads in a law book. Indeed, a judge's human frailty in not being totally objective is often his strength. The passion he or she brings to a decision is frequently what distinguishes the great judge from the mundane.

Fundamentally, wasn't Cardozo really asking what makes a judge? Would rulings be disparate because one worked his way through school, while another was born with a silver spoon in his mouth? Can a judge, born in a communist country, ever really put aside his Orwellian nightmare (or was it a reality?) that Big Brother is upon us, or will he forever be distrustful of government? And if so, is that so bad?

But far more than just the upbringing of a person goes into the mix. Who was the man or woman before he or she became a judge? Was he an academic? A war veteran? Did his prior life (or current life) consist of interests outside the law? And what of her gender, his religion, her race, his sexual status? Can a black judge objectively hear a case where racial discrimination is alleged? Can a female judge command the attention—and the respect—of an Islamic extremist? Does being gay require a judge to recuse himself when the case before him will decide whether same-sex marriage violates the Constitution?

Will conversations around the dinner table and the observations of family and friends translate into how a judge thinks or rules? Can judges who worked in the shadow of the Pentagon or the Twin Towers on 9/11 really be impartial when deciding issues related to that day and its aftermath?

Will the thought of "bad press" (or good press, for that matter) inform their choices? Is she a Democrat or a Republican? Can a church-going judge—appointed to the bench with support from the conservative right—put aside the expectations of others (and perhaps his own beliefs) when deciding the politically loaded question of whether school children should be taught that evolution is nothing more than a theory and that other theories are just as viable? Was she a prosecutor or a defense attorney or maybe both?

And did those experiences make her more drawn, as a judge, to positions typically urged from the table of the courtroom from which she practiced? Or perhaps more skeptical? Does he support charities, and which?

Most important—how does he process all of this "baggage," as it were? Does the judge—*should* the judge—simply look at the case law and decide cases without emotion, without biases, without, what Freud might have called in *The Interpretation of Dreams*, the "residue of the day"? What is the import of the subtle ebbs and flows of each day, or the "great tides and currents," that inform him in his judicial craftsmanship? And, perhaps even more compellingly—are judges unable to empathize or even sympathize with litigants who come before them?

A here unidentified late judge—a brilliant man, revered by all lawyers who appeared before him—once sat on the federal court somewhere in New York. He came to the bench a great liberal, sympathetic—maybe even empathetic—to most every criminal defendant who had suffered through a childhood of poverty or poor parentage. That is, until the day he was mugged at gunpoint in the park across from the courthouse, an incident that drastically changed the way he sentenced, particularly when weapons were involved.

Did this judge acknowledge the differences in his sentencing, before and after the mugging? And was he required to disclose the robbery to those who appeared before him? But what if the change to harshness in how he would sentence defendants, especially for gun offenses, was gradual? And what if it occurred because he was "burned" too often by recidivists, after one too many implored: "If you show me leniency, giving me probation, you will never, ever see me in a courtroom again?" Would we want a judge to be impervious to his earlier bench experiences, both good and bad? A more difficult question, to be sure.

Yes, to that one judge, this incident was—as Judge Cardozo declared—a "reminder that [judges] are subject to human limitations." It surely influenced, maybe even captivated, the manner in which—perhaps the philosophy of how—he would thereafter assess and mete out punishment.

But what of Cardozo's "tides and currents"—the far more profound issues—such as the role of the courts when the other branches of government fail, or come up short; death or mandatory sentences for crime; the state's role as caretaker (or, some might say, dictator) for the downtrodden; the government's regulation of the markets; the (semipermeable) wall of separation between church and state; rights to privacy in a post-9/11 world; and other like issues of great moment?

How does a judge react to events he has experienced, or has observed firsthand? Does he personalize, however subtly, his life experiences when he dispenses justice or seek to maintain objectivity and balance? Does he compartmentalize his life on the bench, perhaps falsely believing that he has separated his decision making from his "real world"? In other words, does he believe his experiences, his background, his encounters have not informed his decisions? Or does she inwardly acknowledge those influences and, having done so, believe that they were properly discarded or addressed?

Put differently, is he truly able—and is it desirable—to exemplify the blindfolded woman who holds in her hands the scales of justice? Should he even try to replicate Lady Justice's model of pursuing justice, blind indeed to all that goes on around her? That is, should he be impervious to all but the counterweights that represent a case's differing views on the scale suspended from her left hand?

At bottom, can anyone seriously argue in opposition to what Cardozo posited, that judges are not—at a minimum, in some subliminal way—influenced by the human dynamic of life, including the subtle biases they picked up along the way? The way in which different judges actually perceive the cases or controversies before them is often markedly disparate. Some judges—"activist judges"—may, directly or with nuance, attempt to engineer change in how they decide cases, when they believe that the legislation or policies don't adequately deal with a particular social or economic ill. And when they do, do they seek to accomplish something far beyond what the litigants before them have actually sought?

I have selected specific (generally, well-known) cases for the free-flowing dialogues that follow from the thousands of cases to which these 13 (alphabetized) judges have been assigned—those that have raised critical questions about justice, policy, precedent, the law, and the way in which the currents and tides of their lives and of our ever-changing society have influenced those rulings. But have the judges been open, even aware, of what experiences have influenced their rulings? And where judges acknowledge awareness of these potential influences—of their "priors," as Judge Posner would articulate it—are they fully candid, to themselves and others, about whether, and to what degree, it has informed their rulings? Or have they contrarily decided, after inwardly acknowledging the "awareness," that they can or did fairly decide the case, so that they needn't publicly reveal themselves?

Indeed, these judges and I might not always agree about what is—and perhaps, what should be—the mindset and role of individuals once they have ascended the bench. Of course, the personal opinions I offer during these dialogues are sometimes expressed in my role as devil's advocate. Those opinions are hardly important, except insofar as they may reflect the opinions of some readers hereof.

Nonetheless, this sometimes disparity in our respective views, which may surface occasionally in these pages, does not in any way detract from one's respect for the master of judicial introspection, Benjamin N. Cardozo—to whose enduring memory I dedicate what follows.

JC
May 14, 2014

Author's Note

The 13 interviews that comprise this volume—all but two conducted during 2013—were tape recorded in the chambers of the respective judges, except for the interview of Judge Hittner, conducted in New York, the interview of (retired) Judge Walker, conducted at his law office in San Francisco, and the interview of (retired) Judge Gertner, conducted at her office at Harvard Law School. Each interview lasted between one and one and one-half hours. The transcripts were then edited by the author slightly for style and, by prearrangement, thereupon provided to each judge for his or her own comments. The judges' edits were minimal and stylistic, and no one changed the substance of the interview or their responses to the questions asked. Each judge was told in advance which litigation would form the basis for the interview. However, none of the interviews were scripted, nor were the judges provided in advance with the questions to be asked.

In short, the interviews were intended to be conducted as extemporaneously as possible.

Chapter 1

Judge Leonie Brinkema

Because, again, in a trial, judges are always balancing. You're balancing probative value against the prejudicial impact that a piece of evidence will have. And so it's like a seesaw, and judges make this type of decision in every type of trial. I was trying to balance things as much as I could.
—Judge Leonie Brinkema, August 28, 2013

Judge Leonie Brinkema, appointed to the Eastern District of Virginia by President Clinton in 1993, was the first female district judge to sit in Alexandria. She is tough, decisive, and no-nonsense, but she is also recognized for her sense of humor, which she has used to diffuse otherwise tense situations in the courtroom.

Her rulings in the Moussaoui *case (discussed in this interview) touched upon innumerable issues. In one hearing, Judge Brinkema barred key prosecution witnesses from testifying, finding that the lawyer for the Transportation Security Administration (TSA) had made "egregious errors" by improperly sharing testimony with upcoming witnesses in violation of the judge's order.*

Judge Brinkema has not shied away from speaking her mind in her opinions. In awarding the Washington Post *attorneys' fees when it successfully defended its right to publish materials that the Religious Technology Center (i.e., the Church of Scientology) claimed were copyrighted, she called the RTC's actions "reprehensible" and designed to "stifl[e] criticism and dissent" of Scientology's practices. In another case, Virginia State employees challenged the constitutionality of a statute that barred them from using their work computers to view pornography. Judge Brinkema recognized the government's argument that workplace pornography decreased efficiency and created a hostile work environment but found the statute—as drafted—unconstitutional (this decision was reversed by the Fourth Circuit). Where a public library allowed its patrons use of the Internet but blocked access to certain sites, Judge Brinkema found that it had improperly censored materials in violation of the First Amendment's guarantee of free speech.*

Judge Brinkema was born in New Jersey. She holds a B.A. and a Masters of Library Science from Rutgers University as well as a J.D. from Cornell Law School. Before attending law school, she studied philosophy at the University of Michigan and New York University. Upon her graduation from Cornell, Judge Brinkema served as a trial attorney in the U.S. Department of Justice's Public Integrity Section before working as an assistant U.S. attorney for the Eastern District of Virginia. She also served in the Department of Justice's Office of International Affairs before entering private practice, during which time she taught at the Northern Virginia Criminal Justice Academy. Judge Brinkema worked as Magistrate Judge in the Eastern District of Virginia until she was appointed to the District Court.

Judge Brinkema sits in Alexandria, Virginia.

The Moussaoui Terrorism Case

The events of September 11, 2001, represent the greatest attack ever from a foreign enemy on American soil. Still, despite what occurred at the Twin Towers in New York City, the Pentagon, and a field near Shanksville, Pennsylvania, America never truly had the satisfaction of closure—or is it revenge?—in seeing those responsible for the murder of thousands convicted. Yes, many years later Osama Bin Laden, who claimed credit for orchestrating the attacks, was killed by an American militia at his compound in Abbottabad, Pakistan; but the 19 hijackers directly responsible for the attacks all—by design and necessity—died in those crashes, making sure no government could "make them pay" for their unspeakable crimes. And, insufferably, they made sure no family member of the 9/11 victims could see justice done.

Nonetheless, despite the sense that all of the hijackers themselves died, the U.S. Justice Department did not relent—it would ultimately bring to justice one Zacarias Moussaoui. Moussaoui was a French-born Islamic extremist. His visits to Afghan training camps run by Osama Bin Laden caused France to put him on its "watch list" in 1998. By 2001, he came to the attention of the Federal Bureau of Investigation when he purchased knives, researched crop-dusting classes, and ultimately enrolled in the Pan Am Flight Academy for commercial flight training. He was arrested on immigration charges on August 16, 2001 (primarily as a means of keeping him out of circulation), and remained incarcerated on September 11.

After the 9/11 attacks, Moussaoui was indicted on six counts of conspiracy, most egregiously to commit acts of terrorism resulting in death. Although Judge Brinkema rejected his earlier attempt to plead guilty, Moussaoui eventually took the plea years after the attack, admitting to his role in Osama Bin Laden's conspiracy to kill thousands of Americans by flying commercial planes into prime-target U.S. buildings, including the White House. Thus, a penalty phase trial by jury was ultimately held in two parts: to first determine if his crimes subjected him to the death penalty and, if so, to decide whether he should be so, permanently and irrevocably, sentenced. At this trial, he would stunningly testify (although the government admitted that it had no evidence to support this claim) that he and shoe-bomber Richard Reid were actually planning to hijack a *fifth* plane on September 11, 2001, and crash it into the White House, but that, because he was in jail at the time, the White House crash plan was never realized. Depending on Moussaoui's story at any particular moment in time—it greatly fluctuated, particularly when he realized that he could receive the ultimate penalty— he would also claim that there was no plan to crash into the White House, but that he was supposed to have been the 20th 9/11 hijacker on one of the four planes.

The *Moussaoui* case, though, would undergo a tortured history from the time he was first arrested on immigration charges to the jury's determination that the death penalty should not be imposed—and even later when Moussaoui, postsentencing, sought to withdraw his guilty plea and conviction. Did the government "drop the ball" when it failed to look at all the information before it in August 2001 and predict that the 9/11 attacks would take place? Did the jury conclude, as Bin Laden would later "announce" from a cave somewhere in Asia three weeks after the jury ruled against death, that Moussaoui had "no connection whatsoever" with September 11 and had simply been "learning to fly"? We shall probably never know whether Bin Laden was actually speaking the truth.

The *Moussaoui* case was—except during several appeals to the Fourth Circuit—on the docket of District Judge Leonie Brinkema in Alexandria, Virginia, from December 2001 until May 3, 2006, when the jury saved him from death. But it was hard to get a handle on what Moussaoui actually did and, alternatively, what he simply claimed responsibility for. Was he the "twentieth hijacker" as he sometimes would claim, or was he merely an Al Qaeda devotee who tried to exaggerate his role and perpetuate a myth that his role was equivalent to the "martyrs" who perished with the hijacked aircraft on 9/11?

Beyond that, what did Judge Brinkema think of the man who appeared before her for five years, the man who brought motions, pro se, such as "Motion to Stop Leonie Brinkema DJ [from] Playing Games with My Life" and his motion to compel the "Government to Apologize to the Muslim Umman for the Insult to the Coran"? Even though Judge Brinkema held him mentally competent to plead guilty to the six-count indictment against him, was there reason to believe, in terms colloquial, that he wasn't quite all there? And, if so, why did she accept his guilty plea?

What procedures did Judge Brinkema put in place for the Rule 11 hearing—to inquire whether Moussaoui's plea was voluntary, intentional, and factual? And how did Judge Brinkema satisfy herself (and the Fourth Circuit) that Moussaoui understood that, if he did not plead guilty, the government had the burden to prove his alleged conspiracies beyond a reasonable doubt and that the consequence of his plea might lead to a sentence of death?

During his years in her court, Moussaoui alternated between a refusal to plead, demands that he be permitted to plead guilty, and pleas of not guilty. He refused court-appointed counsel, insisted on Muslim counsel only, and—when he was permitted to appear pro se with "stand-by" counsel in place—refused to listen to their advice, evidenced most unmistakably by his own testimony, essentially handing the prosecution their proof. Indeed, did Judge Brinkema believe the government would have met its burden to prove Moussaoui guilty of any crime had it not been for Moussaoui's own testimony? Was she concerned when, during the years the case was before her, the government often supported Moussaoui's pro se motions, while his stand-by counsel opposed them?

And how did Judge Brinkema address the myriad issues *Moussaoui* brought to her courtroom? These issues included those that questioned whether Moussaoui could have access to other extremists who might exculpate Moussaoui on the nature of his "role" in the wrongdoing that could help defeat the government's efforts to put Moussaoui to death—and who *may have been* in the custody of the U.S. government (as the government would not acknowledge the identities of those it had detained); those that arose when classified documents were requested but the government refused to provide them, even at penalty of prosecution evidence being suppressed as a result; and those that brought sanctions against the government when, in violation of Judge Brinkema's specific order, a Transportation Security Administration attorney, who was part of the prosecution team, "prepped" witnesses by disclosing the testimony of other prosecution witnesses and, according to Judge Brinkema, lied about it.

And what kind of evidence did Judge Brinkema exclude? How did she balance the government's right to present the evidence that would allow the jurors to put Moussaoui to death against the prejudice to Moussaoui of allowing them to hear the cell phone-recorded pleas, the screams of those trapped in the Twin Towers?

What was going through the judge's mind as all of this was taking place? Did she believe that standing (and often shouting) before her was the lone would-be hijacker who was finally brought to justice in an American courtroom? Would she have gone so far as to actually dismiss the death penalty based on the TSA attorney's misconduct if the defendant had not been a 9/11 conspirator on any version of the facts that Moussaoui chose to present at any moment in time?

How did Judge Brinkema select jurors, given the fervor of the day? How did she maintain the decorum and dignity of the court during the hearings, or after, when the verdict was announced and the press was sure to engage in its own feeding frenzy? Was she concerned about security in her courtroom? Or was she afraid for the lives of the prosecution witnesses, jurors, U.S.

marshals, and attorneys? Did she think she would be responsible if a loved one of a victim attacked Moussaoui? And, importantly, was she concerned for her own safety—then *and* today? Is there any other reason that—years after Moussaoui was sentenced—she does not permit her image to be used, going so far as to request that she be blacked out on the video of her presentation at a 2010 judicial conference entitled "Trying Alleged Terrorists?"

Yes, it would finally come to be that the case would end with the openly contemptuous Moussaoui being sentenced to life in a draconian "supermax" prison. She told him, "You came here to be a martyr and to die in a great bang of glory, but to paraphrase the poet T. S. Eliot, instead, you will die with a whimper. The rest of your life you will spend in prison." When Moussaoui began to respond, the judge instead continued: "You will never again get a chance to speak, and that is an appropriate and fair ending." Her words notwithstanding, had the sentence been up to Judge Brinkema—and not the jury—would she have given this zealot the death penalty? Would she have sentenced him to life? Or did she believe his crimes warranted some lesser sentence?

And, though she denied his motion (and was affirmed by the Fourth Circuit), what did Judge Brinkema think of Moussaoui's postsentence attempt to withdraw his guilty plea upon his surprise that he was not going to be put to death and his disbelief that an American jury could actually put aside their prejudices, be fair, and rule against such an irrevocable sentence? In sum, did Judge Brinkema think—despite the countless issues, appeals, motions, considerations, and concerns—that the "system worked"?

The Dialogue

JC: Judge Brinkema, given that the book's goal is to examine what goes on in a judge's mind but may not be reflected in the record, a good way to start with *Moussaoui* would be to discuss the impact of 9/11 on the world at large, particularly the United States, and more particularly the nation's Northeast Corridor. So, on September 12, 2001 and the days following, did you have a particular view about the state of the world given Muslim extremist terrorism?

LB: Not really. On September 12, the courthouse was still closed. On September 11, while the attacks were underway, I was actually empanelling a jury for a capital murder case involving, ironically, an Afghan victim. I was in the midst of doing a second round of *voir dire* with individual jurors who already filled out a questionnaire. Just then, the marshals came to advise that there had been what appeared to be a terrorist attack in New York, and of course the Pentagon. And the Chief Judge had ordered the court closed. So I had to dismiss the jurors and told them that I didn't know when we were getting back together. The courthouse remained closed the next day, and then we came back the following day.

At that point, all the buildings had not been built around the courthouse, and we could see the Pentagon smoke for days, even weeks after the attack. So that attack was a very visible presence here at the courthouse. To be quite honest, my main focus was getting my capital jury back together to see the impact the attacks would have on my jury pool, and to keep that case moving. I really don't recall having any great overriding concern about future attacks on the nation, given the incredible response here in Washington. We had fighter jets flying over for weeks after that attack. At night you'd hear the jets—a noise we had never heard before. So this area was probably one of the safest since there was such a strong military presence—given the fact that the seat of government was here and we were one of the targets.

JC: Did you have a view about how justice in the United States would be dispensed to Muslims generally given that the population might see *all* Muslims as somehow U.S. haters?

LB: Obviously that was a concern when the *Moussaoui* case went on the docket and I was looking to empanel jurors. I can't say that that was my immediate response because, quite frankly, as I said, I was focused on my capital case. We didn't have any cases involving Muslims or the September 11 events at that point. Of course the *Walker Lindh* case came in first which was assigned to Judge [T.S.] Ellis [III]. So when *Walker Lindh* came in, this Court had a direct involvement in the emerging storm. But I really didn't start to worry about what would happen until I had a case on my docket. I've always had great confidence, frankly, in the jury pool here in northern Virginia. It's such an intelligent pool. And so, I've never detected any real problem with bias. So looking back now, I can't recall having any of those types of concerns before I actually had a concrete case before me.

JC: Was the security in the courthouse changed as a result of *Walker Lindh* case and *Moussaoui*?

LB: Yes. With *Walker Lindh* security changed dramatically. So it was already in place when *Moussaoui* arrived.

JC: On September 12th you couldn't have possibly known that you would ultimately get the *Moussaoui* case?

LB: No.

JC: When you finally did, on the day it was rolled out to you and you now knew what faced you in that case, what was your view of who or what Moussaoui actually was from having read the indictment and some press about him?

LB: Well everyone, including myself, assumed he was the "twentieth hijacker"—that was the label the press gave him. And it was certainly the innuendo, if not the explicit statement in the indictment. Again, there were four planes and three of them had a total of five terrorists. The fourth plane which crashed in Pennsylvania had only four. So the belief was that Moussaoui was intended to be that fifth person on that plane, for a total of twenty. That was the symmetry that everybody had in mind. Accordingly, he was dubbed the twentieth hijacker. That's what I assumed about him when I got the case.

JC: Besides that, did you assume that he was actually a would-be hijacker, even though obviously he was in jail on 9/11?

LB: A fair assumption, yes.

JC: In retrospect, did the fact that you actually believed that then influence how you handled the case?

LB: I don't think so. Not one bit.

JC: Let me probe that. How can that be? If a man is charged with participating in the greatest domestic attack in American history, how could that not influence a judge's handling of a case?

LB: I don't think it changes if one is charged with the most grievous crime or a minor crime. To me, a judge approaches any case the same way. I mean your job is to ensure that the case is tried fairly—that the defendant gets a fair chance to make his case; that the government doesn't abuse the system; and that justice gets done. I really don't think I handled the *Moussaoui* case in that respect any differently from any other. The logistics of trying the *Moussaoui* case were obviously unique. And those are the elements of the case that, as a judge, I find the most interesting. But not in terms of how I approached him. And then it became obvious very early on that he probably was not the twentieth hijacker. When I got to see him in action in court and started to look at the evidence it was pretty obvious that he was not as serious a player as I had first assumed. And that issue permeated the next five or six years, as the case evolved.

JC: We'll soon discuss your view of "who" or "what" he was now that 12 years have passed. But did you, at the time, think he was "all there" in terms of his mental capacity?

LB: Oh yes. He was unique. He was strange. He was probably the first sort of Muslim zealot that I had in court up to that point. And I wanted to be extremely careful to be sure about his "world view" and the way he described it. Plus, it is worth noting, he spoke English with a very thick French accent, and had an extraordinarily clever witty mind. I mean if you read his pleadings you would know that some of his puns were hysterically funny. Frankly, I think he could have written skits for The Daily Show if he'd been of the right philosophical orientation. Very smart.

He was first represented by the Public Defender's office, and he had a decent rapport with them. But it's when they started probing his mental state and suggested that they would try to mount, certainly at the mitigation level, some sort of mental illness defense, he absolutely rejected that. I always thought that he was a man who had a very strong sense of self-dignity in that respect. And anybody who cast aspersions on his mental state got into quick trouble with him.

JC: Was there a competency hearing in the case?

LB: I know that he was not sent for a custodial one. He was always in custody of course. I believe it was Dr. Patterson who evaluated him, yes.

JC: Was that on your order?

LB: Yes, but only because I had to be confident that he was competent to waive counsel. Remember, for many years he was *pro se*. So, I had to make sure that he totally understood what that meant. At bottom, I determined that he was actually competent to represent himself.

I was indeed intrigued by his intellect, and his wit. And he understood some elements of the case better than his own lawyers did. I don't know—but he was a defendant whom I found absolutely intriguing.

JC:　That seems to be on an intellectual level. But what about on an emotional level, given what this confederacy wanted to accomplish? You seem to be looking at the case largely in an intellectual light—"This is an intriguing guy who appeared before me."

LB:　But you have to do that as a judge. Certainly there were emotional elements to the case—the victims. The victims' stories were heart wrenching. I've often told people that if they really want to see a modern morality play in the courtroom, they should look at the transcripts of the trial. The trial only involved the sentencing issue, because he pleaded guilty. So we never had a trial on the merits. But we had the victims. And we had victims testify on both sides. We had victims who testified for the government. They emphasized the aggravating factors of the case—the impact on the victims.

But I allowed the defense to call victims opposed to the death penalty. Nobody can come into court and say "Jury, you should sentence this man to death" or "Jury, you should just sentence him to life." But we also had several family members who came in and talked about the extraordinary life affirming elements of what had happened. In the sense that there was one woman, I recall, whose son was gay and he died. She became very active in the Rainbow movement—using her son's memory as a sort of legacy to improve relations with the gay community. And so there were people who testified on both sides of the issue. Because, ultimately the *Moussaoui* trial, to some degree in my view, became sort of a trial of life versus death. That was the only issue that had to be tried in that case, ultimately. Some of the evidence was excruciating. I kept some of it out, but I had to let some of it in.

JC:　What kind of evidence did you exclude?

LB:　There was one—well, with cell phones, you know how technology has changed things. There was one woman who was in the World Trade Center who had phoned someone to let them know that she was in this building on fire. And it went on for 15 or 20 minutes. Basically if you ran the whole recording you hear her death gasps at the end. You're hearing someone in the process of dying, who is terrorized. Talking about the smoke, and that she can't see. You hear the screams. It was horrible. I allowed the government to play a brief snippet of it. But not the whole thing.

JC: Why?

LB: Because, again, in a trial, judges are always balancing. You're balancing probative value against the prejudicial impact that a piece of evidence will have. And so it's like a seesaw, and judges make this type of decision in every type of trial. I was trying to balance things as much as I could.

JC: At the time you excluded that evidence, had you already concluded, in your own mind, that he had exaggerated his role—that he was not in fact . . .

LB: Yes. I didn't think the death penalty was appropriate for Moussaoui.

JC: So if the death penalty decision were in your hands alone, you would have decided against it?

LB: Correct.

JC: I take it you're not a death penalty abolitionist?

LB: I have serious qualms about the death penalty. But I could impose it if the jury found it. I myself don't know if there's *ever* a case where I think the death penalty is . . . I've not yet had one before me where I thought death was appropriate. I've only had three or four capital cases.

JC: But you wouldn't be making the decision?

LB: No, juries do that.

JC: So, as you sit here now in the quiet of your chambers, when the case was ping-ponging over all those years between you and the Fourth Circuit, what do you think Moussaoui actually did?

LB: I think he was here in the United States definitely being trained for a role in a second-wave attack. I also think that Khalid Sheikh Mohammed ("KSM") and the others were smart enough to realize that he was a bit of . . .

JC: An unguided missile?

LB: Yes an unguided missile, an uncontrollable individual.

JC: As if they were "guided" themselves?

LB: Well, I think KSM was quite brilliant. His was a brilliantly conducted operation. But Moussaoui was a real risk for them—he didn't follow directions. Remember, he was told not to correspond with them, and he was still sending email messages to [Ramzi] bin al-Shibh, which was one of the problems. And this issue came out at the death penalty trial. If the FBI had put all of the dots together—the dots were there, they just weren't connected. And they were connected by some people, but not by everyone. But if they had put it all together and had searched his laptop in a timely fashion, they would have seen email communications between him and bin al-Shibh. And the thinking was that had that been known in mid-August, 2001 there might have been enough time and enough incentive to have put a damper on it.

JC: So what do you think Moussaoui did? Besides going for flight training and buying knives and having a bunch of email communications, what else did he do?

LB: That was it. I think he was being prepped. I don't know how many others—if they did have others here—were being prepped in the same way. But I think he was being groomed to be part of another attack.

JC: So when Bin Laden issued some "announcement" several weeks after the sentence that Moussaoui was not the twentieth hijacker—that he was basically in the States taking flight lessons—the truth was somewhere between those two?

LB: I think that by the end of the case, even the government would admit to the realization that he wasn't the twentieth hijacker. The case flip-flopped. The theory of the case flip-flopped a great deal. By the end of the case, the real theory of the government's case was that he was responsible for September 11th happening. That is because had he not lied to the agents about why he was here and what he was doing, they would have been able to put the dots together. I'm grossly over-simplifying it, but it really shifted to that. And that's what I always thought was interesting and I've never discussed it . . .

JC: You think that was true—that had he not lied 9/11 could have been prevented?

LB: I don't think the lies were the whole of it. I think that, frankly, it was the incompetency of the . . . I don't know whether had the dots been put together, the picture would have been clear enough for action to be taken to stop it. Because I don't know, even to this day—you know there's all that talk about the chatter that was going on. I don't know whether that chatter was sufficient, even if you added information from Moussaoui's computer. Frankly, if Moussaoui had talked to them, if he had been honest and said "Yeah I'm here to learn how to fly a plane because Al Qaeda is talking about using planes as weapons of mass destruction"—if he had cooperated, obviously, I think then they could have stopped it.

But there was going to be an interesting issue. The government had to be careful about this. And I remember talking with my law clerks and saying "Boy if they raise this issue, this case is going to go away." He couldn't be prosecuted for invoking his Fifth Amendment right to remain silent. Could you imagine that theory of the case? But he talked. And what he said were lies. So the government could sort of argue that that was the overt act in furtherance of the conspiracy that he took. Knowing what he knew and then lying to them put them off so that they couldn't put the pieces together.

JC: So you started to use the word "incompetence" before you changed the subject. What incompetence were you referring to—on the part of the government?

LB: Yes. I was very dissatisfied with what they did. I think that Phoenix memo, in my mind, was such a strong piece of circumstantial evidence that there was something amiss with these men of Middle-East origin who didn't seem to have legitimate reasons for learning how to fly planes.[1] The dots were there and some agents were saying we need to put these together, and they weren't put together. And that makes no sense to me, having been a federal prosecutor, where part of one's job used to be to put those pieces together and make a case. It was shocking to me—and I think it was to the House Committee, members of the press. I think even the September 11th Commission had concerns about how this thing was investigated.

JC: Since you concluded that he wasn't—shall I say—"nuts" and was very intelligent, why do you suspect he was saying all this kind of stuff such as that he was planning to blow up the White House?

---

1. Author's note: The Phoenix memo—recommending a worldwide effort to identify those who enrolled in flight school, noting the possibility of a coordinated effort of attacks led by Osama bin Laden—was sent to the FBI main office by an agent in July 2001.

LB: He was a bit of an egomaniac. At times he wanted to portray himself as some infamous terrorist. He certainly vacillated in the *persona* that he portrayed.

JC: Did you ever confront him with that?

LB: I never had any direct interaction with Moussaoui.

JC: I mean confront him on the record and say—"What are you doing? I don't believe some of the things that you're saying. You are hurting yourself"?

LB: He was told that more than once.

JC: But by you?

LB: Remember, he tried to plead guilty. I wouldn't take his first try. I finally accepted it. What can one do if you have a defendant, whom you've found competent, who has gone through an extensive Rule 11 plea colloquy which explained *ad nauseum* the potential effect of pleading guilty, and he insists on pleading guilty. He comes in and says "I did it, I did it, I did it." You have to accept that plea at some point. I have always felt that he was competent.

JC: If he had not pleaded guilty and had not testified in his own behalf (I guess that's an odd phrase in Moussaoui's case) . . .

LB: On the government's behalf. Have you read the transcripts of the two trials? The amazing thing, and the general thinking on my part, from what I was hearing from the grapevine, from the prosecutor, from everyone—had he not testified at the first phase of the penalty trial, it probably would have stopped at that point.

In other words, had he not testified, the jury probably would have found that he was not death-eligible. The reason being that the first phase of the penalty proceeding focused extraordinarily well on the government's failures to do the various things that I mentioned earlier in connecting the dots. And so the picture that was left at the end of that phase was that Moussaoui was clearly not the twentieth hijacker, and that the government really messed up. They couldn't blame September 11 on this guy. And if the jury had made that finding, then he would not have been death-eligible.

He was still convicted on his guilty plea, and then it would have been up to me to determine what sentence was appropriate. But instead he testified, and he came in saying "I was talking to Bin Laden directly." I'm paraphrasing—I'd have to go back and reread my transcripts—but it was clear after his testimony that they were going to find that he was death-eligible. And then we moved to the second phase, which was the aggravating and mitigating factors.

JC: Do you think he would have been convicted had he not pleaded guilty?

LB: That's a very interesting question. I don't know.

JC: You think he actually might not have been convicted?

LB: Of those particular offenses? I mean there were six counts in the indictment, and I can't recall now all six of them but I believe four were conspiracy counts.

Given the breadth of the conspiracy, arguably he could have been convicted of one or two of the conspiracy counts. But it would have been a tough haul for the government, and with 12 jurors you could have had one with reasonable doubt. As was ultimately the case.

JC: Obviously time has passed and your memory has somewhat faded, as would be natural, and your unhappiness with the government has probably dwindled some. Still, at one point you were actually thinking about throwing the case out, when the TSA attorney was prepping witnesses with other witnesses' testimony.

LB: Remember, I wouldn't have thrown the case out. I would have thrown out the death penalty. He was already convicted, having pleaded guilty. So the real question was going to be how do I sentence him for that.

JC: Pardon me, I misspoke, you were actually going to take the death penalty off the table because of that misconduct?

LB: Yes, because I truly felt at that point that the death penalty was not appropriate for him given his overall role in the case. When you're involved in a capital case, whether as a judge, or as a defense attorney, the focus is so oriented towards death, because that is the ultimate punishment. It just permeates a capital case. As a judge, your responsibility is to make sure that that case is handled fairly—and when I say fairly I mean, in my view, you really must make every close judgment call in favor of the defendant. And if you look at the Federal death statute—a brilliantly done statute—the balancing that goes on there is extraordinary. When you think about it, at the end of the day, the government has the burden of proving the aggravating factors beyond a reasonable doubt. It's got to be a unanimous finding. The mitigating factors don't require proof beyond a reasonable doubt. They don't require a unanimous decision. And the jury itself can interject them into the case. They don't even have to be part of the advocacy in the case. That's extraordinary. And it shows that even Congress, with a capital statute on the books, has tipped that balance. Each time you have to weigh something, the balance must go in the defendant's favor in a capital case.

JC: So being the devil's advocate, a skeptic might say that you were using that TSA attorney's misconduct as a means to help take the death penalty off the table.

LB: I don't think I was using it, but the government has an obligation, in my view—and having been a government lawyer for several years, I hold government lawyers to a really high standard which I think is absolutely appropriate in a democracy. And that was such a clear violation of a very explicit order. The conduct wasn't proper. The government's interest, the Department of Justice's interest, in every criminal case is to do justice. Not to get a conviction. And you have to sometimes remind prosecutors of that. And justice can be denied if you over-charge somebody.

Just this morning I got a memo about the new [Attorney General Eric] Holder approach, which I think is great—telling prosecutors that they now should be approaching drug and other types of cases more leniently. I've had problems with some of the prosecutorial decisions for years, as overkill. So I had a government lawyer who adamantly violated a very clear order that's pretty standard in most cases. And certainly in a capital case, it's even more important that the witness coming in is untainted. There has to be a penalty for that. This man's life is at stake.

JC: Do you think a defendant, particularly an alleged terrorist, gets a fair shake when the government can deny him the opportunity to see certain prosecution materials that a defendant in an ordinary case—social security fraud, drug trafficking, credit card scam—would see? Moussaoui was denied the opportunity to see statements by witnesses that he thought might help him.

LB: First of all, it's not just in terrorism cases. In cases of national security of any kind, you have the same problem. And it happens in some very nasty violent crime conspiracy cases. Sometimes, the cooperating witness statements are not—or at least the cooperators' identities—are not revealed. Defendant's counsel may know. So those are, again, those balancing things that go on in the system. That's why a good legal system has to have flexibility to accommodate the specifics of that case. It is difficult, and it does rub up against our concepts of Due Process and one's Sixth Amendment rights when a defendant doesn't have the same access to information as his counsel.

But in some respects, Moussaoui always knew more than his attorneys did. He'd met Bin Laden. He'd met KSM. I believe he'd met bin al-Shibh in person. He knew these people. So often what would happen was he knew more than the others because he'd been on the scene. Another interesting aside, which I've always found just fascinating in *Moussaoui*. I've never had a case—and I've been on the bench for over 20 years—with this line-up. It was not uncommon when Moussaoui was *pro se* that Moussaoui would make a motion and the government would support it. And his stand-by defense counsel would oppose it.

I can't recall the specific motions but there were times when Moussaoui asked for something that was clearly detrimental to his best interests. The government would jump in and say "Yes, that's great, do it." And I'd have Frank Dunham or the public defender's office jumping up, saying "No, Judge, you can't do this." Fascinating. Many times we had that kind of reality . . . I used to describe the case sometimes as feeling like *Alice in Wonderland*—just the complete reversal of roles. And it was my job as the judge to keep the case running fairly. So often, Moussaoui was his own worst enemy.

JC: What do you think of—after the case was over—Moussaoui making a motion to take his guilty plea back, saying, basically, that he didn't realize when he pleaded guilty that he could get such a fair shake from the jury?

LB: I was actually very touched by that. I've quoted that many times as a testament to the fairness of the system. But I must tell you, I pride myself—if there's one thing I think I do well it's a Rule 11 colloquy. And I do believe there comes a point in which an intelligent person, who was truly on notice as to what the ramifications were going to be, who chooses to plead guilty, pleads guilty, and I'm not going to undo that plea. He was guilty of something. Of being involved with these people. Of being here with the intent to do harm to this country. I have no doubt about that. And so for that I rest very comfortably that he was found guilty and he's not walking the streets.

JC: If the sentencing decision were solely yours—say in the pre-Guidelines era—and there was no death penalty issue, what would your sentence likely have been?

LB: Probably 20 to 25 years. Nothing more. I don't think he needs life. Because, first of all, by the time he would get out, the world would have changed. It's a long time to be in prison. I doubt that he would be any kind of a threat.

JC: Don't you think there are some acts that just ring out for a life sentence?

LB: Sure. Khalid Sheikh Mohammed. Frankly, and if you think about it, there are people who, with great justification, can argue that life imprisonment without the possibility for parole is in some respects a far crueler punishment than death. It's almost like a lifetime of death. The conditions under which people like Moussaoui are kept are not pleasant. I cannot imagine what it would be like to live day after day in a very small cell. Not get fresh air. Not be able to hear birds chirping in the morning, or the nuisance of dogs barking. All those things that as human beings we take for granted, you lose. And these people when they're convicted, they don't go to a camp or a Level 1 or 2 institution. They go to pretty tough prisons.

JC: But he's a martyr or wanted to be a martyr. Martyrs want to live the martyr life.

LB: That's fine that he is. But he's still a human being. And I think it's tough for any human being to live under those conditions. I have no idea what he's up to these days. He's in Colorado.

JC: He doesn't write you?

LB: He never has. I've had plenty of defendants write me. A couple of lawyers whom I know who have been at the supermax. I've asked them if they've ever heard anything about Moussaoui. I was told, and this is several years old now, that the prisoners, when they heard on the prison grapevine that he was coming, were all excited. They thought they were going to have this superstar of Islamic terrorism coming in, and were very disappointed about how quiet he's been. So, no, I've not heard a word from him.

JC: When I googled you, I couldn't find your picture other than an artist's sketch of you. And I saw that when you participated in a Ninth Circuit forum, your face was blocked. Why was that?

LB: Quite frankly, I didn't want to become a media person. I didn't want people to necessarily recognize me on the street. "Ooh that's the *Moussaoui* judge."

JC: Anything to do with security concerns?

LB: It's funny—I've never been worried about any terrorist having it in for me. I was more concerned, quite honestly, about U.S. citizens being so outraged at what had happened or if someone had a family member injured or killed, that they might be concerned. So I was more concerned about a sort of domestic potential problem, and never really had it. I think the public by the end of the case was satisfied. And most of the victims from whom I've heard after the trial seem satisfied with the outcome.

JC: If I were to have interviewed you closer in time to 9/11, and the case had been not drawn out over a number of years, would the interview with you have been pretty much the same? In other words, do you think your view of the case, your concerns about security, terrorism, Muslim extremism, would have been the same?

LB: I was never worried about Muslim extremism. The other thing I should tell you is that I am one-quarter Lebanese. My mother's father came over from Lebanon. I never met him. He was dead before I was born. But I had aunts and uncles who were. I have an uncle who is Syrian, and so when I was a kid raised in northern New Jersey I can remember my father or my uncle going over to Atlantic Avenue in Brooklyn and picking up baklava and hummus and my mother made phenomenal kibbeh. So I had some touches with the Arab world that many Americans don't have. And my mother had a very distinct (what one would call) Arab nose. I recall some discussions about when she was a kid of some anti-Arab bias that she and her family had experienced. It never affected me, because if you look at me—most of my background is French.

So I had been exposed to Arab culture a bit. And then when I was in college, I was a philosophy major at Douglass College, which is part of Rutgers. The head of our department was of Lebanese background. He was my mentor. So I had wonderful, positive experiences with people of Middle

Eastern background. And so to that extent I might have felt a bit more comfortable in not worrying about some threat from the Arab world because I knew people from that background. And I thought the ones I knew were highly cultured, marvelously urbane and incredibly civilized.

JC: Did Moussaoui know about your Lebanese background?

LB: I don't think so.

JC: Did he make motions to recuse you on the ground that you're non-Muslim, as he did about his lawyers as non-Muslims?

LB: No. He picked on me for other things, but nothing personal like that. It's funny, I could be wrong on this, but I think at the end of the day, he respected me. I got the least negative press from him, so to speak. The people who got the worst of it were his own attorneys, the people closest to him. He took shots at the prosecution as well. He took shots at everyone—including me. But I never felt that they were that serious. I think, deep down inside, he understood that I was there trying to just make sure everything was done fairly.

JC: At sentence you used a quote from T.S. Eliot that he would—my words—"die without a whimper." Do you use those kind of comments at sentence, or did you just use it for him?

LB: Not often. I used it for him because of the way he allocuted—making all this noise. I just sort of maybe wanted to deflate him a little bit. Because you know, not with a bang but a whimper. That was how it was all ending.

JC: You say you would have sentenced him probably to 20 or 25 years. Are you unhappy that he got a life sentence?

LB: Not unhappy. I can see it can be justified. And there was no choice. I don't waste energy on things that I absolutely can't change.

JC: Is the "book" on you that you're a relatively lenient sentencer?

LB: I think that would be the book. I have been a highly reversed judge in the Fourth Circuit on sentencing issues. I've had trouble with the guidelines ever since they first went into effect. I think as a nation we have suffered extraordinarily from sentence inflation. We sentence far too many people for far too much time. It really is a problem. I'm thrilled it's being addressed by Congress, that they're looking at it seriously. The mandatory minimums have resulted in some horrendous sentences. I doubt that there's a single district judge you can talk to in the country today who wouldn't tell you that there have been sentences they've had to impose that they never would have imposed but for the way the law is set up.

JC: Is the view you have on sentence as a judge different from the view you had when you were a prosecutor? How long were you a prosecutor for?

LB: Six or seven years, something like that.

JC: Were you an aggressive prosecutor?

LB: I think I was a very aggressive prosecutor.

JC: If you had *Moussaoui* as a prosecutor, what would you have done differently?

LB: In the beginning I would have done the exact same thing. That is, I would have assumed he was the twentieth hijacker and I would have pushed for the death penalty. As the case evolved—death cases are so expensive in terms of money, manpower, time—I would have pushed to take death off the table. I don't think I would have been happy pursuing it as a death case particularly after I started getting the discovery, after I had seen what was really going on. I would also have tried vigorously—I was always troubled by this—it seemed to me that Moussaoui's greatest value in those early days would have been to turn him, to flip him.

JC: Taking the death penalty off the table, particularly during the Bush Administration, would have been very difficult to accomplish.

LB: Probably, yes.

JC: So you might have pushed but you would have probably gotten too much push back, right?

LB: Yes. But again, I would love to have known what the intelligence community was saying. Moussaoui could have been an invaluable source of information. Because the sense I have of the back chatter was that there were always some very interesting debates going on in the Executive Branch among the various agencies as to what to do with the case. But by deciding to make a public trial and go through the criminal justice route, it cut off the ability of the intelligence community to really mine him for what he was worth.

I do think that the right approach to Moussaoui would have been to get him to talk. He was a talker. He liked to talk. Someone could have engendered some trust and respect from him. You had to show him respect. I think you always have to show respect to defendants as a judge. But in particular, Moussaoui needed that. And it always troubled me—in terms of thinking about the good of the country—that we didn't try to get more from him. I don't know what they did.

JC: You believe defendants should be shown respect. What do you think Ann Coulter or Bill O'Reilly or their ilk would say about that—a Federal judge thinking that it's very important to show respect to a defendant who, whether he's the twentieth hijacker or not, wishes to cause terrorist acts in the United States?

LB: Because that's how you have a proper legal system. I really don't worry about what the pundits say. I don't listen to that stuff. On either side of the aisle.

JC: Let's assume Bin Laden had not been killed but had been captured and brought here, with the case venued in Alexandria before Judge Brinkema. Would you have handled Bin Laden the same way?

LB: Absolutely. Why treat him differently? He's a defendant. If the evidence is strong enough, he'll be convicted. And the other thing is as a judge—and this is sort of an Eastern District philosophy—I think it's very important for a judge to absolutely control the courtroom. No ifs, ands or buts about it. Lawyers don't control the courtroom. The government doesn't control the courtroom. I do. And so part of keeping decorum in the courtroom is you never want to get into a tiff with a defendant who's being difficult. I show them respect. Most smart defendants will figure out to be appropriately respectful to me. If not, I let them know the penalties that they'll have to pay. And so you maintain control. Part of control is I show respect to the process, to the defendant. And I expect the same back from them. And it usually works.

JC: Let's assume Bin Laden is convicted in your courtroom. Would you find another T.S. Eliot or other quote? What would you be saying to him?

LB: I don't know. That T.S. Eliot thing was not pre-planned. It came to me. It was to me an obvious response to what Moussaoui was saying.

JC: Would you be saying to bin Ladin, "You deserve to die"?

LB: Possibly.

JC: Do you think bin Laden deserved to die?

LB: Bin Laden? Again, I have problems with the death penalty so I don't know. And I'm not sure that flaunting it if a person has been sentenced to death would be the appropriate response. So I don't know.

JC: Well you're saying something very interesting though. You'd have problems imposing the death penalty on Bin Laden?

LB: If the jury has done it . . . The thing about being in my situation, I've never had to impose a death penalty. But if a jury, after hearing the evidence, had voted for death, I would impose it, yes.

JC: Your concern with the death penalty is over the seemingly barbaric nature of it, or because of the concern that the prosecution may have gotten it wrong?

LB: Oh I think there are multiple issues with the death penalty. Among other things, by the way, and it's very interesting—one of the issues that was argued in *Moussaoui*, and it's been argued in other cases, is that if the jury gives the death penalty that's exactly what a fundamentalist terrorist would want. Because that makes them a martyr. And there's a very decent argument, a really pragmatic argument, that one ought not to impose the death penalty on any of these people precisely because it does give them martyrdom. Whereas locking somebody up for the rest of their life in a six by eight cell is not a very glorious type of martyrdom. That's a good argument. And that argument resonates with juries. One can argue whether civilized society should even do that; but nevertheless that really does incapacitate the person and it takes away all the glory. There's no glory in a life sentence. There is, to some degree, with an execution.

JC: Do you think there would have been a benefit in having cameras in the courtroom for this case?

[Long pause.]

LB: I think no—I think it would have put too much pressure on the jury, among other things. I'm opposed to cameras.

JC: Of course no cameras would be focused on the jury or the witnesses.

LB: Even then, I think the cameras would be a problem. I'm opposed to cameras in the courtroom because I don't feel the media uses video correctly. They would only do the sound clips. You know, you'd see Moussaoui—there were moments where Moussaoui was just acting out, ridiculously. So that's what you'd see on the nightly news, and you wouldn't see all the rest of it. I actually would have liked very much to have a radio broadcast of the trial. I think that would have been a very good thing. Again, my concept of balance, a very good compromise. You can still do sound bites and snippets, but it's not quite as dramatic and I would have liked that. But the rules would not have permitted that.

JC: So the takeaway from this conversation is that Judge Brinkema is able to put aside all the outside atmospherics and address the case solely on what takes place in the courtroom.

LB: Yes. And in every case that's the little prep I give a jury. I tell them that they're going to be judges, saying "You should think of yourself as wearing a black robe just like the one I'm wearing because you're going to become a judge for this case. And the way our system works is that you have to make a decision based on what you see and hear in this room. Not on what you see or hear outside of this room. So what you might read [or see] on television, what you might bump into on the internet, what your neighbor might tell you, none of that stuff can be considered in deciding this case. That's how our legal system works."

JC: Other than the record of this case, what did you read about the 9/11 attacks and Moussaoui by editorialists or the like?

LB: While the case was in progress?

JC: Or before. You read the news, obviously.

LB: I read the news. I was home when the last Trade Center building fell. Because, as I said, they closed court, I went home, and I remember I was sitting in my living room. I had a new cat. A little kitten on my shoulder. I was riveted. And my husband who works downtown had called to say they were evacuating the City and he didn't know when he'd be home. So I was waiting for him to get home. My daughter was in college. My son goes to a day program; he hadn't gotten home yet, and so you're there riveted to the TV watching what's going on. So I had that exposure. I read the Times; I read the Post. I saw smoke daily from the Pentagon.

JC: What did you read about Moussaoui while the case was going on or before he was brought before you?

LB: Not a whole lot, because I don't recall there was a lot. I know he was indicted in December 2001. I don't know when it first became public that he'd been arrested and all that. Because it was a "grand jury original." There wasn't a complaint issued. And so frequently with a grand jury original, you don't know a thing about it. I'm not even sure I knew anything about it until I got the call that the case had been assigned to me.

JC: What should I ask you that I haven't?

LB: I loved the logistics of the case. Because they're kind of unique in terms of what a judge has to do. And I think it's important for people who are interested in how to run a trial like this. And to me the logistics were fascinating. Some of the problems we had in the case would not exist today because of technology. But I was very concerned that the trial not become a circus. And of course there were some people who did call it a circus because I allowed Moussaoui to talk a fair amount. And he wrote these scandalous pleadings which ultimately resulted in my revoking his ability to act *pro se*.

But I felt it was extremely important—and I still do—for a courtroom to have proper decorum at all times. We're a fairly formal court here. Lawyers have to stand at the podium when they say anything. We have those types of requirements and so I think that some of the stories that I've told people about the case, things that we sort of had to think through, we were concerned about the media creating a circus. I had a full-time professional press person who helped greatly in media relations. But that was always a great concern. We wanted to make sure that there was enough access for the media to cover the case appropriately but that they didn't upset the process, or create some sort of inappropriate issue.

At the end of the case, one of the concerns that our press person, Ed Adams, had from his experience in other high visibility trials, was that there is this great swoosh as the press all run out of the courtroom to get the scoop on the outcome of the case. And that really is sort of demeaning of the process. So we tried to figure out, how do we announce this verdict without it becoming this sort of crazy media show. We also had an issue, because as you know, this was only the second time in history when a Federal trial was broadcast via closed-circuit TV to off-site locations. The Oklahoma City bombing had been the first case. And the witnesses, the victims who had been watching the trial off site were concerned that they didn't want to be sitting around forever as the jury deliberated, but they wanted advance notice when the verdict came in so that they could be back at the courthouse. So what we agreed was that there would be a delay from the time that the jury announced that they had reached a verdict to the time we publicly announced it in court.

JC: How about dealing with the jury?

LB: With the jury, we did some things that Judge [Richard P.] Matsch in the Oklahoma City bombing case had done. I did not sequester the jury. I don't know if this Court has ever had a sequestered jury. I did have the jurors reporting to an off-site location where they were then picked up by the marshals and driven to the courthouse so that the media couldn't get their license plates or follow them or anything like that.

JC: Was the jury anonymous?

LB: Yes it was an anonymous jury.

JC: Do you think that's somewhat unfair to a defendant to have an anonymous jury?

LB: No I think it's necessary in some cases.

JC: Well perhaps necessary, but still unfair?

LB: Yes, but it's one of those balancing acts. Again, some things are unfair. The issue is whether they are unduly unfair. Do they taint the system?

JC: Did Moussaoui oppose an anonymous jury?

LB: I don't recall that he did, no. I don't think he cared.

JC: But he—largely representing himself—wouldn't have known, maybe, how prejudicial an anonymous jury might be, correct?

LB: He never said anything about it. Of all the things he commented on, I don't recall him ever complaining about it.

JC: What did you tell the jury was the reason for the anonymity?

LB: A question on the jury questionnaire was whether the trial would affect them. I told them we wanted to make sure that they were not bothered, frankly, by the media. I was more concerned about the media, and neighbors, trying to interject themselves because these people went home every night. And the trial was going to go on for several weeks.

JC: Well I must say, when I was a prosecutor and trying a major organized crime figure, Judge Eugene Nickerson—my favorite judge of all time (since deceased)—granted an anonymous jury. He told the jury that the reason for the anonymity was concern over the press bothering them. In truth, he was concerned for their safety.

LB: It's funny, I was never concerned about their safety. As I said, I've never worried about Al Qaeda sneaking over and taking a shot at the jurors. First of all, early on in the case I assessed the fact that Moussaoui was just not a key player. So there was no benefit for Al Qaeda to try to knock off the jury. But I was really concerned about the media. And the media was aggressive. Without going into detail, there was one incident where the press was following the jury van in a *French Connection*-like chase scene.

JC: During the very difficult and tortured nature of this case, did you discuss decisions you needed to make with any mentors or colleagues on whose advice you might rely?

LB: Just my law clerks. The Fourth Circuit was very generous. They allowed me to keep a third law clerk—a *Moussaoui* clerk. I did talk with Judge Matsch who did the Oklahoma City bombing case and I may have talked to Judge [Michael B.] Mukasey, who had the Blind Sheikh [Omar Abdel Rahman] case.

JC: Last question: Is there something, in retrospect, that you would have done differently?

LB: An interesting question. I don't know. The outcome, in my view, was the right one. And given what's happened since, it really was the right outcome—because all sorts of problems developed about the fact that often we were not given accurate information about KSM and some of the others. There was a time, for example—I know I'm on the record someplace saying this—the government kept insisting that there were no videotapes and tape recordings of interrogations of KSM and these other guys whom they'd caught. And Moussaoui and his attorneys had been insisting that they wanted the statements that these guys had made. And they wanted us to put questions to these people because the theory was that they would explain that Moussaoui was not the twentieth hijacker—that he was not part of September 11th, which clearly was mitigating evidence. And the government kept saying "No, there are no tape recordings. These things don't exist." And I remember saying more than once, "Either you're lying or you're inept." Because at that point almost every state police office in the country was recording confessions or statements from serious defendants. So you can't tell me that these high value detainees were not being questioned night and day, and that it wasn't being recorded. I just couldn't believe it. And of course it turns out that I was right. They were being recorded, and the recordings were all destroyed, or almost all destroyed. And all that stuff started coming out after *Moussaoui*. Had he been convicted of a death case and been sentenced to death, the post-conviction litigation would have gone on and on and on. But that he didn't get the death penalty—that changes the nature of the exercise.

JC: Would you have wanted to see KSM in your courtroom?

LB: I think that would have made it a more just outcome. He should have been prosecuted in a civilian courtroom. Yes.

JC: But in your courtroom as a witness?

LB: It would have been appropriate. But it would have been impossible because he was facing his own charges. He would have had a fifth amendment right not to testify. So as a practical matter he was never going to come into court.

JC: But it would have been a more just outcome because it would have presumably supported the defense that Moussaoui wasn't who he said he was?

LB: Yes.

Chapter 2

Judge Denny Chin

We are human beings. And sometimes there is an immediate gut reaction to something. And I wouldn't be honest if I said that doesn't happen. It does happen, most of the time. But we also know enough about the process to keep an open mind.
—Judge Denny Chin, June 11, 2013

Judge Denny Chin was appointed to the U.S. District Court for the Southern District of New York by President Clinton in 1994. In 2010, President Obama nominated him to the U.S. Court of Appeals for the Second Circuit.

As a trial judge, his notable cases are innumerable. In addition to sentencing Bernie Madoff (discussed here and for which Judge Chin acknowledges he will always be remembered), Judge Chin's opinions make it clear that he is not bothered by controversy or public opinion. He irritated many when he decided that Megan's Law (which makes information about registered sex offenders available to the public) could not be applied to sex offenses that occurred before the law took effect (the decision was later reversed).

Judge Chin presided over the criminal trial of Oscar Wyatt, the Texas oil executive accused of paying kickbacks to Saddam Hussein's regime. After Wyatt, then 83, pleaded guilty during trial, Judge Chin sentenced him to one year and a day, which he served in a minimum security prison. (Judge Chin discusses some of his reasoning for that sentence in this interview.) In another matter, Judge Chin denied Fox News's request to enjoin Al Franken from using the Fox slogan "Fair and Balanced" in the title of his book, Lies and the Lying Liars Who Tell Them: A Fair and Balanced Look at the Right, *rejecting the argument that consumers would believe Fox endorsed the book.*

Judge Chin is not one to "rubber-stamp" government requests. He pointedly directed New York City (and Mayor Rudolph Giuliani) to grant a permit to allow the Million Youth March, organized by a group including Khalid Abdul Muhammad, to proceed. Acknowledging that the group had spouted hateful, violent, and frightening ideology in the past, Judge Chin reminded the City that the First Amendment protects even offensive speech.

Judge Chin was born in Hong Kong in 1954; his family moved to the United States when he was two years old. He received his A.B., magna cum laude, from Princeton University and graduated from Fordham University School of Law in 1978, where he was managing editor of Fordham Law Review. *After law school, Judge Chin clerked for Judge Henry Werker in the Southern District of New York. He then went into private practice, worked as an Assistant U.S. Attorney for the Southern District, and returned to private practice—first in a small litigation boutique and later in a labor and employment firm where he represented employees and unions in labor and employment matters—until being appointed to the bench. In addition to his duties as a judge, he teaches a first-year legal writing course at Fordham Law.*

When receiving the Judge Edward Weinfeld Award from the New York County Lawyers Association in 2010, Judge Chin explained that one of the things he would miss most about being a district judge was the opportunity to swear in immigrants as new American citizens. At these ceremonies, he spoke of his grandfather who was born in China in 1896, came to the United States in 1916, and became a citizen in 1947. Judge Chin would show the new citizens his grandfather's naturalization certificate, which hangs on the wall in his Chambers.

Judge Chin currently sits on the Court of Appeals for the Second Circuit in New York City.

Madoff: Why 150 Years?

Rarely has a man committed a crime so profound that he will be labeled with an *ad hominem* term such as "Hitler." When that occurs, it will typically be a war crime or mass murder. Saddam Hussein, Osama bin Laden, Pol Pot. Despite the many individuals victimized, one could not even imagine a financial crime as the predicate for such a moniker. Bernard Madoff was the exception.

Madoff was a seemingly mild man who actually discouraged would-be investors from becoming his clients. Long before he reached age 70, when he was caught, he had constructed a Ponzi scheme. In his own words to his sons, it was "One Big Lie"—a lie of mammoth proportions. The victims were investors—individual, corporate, and charitable—that in many instances literally invested all of their money with him. All of it was gone, except what remained in the personal assets of Madoff's luxurious lifestyle.

So troubled were Madoff's own sons by his nightmarish revelation to them that they themselves turned him in to the U.S. Attorney. He was arrested amid considerable fanfare the very next day. We shall never really know the precise reason for their doing so. Was it absolute disgust with him for having victimized so many, including his own family? Was the arrest Madoff's own desire, which he communicated to them because the Ponzi scheme was about to collapse? Or did they selfishly seek to assure law enforcement that they—employed in the "family business"—weren't complicit?

Whatever motivated Madoff's sons, the unprecedented speed of his arrest for a white collar offense set into motion a panic among his largely aging investors. A trustee was immediately appointed; he would estimate combined losses to the investors as high as $60 billion—a sum unprecedented for Ponzi schemes.

These losses were not only the sums actually invested but also the investors' "expectation" interests. In other words, most investors had reinvested their "profits" believing that their accounts held not only their original investments but also the phantom annual profits that Madoff falsely reported as having been received by them—on which most investors paid their taxes (i.e., for dividends they never actually earned).

Those who withdrew money believing that they legitimately earned it also faced the prospect of a clawback from the trustee of those moneys received and sometimes already spent. For these thousands of good faith investors, not to mention the charities and donors who believed that they had contributed significantly to worthwhile charities, the name "Hitler" easily rolled off their lips. Ironically, some had actually survived Hitler's concentration camps a generation before.

But Madoff didn't end as did Hitler. Madoff was willing to face the music publicly, without demanding a trial. He pleaded guilty to multiple felony counts, with an immediate remand to jail by the judge, thus putting an end to his "house arrest" in the luxurious Manhattan penthouse he shared with his wife.

Given Madoff's crimes and his age when arrested, most any judge assigned to his case would make sure that he would never see the light of day once sentenced. Even if the judge were to sentence him to *only* 30 years in jail—basically, 1 year for each $2 billion of the fraud—Madoff would die well before completing his sentence.

The government recognized that the sentencing guideline for Madoff's crimes was 150 years. The government asked for 150 years or, alternatively, as its sentencing memorandum stated, "for a term that both would insure Madoff would remain in prison for life, and forcefully would promote general deterrence." The 150 years was obviously way beyond the life expectancy of Madoff and all of his victims and literally 125 years above the sentences to which the government pointed in white collar cases (e.g., Ebbers, Rigas, Israel, and Bennett).

Judge Chin, given that the government indicated that it would have been satisfied with a 35-year sentence, then did something unprecedented for a financial crime: he sentenced Madoff to 150 years. Surely the judge wasn't concerned that Madoff was a superman who could defy the odds given his or anyone's life expectancy. Nor, surely, did Judge Chin think that such a sentence would help reimburse the victims. So one wonders precisely what motivated him. Did he want to see the *Madoff* case as the paradigm for "the tough white collar sentence"?

And what other factors did he consider? In an unrelated case, Judge Chin used Google to help with fact finding. Basically, he went outside the court record. Did he also do that in *Madoff*? In deciding on the unprecedented sentence, did Judge Chin look beyond the four corners of the court record? Did he employ the Google search engine for what was surely the most important sentence he would ever impose?

Was Judge Chin moved by external beliefs implicating concepts of right and wrong, other philosophical or legal writings, or concepts of mercy or vengeance? If the death penalty could have been imposed, would Judge Chin have wanted to impose it? Or was he just going by the numbers: the guideline's calculus pointed to 150 years, and that's what he gave? What impact did the victims' testimony have? Did he seek or gain the counsel of colleagues or others?

Typically, when judges impose sentences, they ascend the bench with their mind virtually made up, to be changed only if a particular argument or statement alters the sentence's dynamic while they are on the bench. Was Judge Chin's mind made up here before he listened to the 12 victims who addressed him? If so, what purpose was served in letting those victims cry their hearts out? Was there a role for the victim statements beyond the actual sentence to be imposed?

More directly, was he influenced by Ms. Siegman, who told Judge Chin that after Madoff "announced to the world that he had stolen everything I had," "he refused to say another word to his victims"? Was it that she "shine[s] her shoes each night afraid that they will wear out"? Was it Ms. Fitzmaurice's appeal that "I cry every day when I see the look of pain and despair in my husband's eyes"? Was it the comment of Ms. Ebel, a 61-year-old widow, who told of her "horrible feeling that I had been pushed into the great black abyss, but could not indulge those paralyzing feelings too long"? Was it Ms. Lissauer's remark that "I used to think that it didn't matter if he got 150 years. What would that do for the victims? It wouldn't get their money back"? Or, finally, was it Mr. Ross's citation from Dante's *The Divine Comedy*, that fraud was the worst of all sins, and that the defrauder would find himself lower in the pits of hell than the violent sinner?

Did these remarks influence Judge Chin to impose a sentence far longer than life? Or was Judge Chin completely disciplined and unemotional—a judge who just saw the magnitude of the crime as so grotesque that it warranted a grotesque sentence?

The Dialogue

JC: Judge, before we turn directly to the *Madoff* case, let's explore this: Some years ago I represented the family of a deceased victim of a hit and run driver. The decedent was 60 years old and had left his dental office late one night, and jaywalked across the street. He was hit by a young woman driver who was probably speeding, but not recklessly. She hit him, his body rolled up onto the hood, and was pushed off into the oncoming lane where another driver ran him over. The first driver was about 21 years old. Probably panicked, she sped away from the scene, essentially leaving him to die. He probably died instantly, however, and the other driver stayed at the scene and called for an ambulance. Two hours later the first driver turned herself in. We prevailed on the district attorney to demand a felony plea for this young woman and to ask for jail time. The judge, however, hearing the facts decided to give her probation—not a crazy result given the precedents.

At sentence, however, my client, the widow, addressed the court. She expressed her anger at what the defendant had done and not done. At the last moment, she looked the defendant square in the eye and said: "I will never forgive you. I hope God never forgives you." In some ways, this was the worst punishment she would suffer. I shuddered and for a moment felt embarrassment by that comment, but then realized the widow needed to say that.

Is there a place for that kind of anger in a courtroom?

DC: Well, I think that whether there's a place for it or not, it's certainly there. And I think there probably is a place for it as long as it is received properly. Considered properly. Sentencing is such a difficult process. It's complex, and many things come into play. I think the victim's reaction, the victim's anger, is an appropriate consideration. The judge ought not give undue weight to it; but if a victim feels strongly or doesn't, it's probably something to put into the mix. I have no difficulty with including it in the mix of things.

JC: How about on the judge's part? Is it alright for a judge to feel anger toward a defendant?

DC: That's a little bit harder. I think a judge shouldn't feel anger in that sense. A judge who cares is more likely to get to the right answer, the just answer. So, it's certainly good for the judge to care. A judge who doesn't care—that's a problem. I think a good lawyer tries to get the judge to care. So, in that sense, yes—in the sense that the judge should feel strongly about it, and in that sense I think that's appropriate. To be angry, however, so that it clouds your weighing all the different factors, so that it interferes with the logic and the law, is not appropriate. And so it's a difficult thing.

I had a case where I was accused of being too emotional in sentencing. It was a 9/11 case. The defendant had been convicted of a passport fraud. He probably would have gotten a probationary sentence, but then he got the bright idea of pretending to have been killed on 9/11. And there was a lot of emotion. He was trying to take advantage of this horrible tragedy—really being selfish. Marshals and law enforcement were trying to deal with all of the fallout and here this guy is trying to capitalize on this. And defense counsel essentially accused me of being too emotional. I did feel strongly about it, but I didn't let the emotion cloud my judgment. But I think there is definitely room for these dynamics in the sentencing process—even on the part of the judge.

JC: Have you ever gotten angry? You used the word "emotional," but I'm asking about anger about a particular defendant's conduct. I don't mean the conduct where a defendant might dissemble in a courtroom, but about the underlying conduct that brought them to the courtroom.

DC: I'd have to say no. There are many occasions when I watch the news and hear these horrible stories where defendants rape and murder children. And while personally I'm not a proponent of the death penalty, I might say to myself, "If ever there's a place where the death penalty is appropriate, it's that case." I don't know if that's anger at what the defendant did. It certainly is a strong reaction. But I think when you make the decision in your own case, I think it's important to approach it in a somewhat different way than if you're just a citizen watching the news. You've got to factor in everything—make sure that everyone, including the defendant, the government and the public have an opportunity to be heard. So I think you approach it differently.

JC: My friend Professor Thane Rosenbaum at Fordham says—and I've read you quoted on it—that, essentially, the court process has no soul. That what you try to do is put to the side anger, for example, in order to create a pristine environment in the courtroom. Is there any merit to what he says?

DC: Well, I've been on two panels with him including on his new book "*Payback.*" I was also on a panel many years ago with U.S. Attorney Preet Bharara on Thane's earlier book, "*The Myth of Moral Justice.*" I believe on that panel I said that indeed the law does have a soul. Anyone who's been a trial lawyer over the years will see that there is an important role for emotion in the law. It permeates our rules of evidence. Concepts such as "excited utterances"—concepts that incorporate emotion. Summations to the jury can be powerful, dramatic presentations. And the whole concept of justice necessarily implicates having a soul. I think that if you have a soul you're more likely to achieve justice. There's certainly is a role for it, and it's there. So, to the extent that Thane says it's not there, I disagree. Perhaps he's more blunt and frank about things . . .

JC: Because he doesn't have to deal with the system.

DC: Yes, he's not part of the system. He doesn't have to deal with it. So he says we should have revenge. I say, I don't really want to call it "revenge," but the law does recognize the concept of retribution. Is there a difference between them? Maybe—but there certainly are lots of similarities.

JC: You seem a little uncomfortable with the word "anger." Were you angry at Bernard Madoff before the case was assigned to you, when you read about it in the paper like everybody else? Were you angry at him over his conduct?

DC: I don't think I was ever angry at him. I don't think I was angry at him when I read the newspaper or watched it on TV like any other citizen. I know I wasn't angry at him as a judge. I'm actually more likely to be angry in that sense at a violent crime. On the other hand, in the Madoff case one of the things I thought was that even though it was a financial crime, it wasn't bloodless. There were real victims—not just about money. So maybe there's not as clear a distinction as I might like to think.

JC: When you sentenced him you used the phrase that he was "extraordinarily evil." With no disrespect, that's sort of judgespeak, if there's such a word. I assume, based on the fact that you gave him 150 years sentence, you must have thought this was about the worst financial crime ever.

DC: I might agree with that. This crime went on for 20, 30 years. Thousands of people were victimized. An enormous breach of trust. It's hard to imagine a more egregious financial crime. The words "extraordinarily evil" popped into my head literally maybe just a half an hour before I took the bench. I had of course prepared hard for this and I had my remarks largely prepared in advance. But I was still struggling with the concept of retribution. I even had interns that morning finding me cases on retribution and the concept is that people should be sentenced according to their moral culpability—that a defendant should get his "just desserts." And those concepts are in the cases, and so that's when I thought that what he did, after having read several hundred letters and emails from victims, was extraordinarily evil.

JC: You used the word "retribution" during the sentence and you used it again now. What's the difference between retribution and revenge?

DC: I've struggled with that ever since I've read Thane's book. I don't know if there's a meaningful difference.

JC: So why don't you want to say revenge?

DC: I don't know. I think we're all reluctant to. Revenge conjures up notions of lynch mobs and mass justice and people taking law into their own hands. And so I think maybe it's a matter of degree. Those notions don't sit well with me. The system should take care of these things, not mobs.

JC: Which it did. But yet you don't like even using that phrase. I'm not talking about a bunch of vigilantes like in an old cowboy movie and the sheriffs take the guy out back and hang him. That's not what we're talking using the concept of revenge.

DC: Ira Sorkin, Madoff's lawyer, would say that what was happening was not that much different, that there was a public outcry. A professor from Fordham was quoted in the paper saying that I was pandering to the public with my sentence. So I don't know if there's much of a difference. But, in fact, no one resorted to mob justice. The victims appealed to the court and I felt a responsibility to the victims in doing what I ultimately did.

JC: What were you doing in giving him 150 years? Given the actuarial tables, a 30 year sentence would have done the trick if you were trying to keep him behind bars for life. He was 70 or 71 at the time. So what exactly were you doing?

DC: I wanted to send the strongest message possible.

JC: To whom?

DC: To the public. To others who would engage in similar crimes. An important part of the law is deterrence. A traditional goal of punishment is deterrence. It was certainly part of my thinking that he needed at least a sentence of 25, 30, 40 years by any measure. Anything above that wasn't going to hurt him in the sense that he was going to be in prison for the rest of his life anyway.

To me, doing 75 years, doing 50 years—when I had a potential of 150—would send a message of mercy here. I didn't want to send that message. Moreover, from a legal standpoint, the guideline range was actually 150 years. Anything less than 150 years would have been a below-guideline range. So for those of us in the business, when you sentence someone to a below-guideline range, there's a little bit of a message there, perhaps. I didn't want to send that message. It's ironic, because none of the counts carried a life sentence. And as it turned out the 150 years was perhaps more meaningful than a life sentence in this respect.

JC: Let me ask this. If you had given him 30 or 40 years and instead said these words: "I don't want you to ever see the light of day outside of a prison," would you perhaps have better have sent the message? Might such phraseology not have better helped give closure—if there ever is closure—to the victims?

DC: I don't know. It's not my style. When I sentence someone, I don't typically engage in such remarks or preach in that sense—such as "I don't want you to see the light of day." Some judges do—I guess it's a matter of personal preference. Would it have been more effective? I don't know.

JC: Would it be showing revenge for a judge to say that? There are judges, probably more in the state than federal system, I suppose, who use that kind of phraseology. Although there have been judges in this courthouse too who have.

DC: And I wouldn't say it would be wrong, but rather a matter of personal style. Would it have been more effective? I don't know. It's hard for me . . . I think the way it turned out was pretty effective. And not necessarily by design. If I had had the choice of giving him life, I probably would have. I don't know. But in the end the 150 years really wound up being, I thought, an effective message.

JC: I imagine your obituary will read that you gave Madoff 150 years. Is that something meaningful in your judicial career? You've since been elevated to the Circuit.

DC: Well, I hope that I was not elevated because of the sentence I gave to Bernie Madoff.

JC: I didn't mean to suggest that.

DC: I know. But my confirmation was actually delayed because of the *Madoff* case, in part because there was a thought—to some extent this is speculation—that if I did something that people didn't like it would have made it somewhat more difficult for me. I will, of course, forever be associated with the *Madoff* case, for better or worse. But I don't know that it's going to be because of the number. I would hope that more important than the number was that my goal from the beginning was to do justice, and not to let the case turn into a circus. I wanted it to be conducted in a dignified manner, in a way that was also respectful of Mr. Madoff's rights; that gave everyone a fair opportunity to be heard, including the victims. We weren't sure whether it would turn into a circus, with a mob showing up. I tried very hard to control things. I think people who were there thought that the proceedings were conducted in a just way.

JC: If there were a death penalty available for a white collar offense would the death penalty be perhaps appropriate for this case?

DC: I think not. Interestingly, I went to China last year and interest in the *Madoff* case remained. A woman had been convicted of a financial crime and was sentenced to death. A lot of people asked what I thought of the case. I wouldn't comment on a pending case. But I said that in the United States we don't give the death penalty for financial crimes, and that I agree with that notion.

JC: During the sentence you noted that nobody wrote letters or testimonials on Madoff's behalf, and said that was telling. Why was it telling?

DC: I've done a lot of sentences over the years. Certainly in white collar cases you see letters from family, friends and community attesting to the defendant's good deeds. Here there were none. I think that's because Madoff betrayed many charities that he was involved with. He couldn't make the argument that this was a one-time mistake, because it had gone on for so long. And I think the absence of such support showed how egregious his conduct was.

JC: Years ago I prosecuted a big deal political figure. The judge in that case was Judge [George] Pratt, later of the Second Circuit. He said he was more influenced in according leniency by letters he received—not from politicians or public officials who typically write them—but, for example, from old ladies that the defendant had helped cross the street and the like.

What if there were letters from people—it's hard to imagine someone writing a letter for Madoff, frankly—say, who wrote that he would visit the sick or, in fact, help old ladies cross the street. What effect could that possibly have had on the sentence in this case?

DC: Hard to say what impact it would have had in Madoff. But I once sentenced Oscar Wyatt, a Texas oil man. It was precisely that situation. I received about 200 letters. Many from politicians and prominent people. And like Judge Pratt, I didn't think they were worth that much. But there were a number from ordinary people—someone whose father was dying of cancer and Wyatt invited them to his estate to hunt. Not only did he let them come and use his property, he spent time with them, he had dinner with them, he gave of himself. There was a letter from one of his employees—a relatively low-level employee in his oil company who was hospitalized. He wrote about how Wyatt came to the hospital and sat with him. So it wasn't just using his money or influence. It was giving his time; really becoming personally involved with these folks in a way that touched me. And I wound up giving Mr. Wyatt a lower sentence. Now, if I had had similar letters . . .

JC: Would you then have given Madoff 120 years?

DC: I don't know. I certainly would have considered them, given them weight. And they would have made it harder for me to do 150 years. Not to say that I wouldn't have done it anyway. I don't know. But again, part of the mix that we take in and weigh.

JC: What could Madoff have done or said at sentence or in antici-
pation of sentence that would have changed your view? He did say all the
right stuff—basically what defendants typically say in such cases—didn't
he? What could he have said to you or the victims in the courtroom?

DC: Tough question. I don't know what he could have done. I do think
he wasn't completely remorseful. He was sad, but I don't think remorseful
based on what he said and how he said it. But again, given the egregious-
ness of the crime and all of the other factors, I don't know that I would
have been persuaded to do anything less than 150 years. And again, the
way it was set up as you point out, 120 years wouldn't have made much
difference. 140 years, 105 years.

JC: Forty years wouldn't have made a difference.

DC: But the point is once you make a decision that he should receive
a sentence that he should stay in prison for the rest of his life any number
above doesn't really make that much difference to him. And I don't know
that anything would have persuaded me to let him out after 12 years.

His attorney was really arguing that I do something like 12 years, maybe
20 years, and then maybe he has a chance of seeing the light of day. That's
an important concept to me. You want to give a defendant hope. Something
that will keep him going. No matter how evil. No matter what he's done.
But there comes a point when you say this defendant doesn't deserve that.
And that was one of the dynamics here. I don't know that anything could
have persuaded me to give him a sentence of 12 years or 15 years, where
he might have had a reasonable chance of seeing the light of day.

JC: Am I way off concluding that once he pleaded guilty you pretty
much knew, in your own mind, that the sentence would never let him out
of jail? Did you really need a probation report, submissions from the government, letters from the victims to know that that sentence you would
impose would keep him in jail? Whatever the number, whatever the theory,
whatever the code word—retribution, deterrence, revenge—once he pleaded
guilty he would be in jail for life?

DC: I didn't know. I didn't make up my mind until fairly late in the
process. In part that's the way we're trained. There is a process one must
adhere to, and part of it is to give the parties a chance to be heard. Someone
is convicted of murder. Do I know immediately that I'm going to sentence

him to life? The chances are I know he's going to get something very, very significant, probably life. But again, I'm not supposed to make that decision until I have considered all the materials and given the parties a chance to be heard.

For me, I don't think those are just words. I believe in the process and the process contemplates doing an investigation, finding out if there might be something that could change my mind. I did sentence someone in a murder case, by the way, and I gave him something less than life even though my initial reaction was life, because of the unusual circumstances of that case. You never know. You do want to see the entire picture. Of course, we're human beings. So . . .

JC: That's what I was driving at.

DC: We are human beings. And sometimes there is an immediate gut reaction to something. And I wouldn't be honest if I said that doesn't happen. It does happen, most of the time. But we also know enough about the process to keep an open mind. When we come to oral argument on appeals, we all have a pretty good idea of how we'll come out. Does that mean the lawyer can't convince us? Most of the time the lawyer can't. But there are cases where there's an argument we haven't considered, where perhaps in a close case the argument makes a difference. So perhaps part of being prepared is coming up with a tentative conclusion. But part of being a judge—and when you talk about how judges make decisions—is having to keep an open mind, at least to some degree, until you've heard all the arguments. It's like in a trial. There are highs and lows. Day one goes great for the government, but day two is not so good. You can't make up your mind at the beginning.

JC: Judge, you sat on a very collegial district court. I'm sure you ran into colleagues after the case was assigned to you, who might say about this particular defendant, for example, "Hang him high." Or, "Let him have it." It's inconceivable in a case of that dimension that people weren't saying things to you like that.

DC: Not our culture. I don't believe I got a single comment from any colleague, whether it was "Hang him high" or some other suggestion or hint in the days leading up to this sentence.

JC: Is that because they know you're unapproachable with that kind of thing?

DC: No, I think that's not the culture. In all these years, I never called a colleague to say: "I've got this tough sentencing. What do you think?" And I don't believe I ever got such a call from a colleague. There were times, when you go to the judges' lunch room and kick things around. I don't recall people talking sentencing. Maybe I got one phone call from a junior judge who hadn't done this or that before, and might seek guidance. But it's simply not part of our culture.

JC: It used to be in the Eastern District [of New York] that there were sentencing panels, before the sentencing guidelines. Say, Judge Chin was the sentencing judge, and Judges Nickerson and Weinstein were on the panel. With the probation officer present, the three judges would offer their respective opinions on the proper sentence. That might influence Chin, or not. Do you think that kind of thing valuable?

DC: Would it be valuable to hear what colleagues think? Probably yes. Would I participate? Probably no.

JC: Why not?

DC: It's the nature of it. It's my responsibility ultimately. That's part of what I'm saying, and it's not just me. I've got the guidelines—which of course are based on the experience country-wide—and it reflects the common experience. We have that as guidance. I've got the very detailed, very thorough, very helpful probation report. I have submissions from the government and defense counsel. I see the defendant. I have all of this information already. And the fact is that there's a lot of room for disagreement, so I don't know how helpful the thoughts of colleagues would be.

Before I sentence I would often run it by my law clerks and interns who otherwise didn't participate in my sentencing preparation. I might say—here are the facts, what do you think? But it was more just to hear what individuals who don't really have experience think. It's very much an individualized decision. And on appeal we recognize that there is a fair amount of room for disagreement. So we do defer to the trial judge as long as the sentence falls within the range of reasonableness. But that range is pretty wide.

JC: How about this hypothetical: Assume that Madoff turned out to be a sort of Robin Hood figure. He had stolen all this money in the scheme but, aside from using some for an opulent lifestyle, he took the proceeds and contributed it, obviously without the approval of his investors, to bona fide charities in Uganda or China or Israel (as his victims were largely Jewish). If it turned out that that's what he did—yes, he did keep a fair share for himself—but he actually gave the bulk to charity, how much would that have influenced you?

DC: It would have been helpful to him—it might have made it a little bit harder. But ultimately, of course, it wouldn't have been right. You can't do that. But it would alter the mix, somewhat.

JC: Would it have helped him escape a life sentence?

DC: I don't think so. If you take out all the harm, then it's a different case. But in your example, people are still harmed. Yes, you're taking someone's pot of money that they were saving to send their kids to college, and you're giving it to a hospital in China. That wouldn't make it anywhere close to being right. In fact, he had multiple country club memberships that cost hundreds of thousands of dollars a year. He had—I don't remember how many—two, three yachts with full time crews. He had multiple homes. So in fact it didn't happen that way. A lot of the money was being given to other investors along the way, investors who wanted their money back. He would have to give it back to them from money that he took from other people. And then when things soured there wasn't enough money to cover the people who wanted their money back. So he wasn't using it for those charitable causes. And if he had, I might have seen some letters from people.

JC: So let me take the hypothetical up a notch considerably.

DC: You're trying to make this hard for me here.

JC: Well you're a tough witness, Judge. Let's assume that you're intending to give him effectively a life sentence. And he communicates to you through his lawyer—before sentence or after you've given him a 150 year sentence—that most of money that he has stolen is in offshore accounts that the SIPC trustee, the bankruptcy trustee, the victims, the U.S. Attorney, the SEC will never find. And they each agree that they will never find it. All of those agencies, trustees, and the victims uniformly urge you, saying: "Judge, he wants his sentence reduced to no more 10 years, and will give the money back." What would you do?

DC: If, indeed, he has enough money to pay back victims so that their losses are substantially lessened, that would be an important fact. It would be important because the harm would be significantly mitigated. It would show something about his state of mind, his remorsefulness. And if he had the ability to do that, that would make a difference, and that might cause me to give something less than the equivalent of a life sentence. It still would have been a crime that went on for a long time, and the breach of trust would still have been enormous. But it would have helped a lot in terms of the harm to the victims, his acceptance of responsibility, his effort to try to cooperate and undo some of the damage. That would have been a significant consideration for me.

JC: What about the likely criticism from some quarters that you were letting him buy justice?

DC: I don't know that he's buying justice. It's not the way I would look at it.

JC: Really? He's not buying justice?

DC: Because then he's not deserving of a longer sentence. He is not buying justice because he's actually making up for some of what he did. The harder question is that Madoff surely wanted to do that, but just didn't have the means anymore. And so then what? I don't know.

JC: Would you ever give thought to talking to victims after the case is over and telling them, "Hey, we did the best we could under the circumstances. This is the way the system works." It might help them deal with the feeling that the system is somewhat effete—it's just doling out a long sentence, but not really accomplishing much. Did you ever think that that might be a valuable component, something that Professor Rosenbaum sort of talks about?

DC: I don't know that I would do it. I would certainly try hard to give every victim who wanted it an opportunity to be heard as part of the process. The opportunity to speak. And my comments, of course, are directed to them in part, but that's on the record as part of the process. Now would I afterwards, off the record, go talk to victims? I'd be reluctant. Does it become an *ex parte* conversation whereby the defendant is deprived of an opportunity to participate? It would almost have to be an informal thing. And I'm not sure that I would do it for that reason. It's hard to draw the line. I'm comfortable speaking to you today on the record. I'm comfortable talking to Ben Weiser of the New York Times. I'm comfortable being on Professor Rosenbaum's panel. But I'm not sure that I would want to address a room full of victims. There may be some emotional people, there may be angry people still who thought maybe I should have eliminated the SEC as an agency. So who knows?

You've just got to think about these things. I don't know what the Marshal's service would think. There are judges who regularly go to prison to talk to prisoners. I do see part of my role as a judge as being out there and talking to the public, in particular young lawyers, bar association speeches. I'm just a little reluctant to go address a group of victims, in the *Madoff* case, for example. There's also ongoing litigation, so I don't know.

JC: In the unrelated so-called yellow rain hat case, *U.S. v. Bari*, you were deciding a supervised release revocation proceeding, and there was some factual issue in the case. You asked your clerk to Google the frequency of the use of yellow rain hats in New York, seeing it relevant to your factual determination. The defendant argued on appeal, albeit unsuccessfully, that you had improperly gone beyond the record to search out that fact.

That said, were there facts in the *Madoff* case or opinions by journalists that you read that may have subtly influenced your views of the case? In the yellow rain hat case, you told the parties that you had done that, so they had a chance to explain why your research was in error. In *Madoff*, though, was there something you saw or read that could have subtly influenced your thinking?

DC: Not to my knowledge. Again, we learn that our decision making should be based on the record before us. If for some reason I want to expand on that record, I would certainly tell the parties about it to give them a chance. If I hadn't done that in the yellow rain hat case I might have been reversed, but my instinct always is if there is something like that . . .

JC: But, frankly, if you hadn't told the parties in the yellow rain hat case what you did, the parties wouldn't have known about it.

DC: That's true. But part of my decision making process is that if I have a thought I do want to share it with counsel and give them a chance to tell me that I'm wrong—to give them a chance to do their own Google search. In the *Madoff* case, of course I was reading the newspapers and watching the news reports. I don't know if there were editorials, but there must have been some editorials before the sentencing. And yes, I read those things. I don't stop watching the news or reading the newspapers when I've got a case pending. But I can say with confidence that my decision was based on what I read as part of the case.

Over the years I've had a lot of high profile cases. Megan's Law, Million Youth March, the Google Books settlement, where there's lots of stuff written about these cases. And I enjoy reading it. I also know that reporters don't always get it right. Something will happen in my courtroom, and it will be reported on the next day, and it's not quite right sometimes. So you take it all with a grain of salt.

JC: Do you ever take the opportunity to say: "I read something about something that's going on in my courtroom, and what they wrote is wrong?"

DC: I usually don't get involved. I don't respond to comments. There are crazy people writing comments online. I don't do that. One sort of grey area, particularly these days with the internet, is reading a Law Review article. Now you have lots of Law Review-type columns. I've got Aereo now. The copyright case. There is tons of stuff being written about Aereo by copyright professors, and I enjoy reading that stuff. Will they give me ideas? If a professor writes a law review article that gives me an idea, is it wrong to consider that? I don't think so. I think that's a little bit different.

But you'd have to plug it into the case and all of the other briefs. It's a little different now because on appeal I can't just say to the lawyers: "Look, I've read this law review article yesterday, what do you think?" If I'm on trial I can do that. I can help make the record and now the record is what it is. That kind of thing, I think, would fall into the category of law review, law journal article, which I think traditionally we've always been able to take account of.

JC: Let me ask one last question which derives from my own practice. I once had a case with a then young prosecutor in this district, now a distinguished judge. He was interviewing my client as a potential cooperator. The client was somewhat odd. I called the prosecutor the next day to see how it went. He said: "Well, it was somewhat interesting, but your client is a freak." The prosecutor's colleague was on the line and tried to poo-poo the comment lest I be bothered by its directness. I told them both not to be bothered, because I ideally want a prosecutor to tell me exactly what's going on in his mind. If he tells me what's going on in his mind, I can deal with and maybe change his mind somehow or other. Should judges do that—say exactly what's on their mind so that the lawyer can try to refute it?

DC: It depends on the circumstances. In some courts, judges release draft opinions and they give the lawyers a chance to comment on them. Not here, but out west in some courts. I wouldn't do that. I think I'd want to issue an opinion, and that's it. If someone wants to move for reconsideration because I got something wrong, that's fine. But I don't think I would release a draft and let lawyers comment. I think it's good for a judge during oral argument to, within reason, give some preliminary views and give the lawyers a chance to address them. If I have concerns, I like to focus. So part of the process of helping the lawyers focus is giving them some idea of what's troubling you—perhaps your tentative thinking. So I think it's a useful thing.

JC: So in *Madoff*, his lawyer had asked in his papers for a 12-year sentence. What if you were to tell him when you got on the bench: "Mr. Sorkin, I've got to tell you going in, you're way off with that. That's not happening. You need to up the ante considerably. In fairness to you and your client, I need to tell you that what you're proposing is just not going to work."

DC: I wouldn't do that. Sentencing is a little bit different. There are some sentencings where I might say I'm inclined to do this. But that usually would be, I'm inclined to be at the bottom of the range, or I'm inclined to impose the mandatory minimum. So you're not going to do any better than that, in that sense. Like in the old days when the guidelines were mandatory I could say based on what I've read that I'm inclined to be at the bottom of the range. That's a little bit different from this scenario. I wouldn't want to say to counsel, "By the way, I'm thinking high end."

JC: Why not?

DC: It doesn't sit right with me. I'd want to give him a chance to be heard before I reached that conclusion. Whereas it's different if it's the government. The government could make arguably the same argument, but there you're giving the benefit of the doubt to the defendant. So I see that as a different circumstance.

JC: Like I said, Judge, you're a tough witness.

Chapter 3

Judge Martin Feldman

[N]ot all trains are dangerous. Not all airplanes are going to crash. I looked at the tragedy of the DeepWater Horizon as a horrible incident in an industry in which, statistically, it was immensely rare for something like that to happen. And that's how I approached the case.
—Judge Martin Feldman, April 17, 2013

Since being appointed as a U.S. District Judge for the Eastern District of Louisiana by President Ronald Reagan in 1983, Judge Martin Leach-Cross Feldman has presided over many important matters. Notably, less than two years after being confirmed, he denied a Ukrainian seaman's request for asylum in an opinion issued only days before President Reagan was to meet with Soviet Union President Mikhail Gorbachev in 1985. Conservatives criticized his decision, decrying it as the end to the Reagan Revolution.

Demanding, smart, and exacting in the courtroom, Judge Feldman writes scholarly and comprehensive opinions so that his readers (including the Fifth Circuit Court of Appeals) understand his rationale, regardless of whether they agree with it.

None of the cases he presided over in 27 years on the bench drew as much attention and amassed as much controversy as his opinions in the DeepWater Horizon case. Not only did he enjoin the Obama administration's six-month moratorium on deep-sea drilling, but he also refused to recuse himself in the face of aggressive assertions that he held stock in, and was thus beholden to, the oil industry.

Born in St. Louis, Missouri, in 1934, Judge Feldman relocated to New Orleans to attend Tulane University and Law School and has worked in New Orleans since. Upon his graduation from law school in 1957, he became the first law clerk to the legendary John Minor Wisdom, who had been appointed to the Fifth Circuit by President Dwight D. Eisenhower and is credited as being one of the Southern judges who helped end segregation.

After his two-year clerkship, Judge Feldman spent more than 20 years in private practice in New Orleans, traveling the country representing businesses primarily in antitrust, securities, and tax litigations. He also served as a Reserve Captain in the U.S. Army Judge Advocate General's Corps from 1957 until 1963. Judge Feldman is a regular lecturer and a member of the Advisory Committee of the American Association for the Advancement of Science and was for decades chair of the Fifth Circuit District Judges Committee on Pattern Jury Instructions.

In 2010 Judge Feldman was appointed by Chief Justice John Roberts to serve a seven-year term on the controversial, 11-member, Foreign Intelligence Surveillance Court, which operates in secrecy to review applications for warrants related to national security, such as those that involve foreign terrorists.

Judge Feldman sits in New Orleans, Louisiana.

DeepWater Horizon

When a judge is assigned a case, particularly one of national interest, and there is public controversy over his presiding—even if the public sentiment favoring recusal (i.e., that the judge remove himself from the case) might be unwarranted under applicable law—should the judge nonetheless exercise the discretion to step aside, difficult as that decision might be?

On April 21, 2010, America woke up to a nightmare—one of catastrophic proportions. The night before, just before 10 p.m., CDT, DeepWater Horizon, an ultra-deepwater, semisubmersible offshore oil rig operated by British Petroleum (BP), which was drilling in the Gulf of Mexico, suffered an explosion, igniting a fireball visible from 35 miles away. Eleven crew were killed immediately.

But it was not the horrible, almost unimaginably painful, deaths of those crewmen that caused the great turbulence with which the Obama administration and the courts would be forced to deal. Rather, it was that the resulting fire could not be extinguished, such that two days later DeepWater Horizon sank—leaving the well gushing 5,000 to 60,000 barrels per day and causing the largest offshore oil spill in U.S. history. While the president and his environmental team stood on the sidelines seemingly helpless, the oil spill would continue until July 15, when it was temporarily capped.

It was not until September 19, 2010, over five months after the initial explosion, that DeepWater Horizon was declared permanently dead. Putting aside the overall devastation and environmental impact, the financial cost to businesses in the Gulf states remains incalculable even today.

The DeepWater Horizon crisis, however, did not arrive in a vacuum. Since 1990, each U.S. president had vacillated on the complicated issue of offshore drilling given the competing concerns of environmental security and energy independence and the attendant political influences, particularly in the wake of 9/11. In fact, on March 31, 2010, just 20 days before the explosion, President Obama had announced that he was opening new areas in U.S. coastal waters for offshore drilling for gas and oil.

It was ironic that he did so, given his administration's seeming inability to stop the BP "spill," to the dismay of America, and particularly the Gulf states whose shores were rapidly becoming thick with bands of oil slick. The president needed to act forcefully. So on May 30, 2010, after the spill had continued unceasingly for 40 days, Interior Secretary Ken Salazar issued a six-month moratorium on *all* deep-water offshore drilling on the Outer Continental Shelf. Given the impact of such an extraordinary injunction on drilling in the region—way beyond a ban against BP—a lawsuit to invalidate the moratorium was inevitable. Plaintiffs would surely bring that lawsuit in a Gulf state, strategizing that judges in that region would be more sympathetic to a claim that the moratorium was an overreaction to the BP spill that would paralyze the local economy so heavily dependent on oil and gas drilling. Specifically, that lawsuit would argue that the secretary did not have the authority to issue the ban.

When the case was randomly assigned to Judge Martin Feldman in New Orleans, Louisiana, it immediately seemed on its face to favor the plaintiffs—that is, Hornbeck Offshore Services, LLC and 40 other companies involved in the oil and gas drilling industry. Hornbeck owned and operated a fleet of vessels that support deep-water exploration, holding contracts with nearly all of the operators of the 33 wells closed by the moratorium.

Judge Feldman had attended law school at Tulane University, clerked on the Fifth Circuit in New Orleans, and practiced law there. Not a native, his roots were nonetheless deep in the Gulf Coast. Perhaps most comforting to the plaintiffs, though, Judge Feldman—not that a judge can or should be judged as to how he will decide cases by who selected him—was appointed to the bench by Ronald Reagan, a doctrinaire hardliner who opposed excessive governmental regulation. Going into the case, then, Hornbeck et al. seemed well positioned with Judge Feldman—surely better than if their case were filed, for example, in Montana, San Francisco, or Boston before a judge with no roots in the Gulf, or one appointed to the court by President Carter, Clinton or, indeed, for that matter, Obama. The government's lawyers could not have been pleased.

The results reinforced their concerns. On June 22, 2010, Judge Feldman granted plaintiffs' preliminary injunction motion and ordered that the administration could not enforce the blanket moratorium. In response, the administration rescinded the moratorium and issued a new one, which Judge Feldman likewise rejected. Dispensing with the government's claim that issues surrounding the first moratorium were moot because it had issued a second, superseding, moratorium, Judge Feldman said this in a September 1, 2010, decision:

> Because this Court has determined that the process leading to the first moratorium lacks probity; because this Court has determined that no rational nexus exists between the tragic DeepWater Horizon blowout and placing an attainder of universal culpability on every deep water rig operator in the Gulf of Mexico; because this Court has determined that the first moratorium is invalid in law; and because the Interior Secretary's second moratorium arguably fashions no substantial changes from the first moratorium, the government has failed to circumvent the voluntary cessation exception to mootness.

Accordingly, the defendant's motion to dismiss or alternatively for a stay, is DENIED without prejudice.

In other words, Judge Feldman would not permit any moratorium on drilling to remain in place. Thus, the moratorium was at an end. But that was not enough for the plaintiffs. Upon their motion, Judge Feldman found the government in contempt and responsible for more than $500,000 in legal fees (this determination was subsequently reversed by the appellate court in a split decision).

When Judge Feldman set the initial moratorium aside on June 24, 2010, questions had been raised about his remaining on the case when it turned out that he owned stock in Allis-Chalmers Energy Inc.—a company that services deep-water drilling operations in the Gulf and elsewhere. In fact, six Democrat U.S. senators wrote Senator Patrick J. Leahy, Chairman of the Judiciary Committee, complaining that Judge Feldman's opinion showed "a high level of support for offshore drilling . . . suggesting that oil and gas drilling was 'simply elemental' to Gulf communities." They expressed concern that his ruling "may have been influenced by his extensive stock-holdings in energy and oil companies that would be financially impacted by the moratorium." And that Judge Feldman sold stock in Exxon Mobil just hours before the moratorium ruling also troubled them—purported evidence of his own recognition of his conflict.

These senators, though, didn't end their complaint with Judge Feldman. They quoted an Associated Press story of June 6, 2010, that 37 of the active or senior judges in key Gulf Coast districts in Louisiana, Texas, Alabama, Mississippi, and Florida "have links to oil, gas and related energy industries"—including stock or bond ownership in BP, PLC, Halliburton, or Transocean—and that they receive royalties from oil and gas production wells. The senators called for an investigation of what they believed to be a widespread conflict, and demanded that a protocol be developed so that judges who derive income from companies that benefit from offshore drilling not decide cases that will affect the future of such drilling.

Notwithstanding this outcry, the government never sought Judge Feldman's recusal; that was left to various environmental groups who intervened in the case and demanded that he step down so another judge could decide the issues. Judge Feldman saw no need to do so and denied the motion summarily in a one-paragraph order. That decision was never reversed or even appealed.

The issue is joined thus: Put the niceties of recusal standards aside. Also, put aside whether Judge Feldman's decision to not disqualify himself was totally justifiable on the law: he truly believed and articulated on the record that he could be fair to both sides notwithstanding his former stockholdings in "Big Oil."[1] Nonetheless, why would a thoughtful judge, in the glare of the spotlight over handling a monumental case (and the inevitable and seemingly never-ending press) decide to keep it despite seemingly reasonable questions about "appearance"? He would surely know that if his decision held for a party with which his personal interests seemed to be financially allied, it might be viewed as suspect by an appellate court, and by the public at large, precisely because of the "appearance" issue that he himself allowed by denying it.

Should a district judge yield to arguments that hearing a particular case may create an appearance of impropriety and disqualify himself, especially if he has not yet expended any meaningful time and effort into the case when he became aware of the "conflict" question? Should he do so even though he has no question in his own mind that he can be fair? Should it matter to him that a district judge's decisions—particularly on factual issues—deserve a considerable amount of deference on appeal? Was he concerned about how his colleagues would react if he stepped aside? And how much did Judge Feldman—a long-tenured judge with extensive experience—perceive all of this when there was a public outcry over his presiding over this critical case?

The Dialogue

JC: Judge, before we talk about the DeepWater Horizon Moratorium case, I was wondering this: You practiced for a fair amount of time before

---

1. Judge Feldman held stock in Exxon, which he did not know about and sold before he issued his opinion.

you were appointed to your judgeship. I wonder if you had the same experience as have I and others who litigate. That is, once a case is filed by you or your opponent, but before you learn which judge is assigned, there exists an almost surreal moment awaiting that assignment. The judge assigned can affect very significantly not only the tone and tenor of the litigation, but maybe the actual result. It's almost a game of Russian roulette. In some criminal cases, for example, especially where the sentence means everything, depending on which judge in the courthouse is assigned, the sentence can range from one end of the spectrum to the other. Was that your experience when you practiced?

MF: Yes. We always thought about who the judge might be of course as part of the assessment of litigation risk. My work was basically on the side of a company in the field of antitrust and securities litigation. Most of my work, with one exception, was in Federal courts somewhere around the country. I did some tax litigation too. Practicing law before the internet age, we didn't have the instant information feed that you have now. We were always interested in who the judge might be as a function of litigation risk. I can't speak so much for state court litigation because I didn't do that much. Most of my work was in Federal court; and even though the bench was smaller than now, we always paid a lot of attention to who the judge would be. Whether a judge kept a timely schedule, whether we could look forward to that being kept. Because if you're a busy litigator and a judge is not known for keeping to the schedule they'd set then you've got to go worry about something else and not that case. So mainly to the extent of making some risk assessment.

JC: Besides the procedural aspects of keeping to a schedule and the like, the judge who would be assigned to a case could really make a huge difference in the ultimate handling of the case and the result in the case, don't you think?

MF: Yes, I do. I don't know if the concern was as prominent then as now. There is a greater diversity now on the Federal bench than then. Most of the judges who I came across were typically cut from the same cloth. They were either a little to the right or left of center, but they were pretty much the same. I did do some white collar crime cases too—tax fraud, construction fraud, stuff like that. In that area, yes, the judge made an abundant difference. Because sentencing was so open-ended you had judges who were all over the lot. That's for sure.

JC: In some state systems there's actually a preemptory challenge allowed to litigants—that if X judge is assigned to the case, a litigant can say "You know what, I don't want X." And it goes back into the wheel and whoever comes out becomes the judge, unless there is some particular ground for recusing him too.

MF: I never had the benefit of that when I practiced law.

JC: Would that be something worthwhile in the Federal system?

MF: It certainly smacks of forum shopping, which I don't like. I would be disinclined to support that.

JC: You were appointed by President Reagan, who was well known for being anti-government overregulation. Was there a so-called litmus test presented to you when you were being cleared by the Justice Department?

MF: No, I was not asked a single substantive question that pertained to being a federal judge. The President called me on September 8, 1983. I had been in Washington maybe once or twice at the Justice Department with the attorneys who reviewed nominees. After the President called me, a month and four days later, I took the oath of office.

JC: Given your appointment by President Reagan and his philosophy concerning big government, would a litigant be wise to be somewhat concerned if you were assigned to his case where a claim of overregulation would be the principal issue in the case?

MF: I don't know what the concern of lawyers or litigants might be if a case is assigned to Feldman. I would hope that they know that no matter which President appointed me or what issue would be before me, that I will be nothing but fair and impartial to both sides. Now, obviously there are a lot of normative issues in the law. Laws are made by humans who are flawed, and there are judges who have to decide those issues. And maybe we're flawed too. But I and the judges with whom I'm friendly, don't sit down and say "Well, this is a case involves regulation. I'm against overregulation. Therefore, before I even look at the facts, read the briefs or consider the arguments, this is how I'm going to vote." I don't do that and I would hope that lawyers know that.

JC: So let's turn to the DeepWater Horizon moratorium case [the "Moratorium," hereinafter]. When that case was assigned to you, you knew that this was the biggest energy case in the country at the time, and that the considerations were absolutely significant. Weren't you concerned about the potential consequences if you declared the six month Moratorium invalid, as you did, and a similar tragedy occurred again?

MF: No. And the reason, as I explained in my opinion, was that not all trains are dangerous. Not all airplanes are going to crash. I looked at the tragedy of the DeepWater Horizon as a horrible incident in an industry in which, statistically, it was immensely rare for something like that to happen. And that's how I approached the case.

JC: Yes, but at the same time, if something so horrendous had reoccurred, that would surely be the judgment about you for the rest of your judicial career. That would be your obituary—that you invalidated the Moratorium and resultantly tragedy struck again.

MF: I would feel awful about that, but not because of a bad obituary. I have life tenure. I took an oath to be fair and impartial to the rich and the poor. And that's the way I approach every case. I would have felt terrible, but I would not have been intimidated into not deciding the way I decided simply fearing what could happen down the road.

JC: When this case was rolled out to you, you knew that the President and his Administration were in a tight spot—that they had not been able to repair the blowout. Given those circumstances, why didn't you feel that the President and Secretary Salazar were entitled to more deference? Obviously their experts, to some extent, believed that the Moratorium was essential. Why didn't you feel the need to accord the President such deference?

MF: The credibility of the experts' reports themselves was a big issue. Credibility is always an issue for a district judge. There had been some misrepresentations, not once but several times in my court, to me, about peer review. These were misrepresentations to me in open court by underlings at the Justice Department, in the presence of the personal counsel to the Interior Secretary.

JC: Describe those misrepresentations, if you recall them.

MF: I recall them vividly. When the so-called report came out that justified the first Moratorium there were statements saying that all these things had been peer-reviewed by some eight scientists, who later publicly said "We not only didn't peer-review them, we're not in favor of the Moratorium." Second time around, the representation was made that "What we meant was that the data was peer-reviewed but the substance of the report wasn't." That was untrue. And finally, it came out that someone on the White House staff actually changed the report and added, without basis whatsoever, that it had been peer-reviewed by eight scientists.

So there was a large, very serious question of credibility. Beyond that, after the first Moratorium there was argument in the Fifth Circuit in which, I'm told—I wasn't there—by one of my staffers who was, that one judge on the Fifth Circuit said "You don't seem to care what the Federal judiciary does." The response was "We don't." I confronted counsel in my second hearing and asked about that. The only response was "We weren't at the Fifth Circuit argument."

JC: What could they have meant by "We don't care what the judiciary does?"

MF: Mr. Salazar, the Interior Secretary, was already publicly making statements that he intended to put a second moratorium in place.

JC: Do you think the government was operating in bad faith or making the situation appear worse than it was?

MF: I don't know that. All I know is what I know from the case that was before me. Serious misrepresentations were made which affected the credibility of the basis for the Moratoriums themselves.

JC: Why do you think the President and Secretary Salazar wanted the Moratorium?

MF: I don't know. I'd have to make a political judgment, and I'm not willing to do that.

JC: Don't make the political judgment—just please explain what possibly could have been going through their minds.

MF: I don't want to speculate. I don't want to accuse the President and Salazar of something that may or may not be true. And that would just be my personal opinion. So it's not relevant to my duties as a Federal judge.

JC: Did you have the impression that they wanted to be able to say for the Administration, "We wanted a Moratorium, the courts said no, that the Moratorium was no good. We tried hard to avoid a reoccurrence and the courts wouldn't allow it. You can't blame us." Was that their goal?

MF: I don't know what went through their minds. What I've said publicly in my opinions was that the conduct and the attitude of the Interior Secretary was very dismissive of the Federal judiciary. I still believe that. Whatever their political agenda was, whatever they hoped to sell to the public, whatever they hoped to say about Judge Feldman, and they said pretty nasty things, makes no difference to me, and I have no opinion about it. I won't speculate as a private citizen about their motives. As a Federal judge I found that the evidence lacked a good deal of believability. That's what I based my opinions on.

JC: Should the government have done something different than they did? We can assume, can't we, that at least part of what they were trying to do was to avoid a reoccurrence?

MF: That's what they said. But the data, as I best recall, showed that shallow water drilling, which went unnoticed in their activities, had the same issues that deep water drilling had. As a matter of fact, in November of that year, there was an explosion out here—a shallow water explosion. So I don't know what their agenda was. They had been accused of being anti-oil industry, being "green," not wanting the oil industry to succeed. I have no idea. All I know is that I was satisfied from what I heard in several court proceedings that they had not been forthcoming with me and that their presentation lacked credibility.

JC: Did you give any thought to bringing the parties into chambers and saying, "Guys, you're pushing this too far. Why not narrow the Moratorium to something I might approve?"

MF: Nobody requested a settlement or status conference. It's hard to remember all of the conferences I've had in this room, but I don't recall anything like that. Even in meeting with the lawyers in the two cases, I don't recall that ever coming up. Nor did I sense—because I often become active in settlements—any desire on the part of either side wanting to do anything but fight to a resolution.

JC: So if a party said "Judge, we'd like to talk to you?"

MF: I will always do that.

JC: Had they shown interest, what would you have recommended to the government to accomplish its purported goals, and what might pacify the plaintiffs?

MF: I don't know. Some of these settlement conferences or mediations take varying turns depending on the agenda of each side, or how each side sees their litigation risk. And that's how I assess whether a case can be settled. I have a reputation for having some skills in mediation. But I had no sense that that was of interest to either side. To be fair to the government, I didn't sense that Hornbeck was interested either. And I certainly didn't get that sense from the government. My sense was that the government was on a mission, and they were going to see it through. But I would have certainly explored the possibility of resolving things amicably if I had had any sense that the parties wanted to.

JC: I take it you were reading editorials that were critical of the court not approving the Moratorium?

MF: I've had 30 years of favorable journalism and unfavorable journalism. I can honestly say that I've never read a piece, nice or un-nice about me, that has ever reflected much beyond ignorance. So I don't pay any attention.

JC: Even the nice ones?

MF: Even the nice ones. I don't pay any attention to the media. None whatsoever. I think their understanding of what we do is sadly limited. They go for bullet points and not substance. Good or bad. Some of the media wrote stories about me that I owned oil stocks. Well, I owned oil stocks that had nothing to do with the case. And in the one instance I did, when I had the case under submission, my broker called me to let me know that I owned Exxon. I told him to sell at the opening of the market while I was still working on the opinion. I didn't even know how much of it I had, or whether I had made a profit or loss. I just said "sell"—because I can't own anything that is affected by the litigation. But that didn't stop Time magazine or papers in Detroit or wherever from saying "Oh, he's a toad of the oil industry." They're all ignorant, and I don't pay any attention to them. None. Absolutely none. Nice or un-nice.

JC: But in addition to the articles, the "Green Groups" sought to intervene and seek your disqualification. The government didn't seek your disqualification. Did you have any understanding as to why the Green Groups, the Sierra Club and others did, but not the government?

MF: And some of the environmentalists did not. Some did. I think the ones who did were forum shopping—looking for someone whom they thought would look more favorably upon their causes.

JC: What about the fact that there had been a hoopla about your stock ownerships, even though not directly related to the plaintiffs and the litigation?

MF: And which, by the way, at the time of the case I did not own.

JC: Yes. But there is an "appearance" question about your refusal to recuse yourself, which you did in very short summary order. Did you consider that because Rachel Maddow, for example, and other commentators were calling for your scalp, that maybe it was better to just put the case back into the wheel and let a colleague handle it, rather than have your judgment questioned in the public eye?

MF: Let me make two very clear points. Number one, I don't care about the public eye. Number two, to recuse myself just because it might be inconvenient to read, hear or see things being said about me would be unfair to my colleagues. And so the answer to your question is flatly no. That's not something I would ever consider or even worry about. Within two years of my appointment my first important case to decide was one against Ronald Reagan—the Ukrainian Seaman case. A week before Reagan was going to meet Gorbachev. I don't care about public perceptions. And I don't care about the media. Period.

JC: That's noble, I suppose. But do you think that that's a view shared by most of your colleagues?

MF: You'd have to ask them. I'm speaking only for Marty Feldman and how I feel about the oath I took. And how I feel that all Federal judges should be. Not just me. How do they feel? I know some pretty wonderful people on the courts and I think they feel the same way I do.

JC: When you have an important case in the public domain, such as the Moratorium, do you confer with a confidant, maybe a judge or lawyer you respect, and say: "I'd like to pick your brain. What do you think about this?"

MF: No.

JC: Would that be wrong?

MF: It's not something I feel I need to do. I don't think it would be wrong but it's just not something I do. I'm satisfied that the oath I took was my oath and I'll do the best I can. That's a reason we have courts of appeal—even though sometimes I don't agree with them—to set me straight if I've done something that I shouldn't have done. But, for me, my decisions aren't a matter of group think. I have some very close friends who are lawyers, very close friends who are Federal judges, including some members of the Supreme Court. But no, I don't do that.

JC: Let me talk in contemporary terms. Just two days ago we saw this horrendous tragedy at the Boston Marathon. Suppose the President or the appropriate cabinet secretary—say, Homeland Security—imposed a moratorium on all marathons for the next six months because marathon races are so hard to secure, until we figure out who's responsible for this. You probably believe that that would be an invalid action by the government.

MF: Not necessarily. I'd take a look at the briefs and the administrative procedures act; I'd take a look at how the regulation was promulgated and consider the risks as I did in the DeepWater Horizon case. And then I'll make a decision. It might be that, speculating about that sort of fact situation, it might be perfectly proper. I don't know. But I don't give advisory opinions.

My point is that I really diligently try not to form a speculative opinion without looking at the briefs and considering the law. Considering the conduct in the case you're posing, and in the Moratorium case, it all hinged on some provisions of administrative law. And then I make a decision. But I wouldn't just sit here arbitrarily and say "No, that would be wrong." Because it could be right—it definitely could be right.

JC: So what you're saying is you weren't bothered by the whole idea of a Moratorium, but that basically the facts presented to you just didn't support it?

MF: And that some of the evidence simply wasn't credible.

JC: And you were willing to stand up to the public flak simply because the government hadn't made its case?

MF: Absolutely. As I did when I ruled against Ronald Reagan, a week before he went to meet Gorbachev in Reykjavik and the entire Conservative world came down on my head.

JC: What exactly was the Ukrainian Seaman case?

MF: In 1985 a seaman jumped ship here in the Port of New Orleans. The Ukrainian seaman on a Russian merchant ship asked for asylum. He was denied it and put back on the ship. He jumped ship again, asked for asylum again and then was forcibly put back on the ship. I had a cooling off period. The CIA and the National Security Council all came down here. The guy was taken off the ship. He went to the Naval Station in Algiers Louisiana, was fed and slept. For 24 hours he was interviewed, and said he wanted to go back on the ship.

The whole Conservative world said "Russians. Soviets." Jesse Helms of North Carolina said: "The guy's a KGB plant. He's doing this intentionally to embarrass Reagan. You can't send him back. He'll be killed. You've got to stop the ship." I decided that declaring war was not my responsibility. It was the responsibility of the President and Congress, and if the ship ran, it was going to get shot out of the water in the Port of New Orleans. But that it was up to Congress and the President, not me. I let the ship go and I wouldn't take him off the ship.

The whole Conservative world wanted me to intercede, take him off the ship and show those communists. U.S. World Report wrote a story about me saying that the Reagan Revolution is over. Now it's a matter of evolution and not revolution. So that's a very long-winded way of saying I don't give a damn about the media or public perceptions. And I frankly think no Federal judge should.

JC: That's fair enough. However, part of the recusal statute raises the question of appearance.

MF: If it's a viable, valid issue, yes it certainly should be taken into consideration. But in the Moratorium case, I owned no stock that would be affected by my decision. And the only instance in which I did own stock—which I didn't know it at the time, my broker called me 10 o'clock at night, and I ordered him to sell at the opening of the market. I didn't even know how much I had. I didn't know whether I made or lost money. I just happened to remember that reading an exhibit that said that of the 19 companies that had rigs out in the Gulf, Exxon Mobil was one, and I owned a small amount of Exxon Mobil. I didn't feel that there was any valid appearance issue because I didn't own any stock in any company that would be affected by the Moratorium. That's the way I felt.

JC: When you deal with a legal issue, say, the validity of the Moratorium, are you influenced by the likelihood that the government will get a quick appellate review? In other words, "This is my decision. Take an appeal. If I'm wrong, I'm wrong, and I'll comply."

MF: That's exactly the way I feel. I know that any controversy will be appealed. I think in the DeepWater case I wrote solid, scholarly and restrained opinions. If the Fifth Circuit thought otherwise that's their responsibility, and my responsibility is then to do what they tell me to do. I feel very strongly about that. And remember, I started my career clerking in the Fifth Circuit for John Minor Wisdom. I was his first law clerk.

JC: But when you, or other judges, can rely on the Circuit which will decide such a case very quickly, doesn't it sort of let district judges a bit off the hook, because they're not making the final decision.

MF: I've never felt that way: My responsibility is my responsibility. That's why I write a lot of opinions.

JC: Explain that.

MF: I write a lot of opinions for several reasons. Aside from the fact that I enjoy writing, I write for the community. It should know the reasons behind a judgment. And I write for the Court of Appeals—so that it will accept my reasoning, which I hope is clear enough to convince the panel. So sure, I have that in mind. Absolutely. That's why I write a lot of opinions. I think the Court of Appeals should know exactly why I decided the way I did, with as much clarity and scholarship as possible. I want them to respect me, so that my decisions will be viewed favorably.

JC: So when you said earlier—in terms of the public outcry that might exist over a position you take in a case such as the Ukrainian sailor or the Moratorium—you believe it's the duty of the Federal District Judge to have an "I don't give a damn" attitude about potential criticism—his or her job is to decide the case on the merits, and if the public or the commentators don't like it, well, too bad?

MF: Yes.

JC: I walked down the hall in this Courthouse earlier, and saw Skelly Wright's portrait on the wall. I'm sure there are many folks in New Orleans who were very unhappy with some of his civil rights decisions, or those of John Minor Wisdom.

MF: Absolutely. I practiced before Judge Wright, an extraordinary judge, as was John Minor Wisdom.

JC: Did they too articulate it in those terms?

MF: John Minor Wisdom kept a crank file during the civil rights days. I clerked for him from 1957 through 1959. Every time he got a letter about civil rights calling him whatever ugly things they called him, he just put it in the crank file. He didn't care. He did what he thought was his obligation—under the oath he took—to do. Period. I learned a great deal from one of the greatest human beings in the world. A lot of what I learned when I was 23 years old, clerking for him, you're still listening to right now.

JC: The reader will not see what I just saw: You present as a tough guy, but your eyes well up and tears run down your cheek when you simply mention Judge Wisdom's name.

MF: Right. What you're hearing from me today is pretty much John Minor Wisdom rewarmed 50 years later.

JC: Your critics over the recusal denial in the Moratorium case argue that your stock ownership in oil and gas industry, if not directly in the stock of the litigants in the case, might have influenced your decision, because you had an economic interest in the industry.

MF: They could speculate that, but it's an irrational, remote speculation, with no reason to believe it. Because I like brown, given that this conference room is all brown, doesn't mean if the color brown is somehow indirectly related in some litigation months away I have to recuse myself. Recusal is an arrow in the litigator's quiver. It's irresponsibly asserted, and at times it's responsibly asserted. And sometimes there's a double standard. For example, my friend Vaughn Walker, at the same time I was deciding the Moratorium cases was deciding the Prop 8 case in California. I remotely owned stock in some oil companies. Vaughn is openly gay. I'm not saying he should have recused himself. Nobody in the media or the bar, as far as I know, raised an eyebrow about that.

JC: Really?

MF: He's a fine judge. I'm simply using that as an example of a double standard. I don't think he should have been asked to recuse himself, and I don't think I should have been asked to recuse myself.

JC: In terms of a recusal, if you had owned $10 worth of Hornbeck's stock and . . .

MF: And had not recused myself? I would have been wrong, if I had owned one dollar of Hornbeck. Because the ethical construct is if you own any part of anything that will be affected by the litigation then you must recuse yourself.

JC: Does that rule make sense? Because if you owned $1 worth of Hornbeck stock—and the entire world would agree that that *de minimis* ownership would not influence your opinion—you would have to recuse, but if you own $15,000 worth of stock in the industry that will be indirectly influenced by your decision, you needn't?

MF: Maybe not. But that's the rule. And all I can do is go by the rule. I thought it was ridiculous, and pretty clear to me that they were forum shopping. As a matter of fact, as I mentioned, some environmentalists did not want me to recuse because they felt I'd do a good job one way or the other, including the head of Environmental Law section at Tulane and some professors there. The people from Georgia never came back to court. So, I felt it was frivolous.

I knew I could be fair and impartial. I would have hoped that some of the submissions would have less misrepresented about me. I don't know whether some of those people who were seeking my recusal were party to those misrepresentations. But I knew that it was my responsibility to decide the case. And I didn't give a damn what ignorant reporters were saying, or TV people who were using bullet points with no substance behind them. I have never ever bothered about the good side of the media or the bad side of the media.

JC: You were aware that some U.S. Senators had also asked for an investigation into the fact that about 25 or more judges within the Circuit owned stock in the industry?

MF: In the Ukrainian Seaman case Senator Jesse Helms tried to talk to me personally—which was inappropriate. I wouldn't talk to him. If I thought anything was wrong on my part in the Moratorium case requiring recusal I would have acted accordingly. But I don't know whatever became of the Senators or whatever they thought. Whatever investigations people were seeking at the time had a political agenda.

JC: Have you ever been asked to recuse yourself and did so, or did so *sua sponte,* over an appearance issue?

MF: That's more complex a question than you make it out to be. First of all, we have a computer system that kicks us out of cases when there's a question of direct ownership. Quite frankly, I didn't even know I owned oil stocks. I'm blessed—I own a lot of things. And I don't know what I own. I really don't. There have been instances in which I don't know what bank stock I own where I've been looking at a pleading and I see a bank but it's not the bank I own but a similar name. I'll go to my secretary and ask her to call my investment people to find out if this is related to the bank stock that I own. And if it is, I recuse myself. If it's not, I don't. So I have done that maybe a dozen times.

JC: So to your critics who would say that the reason why you hung on to the case was because you wanted to protect an industry in which you and your community have a vested interest, you would say that's bunk?

MF: Total bunk. And I know that there are people out there who said that I was their hero. Also, total bunk. I received some accolades on the Saturday after the first decision came out and I told the people who were applauding—I happened to be in a public place—to not applaud: "I'm just doing what the Founding Fathers expected me to do." Yeah, total bunk.

JC: If you knew when the case was first rolled out of all the flap about stock you do own but didn't know about, would you have thought it better to just throw it back into the wheel? After all, you have many colleagues down the hall who could handle it.

MF: I would never do something like that. I just wouldn't do that.

JC: Do you rely on the "duty to sit" concept, or some broader view of your judgeship?

MF: I think it's my duty to decide cases when I can be fair and impartial—unless the appearance of bias is rational and valid, in which case I would recuse myself and have done so in the past. But I just don't believe in kicking the can down the road. I know it happens. I've taken a case recently in which I think the can was kicked down the road, and I could have sent it back to the judge who kicked it, but I didn't. I kept the case. And it's going to be a very controversial one. But I feel very strongly that

that's why the founders created the federal judiciary, and that's why they gave us life tenure.

JC: You were recently reversed on a contempt finding against the government relating to the Moratorium. After a case is reversed by the Circuit, do you ever talk to the judges who reversed you?

MF: No.

JC: For what reason?

MF: I just don't think it's appropriate. I've done it once. Years ago, a panel of the Fifth Circuit reversed me in a trial in which I had let in some impeachment evidence. And there was zero verdict for the plaintiff. There were films of the guy lifting heavy things and he claimed his back was bad. I got reversed. I told the panel that I thought that it was a screwy opinion, but because I talked to the panel I recused myself from the retrial. Another judge, a Democrat by the way, a perceptively much more liberal judge than Feldman, in a jury trial reached the same result. That's the only time I ever had anything to say to a panel. And I said it because they said that they felt that I had not given the plaintiff a fair trial—which I found not only wrong but insulting. So I did say something then. Other than that, never.

JC: You said before that the case was moved to a judge more "liberal" than Feldman. What does that mean, to be more liberal than Feldman?

MF: Whatever the public thinks that is. I don't know.

JC: What do *you* think it means?

MF: I think the perception of me is that I'm tough in criminal cases, that I'm generally a tough judge when it comes to schedules, and that there are other judges who might be more relaxed about those things. And I think the huge mistake that some people make, including our now extinct newspaper, is that the judge in a case is so-and-so, appointed by Barack Obama, or the judge in this case is so-and-so, appointed by Ronald Reagan—as if, "Aha! We know how that judge is going to rule because of the president who appointed that judge." And that's just plain stupid. So I'm shadowed by shallow public perceptions. When I use words like liberal and conservative it's whatever other people think they mean. It's not what I mean.

JC: But sometimes—I'm not saying it's so in your case—the president who appointed the judge might indeed influence a decision in the case.

MF: Well you know, Scalia—we might as well be open about this . . .

JC: Let's talk about *Bush v. Gore.*

MF: I'd talk about that all day long because it was *Gore v. Bush* first of all. And it was Gore who brought the case and the first vote was seven to two. So it wasn't what the people out on the street would call a political vote. The disagreement among the justices in *Gore v. Bush* was remedy, not relief. So I'll talk to you about *Gore v. Bush* all day long. I have to be transparent. My best friend in the world is Justice Scalia. We've been friends for 30 years. We were appointed within a year of each other to the Federal bench, and three years later he was appointed to the Supreme Court.

He has made the point, and I agree with it, that in our process the presidents know who we are, or at least they think they know who we are. Obama knows what kind of Federal judge he wants even though they might not bring people in and say "Were you for *Roe v. Wade* or against it," because I don't think that happens. Or how do you feel about this or that issue. Justice Scalia makes the point that they know who we are. They have an idea of what they want, and that filters throughout the Federal judiciary. Our senators know. In my case, for example, I was counsel to a governor with whom I never agreed politically. He supported Reagan when I was supporting Nixon. He supported Goldwater when I was supporting Rockefeller. But I like to think he knew I was a damn good lawyer and an honest and reliable guy who would give good effective advice, and would be a credit to the Federal judiciary. So that's why I'm sitting here right now—because of a guy who never agreed with me about anything.

JC: But you did just raise something. President Obama would generally know what he's getting in the guy he appoints.

MF: You would think he knows.

JC: So if, right after he became president, he appointed a man or woman to the Eastern District of Louisiana and the Moratorium case got wheeled out to him or her, don't you think the Obama Administration would be going to court with a lot more confidence with that judge than with Feldman sitting on the case?

MF: That's one of the fallacies of the human condition. I think they would *think* they had a better chance, but that doesn't mean they would.

I'll tell you a story but I'll have to keep the name of the judge anonymous. Right after one of my colleagues was appointed by President Clinton, I got a call. Can we go to lunch? Sure. I need to talk to you about a case. Sure. This judge had a civil rights case. There was a motion for summary judgment and the judge felt that it was a good motion, but emotionally the judge didn't want to grant it for the defendant. So the judge called me. Wanted to talk through the case. Some judges do that. And that judge picked me because that judge thought that I would give a balanced view because of my experience with that type of case. This judge was appointed by Clinton, I was appointed by Reagan.

That judge ended up granting summary judgment, even though the judge's entire career and law practice was the exact opposite. Exact opposite. The President may think "Oh, we've got one of our appointees." I know his three appointees and am very close with them. Let me tell you this: President Obama shouldn't feel too confident about any result before any one of those three colleagues. So yes, that happens. There is a public perception, but it's a lazy perception in my opinion. And it's a perception that's fueled by the media at times, and by their lack of understanding of the judiciary. But it's there and like I said, the media will say, Feldman's got this case. He was appointed by Reagan. So and so has got this case, she was appointed by Obama, as if that has anything to do with the actual truth of how the court will approach the issue, as opposed to the public perception of how we approach the issues. That's the best way I can explain it

JC: So if in the Moratorium case you were running into flak from your house of worship, if any, your golf club, your rotary club, your neighbors and whatnot, over how you might decide a case, your attitude would be the hell with them?

MF: Exactly.

JC: No one, sir, will ever challenge your directness.

Chapter 4

Judge Nancy Gertner

You have to make credibility determinations. What's a credibility determination? You're listening to someone in the context of your life, that's the only lens in which to view them. And you're deciding if what they say makes sense.
—Judge Nancy Gertner, January 19, 2014

Judge Nancy Gertner, now retired from the bench, was appointed to the U.S. District Court for the District of Massachusetts by President William J. Clinton in 1994 upon the recommendations of Senators Edward M. Kennedy and John Kerry. An unabashed feminist and unapologetic liberal, Judge Gertner's reputation while on the bench is that she was fair, nondiscriminatory, and passionate in her devotion to justice.

Her 250-page comprehensive opinion in the Limone case, discussed here, is perhaps the pinnacle of a judicial career devoted to a detailed attention to the facts, law, and justice.

When deciding whether an employee of 22 years had been the victim of age discrimination when she was suddenly denied raises after being called an "old shoe" and asked, by her manager, when she was going to retire, Judge Gertner issued a decision that discussed the complexities of determining whether discrimination has taken place, noting that it is rarely direct and often involves an understanding of the relationships of the parties.

Her decision that a jury verdict was unconstitutionally excessive and violated due process in a case brought by Sony against a college student who illegally downloaded and shared music files in violation of the Copyright

73

Act was both applauded and criticized. Judge Gertner had reduced the jury's $675,000 award in favor of Sony to $67,500, noting, among other things, that she did not believe Congress contemplated such damages would be applied to college students who shared files without pecuniary gain. She stated that, while she did not condone the student's actions, the damages permitted under the Act and awarded by the jury were wholly out of proportion and grossly excessive given the facts. The First Circuit remanded and, upon Judge Gertner's retirement, another judge found the jury award appropriate; the First Circuit affirmed.

Outspoken as a judge, Judge Gertner has not hesitated to speak her mind since leaving the bench. In a January 2013 interview, she criticized the harsh and unrelenting prosecution of a 26-year-old Internet hacker who faced a 35-year prison sentence for downloading articles from a subscription service with the intent of making the content free to the public. Judge Gertner challenged the prosecution, noting that "[J]ust because you can charge someone with a crime, just because a technical crime has been committed, doesn't mean you should."

Judge Gertner was born in New York City, where she was both high school cheerleader and valedictorian. She attended Barnard College and, in 1971, received a Masters of Arts and Juris Doctor from Yale, where she was an editor of the Yale Law Journal. *She clerked for Judge Luther Swygert of the Seventh Circuit Court of Appeals immediately following graduation. While in private practice from 1972 through 1994, she taught at Boston University School of Law and Harvard Law School, where she is now a member of the faculty. She was a visiting lecturer at Yale Law School from 1998 until 2011. Judge Gertner has been the recipient of many awards for distinguished judicial service and judicial excellence. Notably, following Justice Ruth Bader Ginsburg, she is only the second woman to receive the Thurgood Marshall Award from the American Bar Association's Section of Individual Rights and Responsibilities.*

The title of her book, published in 2011, perhaps says it all: In Defense of Women: Memoirs of an Unrepentant Advocate. *She is currently writing a book on judging, working title* Not Activist Enough, *to be published by Beacon Press.*

Having retired from the bench shortly after reaching senior status in 2011, Judge Gertner teaches at Harvard, practices law in Boston, Massachusetts, and is Special Counsel to Neufeld Scheck and Brustin, LLP, a New York–based law firm.

Upbraiding the FBI

For most of middle America—maybe even America at large—the Federal Bureau of Investigation was, for much if its history, considered the paradigm for what law enforcement should be. It was above reproach. And its director, J. Edgar Hoover, who had served first as Director of the Bureau of Investigation (the FBI's predecessor) and then Director of the FBI from 1935 until his death in 1972, was synonymous with the agency and its austere reputation.

Yes, there were stories, some of which became legend: Hoover threatened to expose President John F. Kennedy's amorous adventures in order to maintain his authority; Hoover illegally wiretapped Martin Luther King Jr., the justification being that King's confidantes included communists or communist sympathizers; and, notoriously, Hoover assembled files, not only on common "subversives," but on governmental officials and critics, which allowed Hoover to demand (perhaps extort) almost unfettered power.

These stories aside, Hoover and the FBI fervently fought crime—and Hoover's attacks on organized crime, in particular, were relentless. Indeed, it was his highly publicized capture of several notable 1930s "gangsters" that expanded the authority of the Department of Investigation and allowed Hoover to lead the FBI as the preeminent domestic intelligence agency in the world. That holy war on organized crime, particularly in the Massachusetts/Rhode Island area, continued for decades and, in the 1960s, focused on "The Office," the family led by purported mobster Raymond Patriarca. Through illegal wiretaps, the FBI came to learn not only about crimes members of The Office had committed but also about those that were about to be committed. And the FBI used this information to "flip" participants, a common practice then and now. No one, however, anticipated that the FBI actually protected some informants by participating in "framing" people for murder. Such corruption—and there is no other word for it—would be the antithesis of what the FBI had purportedly stood for all these years.

The scandal over the FBI's handling of informants in the Boston office of the Bureau came to light when, during the 1995 trial entitled *U.S. v. Salemme*, before Judge Mark Wolf in Federal District Court in Boston, evidence emerged of a corrupt—again, no other word will do—relationship between members of the Boston office and two Boston gangsters of the notorious Winter Hill gang, James J. "Whitey" Bulger and Stephen J. "The Rifleman" Flemmi. As the investigation burgeoned, the Suffolk County District Attorney's Office, which had been spoon-fed the wherewithal to have brought the prosecution in the first place, took a closer look at the 1968 convictions of Peter Limone and others—all of whom had repeatedly declared their innocence—for the murder of one Teddy Deegan. The convictions rested largely on the testimony of FBI informant Joseph "The Animal" Barboza, a killer himself many times over.

These were no ordinary murder convictions, and Barboza was no ordinary prosecution witness. His cooperation had been solicited by prize FBI agents who promised him support for leniency and sponsorship into the then newly emerging witness protection program. The problem was that Barboza's story was false, and anyone with the skillsets of his handlers (or perhaps anyone at all, had they had access to the FBI's records and prior Barboza witness statements) would know it. Barboza's story constantly changed in the manner of a chameleon to suit the needs of the day—and it changed in response to information provided by his handlers. When Barboza's version of events contradicted evidence the FBI knew that Limone's counsel had, Barboza's recollection somehow changed, taking that evidence into account.

But, most disturbingly, as it would turn out, the scandal was not limited to a coterie of wayward FBI agents in Boston—but in telexes directly to J. Edgar Hoover himself. To be clear—Hoover apparently knew about Barboza's lies and that people innocent of the murder would be convicted. Yet Hoover, remarkably, would do nothing to prevent the miscarriage of justice that was occurring by virtue of Barboza's insidious, and suborned, perjury—designed to protect Mafia chieftains whom Barboza warned the FBI he would never "give up." Instead, Limone and two of his codefendants were first literally sentenced to the electric chair, later commuted to life in prison when the U.S. Supreme Court finally declared the death penalty unconstitutional in 1972. And while the defendants were at the time scheduled to die for a crime they did not commit, the Boston office FBI agents were congratulated and promoted for their "fine work."

When the Suffolk District Attorney—who had no knowledge of what was actually in FBI files when it prosecuted Limone and his codefendants so many years earlier (a remarkable concept itself)—finally petitioned for their release, two of the defendants had already died while in prison; one had served 31 years and Limone had served 33 years. They missed every family event for three decades—birthdays, communions, graduations, confirmations, funerals, and births.

A lawsuit was filed by Limone, three other defendants (or their estates), and their families against the United States, although in actuality it was against the FBI. The facts were startling; the FBI's conduct was unimaginable to all but the most ardent conspiracy theorists. Limone and his coplaintiffs, of course, could not get back all those years. But under the Federal Tort Claims Act, they could seek financial redress for their loss of liberty, their pain, and the pain of their loved ones. This suit—and the indisputable facts it brought to light—was bad enough for the FBI.

But from the FBI's point of view, what about the fact that the case randomly landed on the docket of Judge Nancy Gertner, who was appointed to the District Court by President Clinton on the joint recommendations of Senators Edward M. Kennedy and John Kerry and who, before being appointed to the bench, had been a criminal law and civil rights activist for 25 years?

The government likely recognized, given Judge Gertner's years on the bench, that she would treat all litigants before her fairly; however, her background might have made the government shudder. As a lawyer, she represented feminists, radicals, an anti–Vietnam War activist accused of killing a police officer; she took every abortion case she could. Not to mention that Judge Gertner's husband, John Reinstein, was then the Legal Director of the American Civil Liberties Union (ACLU) of Massachusetts. Indeed, when interviewed for her nomination, Ms. Gertner challenged Senator Kennedy to seek the appointment of an activist (such as herself): "If you value the things you say you do, at some point—not necessarily me—you need to propose a civil rights lawyer as a judge, to validate this career path." In other words, one can presume that the government, as a litigant before her on this case, could not have been pleased.

But beyond that, and even if a finding of liability against the government for the Barboza frame would be a slam dunk no matter which judge would be drawn out of the wheel given the overwhelming evidence supporting the FBI's ongoing knowledge—and outright suborning—of Barboza's perjury, could the government possibly want as its "draw" a judge who had earned her stripes as a lawyer who—perhaps occupationally—was suspicious of law enforcement?

Judge Gertner heard 22 days of trial, which consisted mostly of documents—many of the witnesses long gone. In her 250-page painstakingly detailed opinion, she awarded Limone, his coplaintiffs, and their families more than $100 million for their time lost in prison, a decision reluctantly affirmed by the First Circuit, although with some modifications to Judge Gertner's application of the law. Why "reluctantly"? In affirming, the Circuit went out of its way to say that none of the affirming judges, had the trial been before them, would have awarded anything near what Judge Gertner did. One wonders why the court felt the need to say that, what it hoped to accomplish by such a pronouncement, and what Judge Gertner might have thought about such a comment, or what she thinks about it now. Or did it matter to her, particularly given that her $100 million award was affirmed? Was this the first time she had been criticized—slapped on the wrist, perhaps—by the Circuit? Or is the Circuit known for admonishing its District Court judges so that any such slap is, how can we say it, par for the course?

By awarding what some would think is an astronomical sum to parties who, prior to their imprisonment, in the instance of some, were far from choirboys, one would have to wonder whether Judge Gertner was getting even. Was she settling scores, recalling her years as a defense attorney when, sometimes, law enforcement just plain lied? Did she perhaps think about every government abuse she witnessed as a judge? Had she come across FBI abuses earlier in her career? And did she discuss these issues with her husband, himself a capable and prominent civil rights attorney?

Or, after reading and hearing all the parties had to offer, did she simply believe the FBI had gone far beyond what could be tolerated? Quoting Justice Brandeis to conclude her opinion, Judge Gertner reminded all: "If the Government becomes a lawbreaker, it breeds contempt for law; it invites every man to become a law unto himself; it invites anarchy. To declare that in the administration of the criminal law the end justifies the means—to declare that the Government may commit crimes in order to secure the conviction of a private criminal—would bring terrible retribution. Against that pernicious doctrine the Court should resolutely set its face." [1]

At bottom, what influenced Judge Gertner? Did her past as a criminal/ civil rights lawyer viscerally inform her thinking and actions as the judge presiding? Did her husband's position at the ACLU guide her in any way? And did Judge Gertner's experiences as a woman—a woman admitted to practice at a time when the legal profession was less than welcoming to women—inform her decisions, whether in *Limone* or in other cases before her?

The Dialogue

JC: We're sitting in your office at Griswold Hall on the campus of Harvard Law School. Probably the pinnacle of legal academia—a place where one studies and analyzes how the law is implemented in the United States, in the real world. And, I understand, you're actually writing a book on judging. Do you think your view today of how judges decide cases differs now from your first day on the bench, or from when you were a judge for, say, five or ten years?

NG: Did it change over the period of 17 years that I was a judge? Yes and no. At first, I had a hard time figuring out how to be "me" in the job. It was not a question of experience, not understanding the issues, the procedures, the law. I had done criminal trials and appeals that touched every aspect of the system. It wasn't a question of understanding the facts of a case, nor a question of engaging in the issues. I was trying to figure out how

---

1. Olmstead v. United States, 277 U.S. 438 (1928).

I could—how do I describe this? I knew what criminal justice was like in the United States. After all, I had been a criminal defense lawyer. I knew, for example, that police officers sometimes lie. I knew that defense lawyers were sometimes racing through the case to complete it, and not really knowing that much about their client. I knew what the Boston municipal court looked like. I knew what the Supreme Court looked like. The question is how you deal with that knowledge as a judge. How do I deal with my past? It wasn't just a past of advocacy—it was a past of experience. And there was some discomfort around how I would handle it.

In my first motion to suppress, the police officer took the stand. I knew that officers sometimes lie, and sometimes they tell the truth. I had that swirling around in my head. I absorbed his testimony and I realized I completely believed him. And that was sort of a moment of being a judge. I knew what my experience had been. I could envision a distortion in the system, but I also knew that I had the intellectual honesty to say, "This guy is telling the truth."

The better example involves the sentencing guidelines. I had been a lawyer before the guidelines were in full force. So what do you do the first time you have to sentence someone to a term that is completely out of proportion to anything you think any civilized society should allow? At first, I didn't feel it was legitimate to scrutinize the guidelines, to scrutinize the case to see if there was anything wrong with it. I thought it was illegitimate to dig for a way out of this incredibly onerous regime. And over time, I began to realize that there was nothing wrong with that. Nothing wrong with my looking into a case to determine what I thought was fair—so long as I would be honest with myself when the law didn't support me. So long as I could take who I was and look at the cases and say, "This is what I thought. This is what I think is a fair outcome. This is where I think the law ought to be." But be intellectually honest enough that, after I determined that the law was not where I thought it should be, I would say so. And I could relax in the job once I knew I could do that.

JC: You used an odd expression at the outset. You said you wanted to be sure that you could be "me."

NG: Right.

JC: What does that mean?

NG: There was a considerable—not criticism. I had very little criticism in my confirmation process, at least in Boston. But there were people who would say "How can an advocate like you become a judge?" I thought a long time about that. You don't ask that question of prosecutors, whom we assume can move to neutral. You don't ask that question of big firm lawyers whom you think never had an opinion about anything. But, for me, that was a question.

So I asked myself that question as well. In an abortion case, I knew exactly what I believed. If I had a death penalty case, I knew exactly what I believed. And I had to figure out how to deal with those feelings and positions and inclinations and be a good judge—be a fair judge, and be true to my oath. That's what I meant. One of the cases I was known for around here was a death penalty case. I thought the death penalty was wrong. But the way those beliefs would translate into my judging was that I wanted to make this the fairest trial that anyone ever had. That was one way to bring my experiences to bear.

Or, assume in a criminal case, that there was a sentence that I thought was fair, but I could not accomplish that result through the guidelines. I would interpret the guidelines, I would read every case, the legislative history, the rationale for the guidelines, but there were times I knew I couldn't get to the point I wanted to be. So I knew where I started—and perhaps I knew precisely because of my history of advocacy. But I also knew the law, and I would struggle with it. When I realized I could count on myself to not distort the law for my personal positions, that I would be intellectually honest about what the law demanded, then I could relax on the job. That's what I mean by being "me."

JC: You said before that you knew that from time to time—maybe "frequently," my word—police would lie in testimony, and there were problems with defense lawyers not being sufficiently attentive to their clients. Would you say that you had a dim view of how the criminal justice system works?

NG: Oh, surely. My book talks about this. I knew how hard it was to make the system fair. I knew how much work I had to put in to make the system fair. I knew that the default position was the assumption that the person was guilty, and that he or she would plead guilty. In those days, it wasn't the default position that they would go away for nine million years; but I knew how hard it was to make the system fair, particularly for people of color and people who were poor.

JC: Do you think—and this is, of course, a generality—that judges come to the bench with some kind of "agenda" in terms of how they view the system? Whether it's in a prior life as a patent lawyer, or in your case a criminal defense or civil rights lawyer?

NG: "Agenda" is the wrong word. You come with your experience. In the course I teach on judging, we've been struggling with how experience figures into judging. It is an illusion to believe that it does not figure in. You have to make credibility determinations. What's a credibility determination? You're listening to someone in the context of your life, that's the only lens in which to view them. And you're deciding if what they say makes sense. Credibility determinations are necessarily in the context of your life. So, for example, I've run into judges who have basically believed that the civil rights laws are unnecessary—that discrimination is over. So if a woman gets on the stand (or reports in an affidavit) that "this man said this outrageous thing to me," a judge could well find her testimony not credible—particularly a judge who had never been in that situation.

After the *Iqbal*[2] and *Twombley*[3] decisions by the Supreme Court on the civil side, judges are now required to evaluate the plausibility of allegations. Well, that's an experiential issue. And, as I said, I had an easier time because my background was clear to me. Still, at every moment over the past seventeen years I would struggle with every case, its issues, my oath, and the influence of my experience. I worried about judges who somehow believed that they had had an operation the minute they became judges that eliminated all their preexisting opinions, wiped out their memories. But issues of plausibility, credibility, all the weighing and balancing tests, even the procedural questions—how far to delve into a legal issue before you're satisfied that you understand it—require judgment, the judgment of human beings.

Right before I left the bench I had a case of a woman prisoner who claimed that a guard had had sex with her. Not a rape, no violence—but

---

2. Ashcroft v. Iqbal, 556 U.S. 662 (2009).
3. Bell Atlantic Corp. v. Twombley, 550 U.S. 544 (2007).

that they just had sex. And he had an enormous amount of power over her; consent in this situation was arguably ambiguous. She sued the officer after she left prison and then, in addition, sued the supervisors. The officer went to jail, but the question was the supervisor's liability. My law clerk came to me and said that there are cases across the country that dismissed these allegations. I said: "What?" "They dismissed these allegations. In fact, Judge, you could dismiss it if you wanted to." I said that the case law made no sense, Let's look at the facts. Virtually all of the cases involved male prisoners and female guards—with an implicit judgment by the judges that these encounters were no big deal. The men probably liked the sex. So, who cares?

So my point here is that when I read these cases, I was absolutely not satisfied with the analyses. Because I knew what prisons were like. I knew what women's prisons were like. And I wasn't satisfied until I understood the case law, and until I thought that there was an alternative. I concluded that the case should not be dismissed, that the issues were sufficiently complicated and that a jury should hear them.

Judgment comes in at every stage, from procedural issues to balancing and weighing tests. And it's an illusion to believe that there isn't judgment.

JC: But isn't it possible for a judge to be appointed to the bench whose life before was so circumscribed, and disengaged from the real world, that he or she can be more objective than, say, you, having been an aggressive defensive lawyer?

NG: I'm not sure "objective" is the right word there. There's a set of values that they apply that are just different than the values that I'm applying.

JC: They have less "baggage." How about that?

NG: No. They have unexamined baggage. We select judges in their 40's and early 50's. Unless you've lived in a cave, you take positions. So let's take someone who's been a big firm lawyer all his life—a white man who never experienced discrimination. He has a view of what the world is like which is implicit, not explicit. And it may be that because he had no trouble getting through his life, he doesn't see problems that anyone else has. It's different in Europe where judges are appointed in their 20's and they're essentially cultivated to be judges. We appoint people who have lived.

JC: So for example, Judge Posner wrote in his newest book, *Reflections on Judging*, that his parents were "very left wing." And remarkably, that they were admirers of Joseph Stalin and that the day that Stalin died was a "day of mourning" in his parents' home. He also says that his mother was one of the witnesses subpoenaed before the House Un-American Activities Committee, and she actually took the fifth amendment when asked if she had been a member of the Communist Party. Now, I haven't studied Judge Posner's fifth amendment jurisprudence, but assuming he had to decide a fifth amendment assertion, mightn't there be a risk that he (or any judge similarly situated) could potentially be overly influenced by his own life experience?

NG: I think it's a process question. So, if he approaches a fifth amendment case understanding the consequences of taking the fifth and that makes him look more carefully at the law, that's a good thing. And if *I* understand what it's like to go to jail—as a young lawyer, a door got stuck and I was actually stuck in the entry way to the jail for something like a half hour. If that, actually, makes me really careful about taking away someone's liberty, what's wrong with that?

In other words, if in the case of Judge Posner—if you take your body of experiences or even the absence of experiences as your previous hypothetical was, and you try to work it through and take it into account in evaluating the law, but understand that there are moments that there isn't a one-to-one correlation between what you want to see happen and what's going to happen, if it makes you examine it more carefully, there's nothing wrong with that.

I was just doing commentary on the new civil rules of discovery and the committee wants judges to evaluate whether the discovery sought is proportional to the harm involved in the case. I can't tell you the number of times as a judge that I have heard "This case is only worth $10,000. This is *de minimus*." Where I come from that was not *de minimus*. I did not come from money—my father was in the linoleum business. Now, is there something wrong in my saying "Gee there are people in this world for whom this is a lot of money. And I think the discovery should be proportional to their view of the money as opposed to my view of the money or some other judge's view of the money?" So I guess what I'm saying is this—you are aware of your prejudices or your biases or your experience and you struggle with them, and the best we can hope for is a good faith struggle.

JC: So let's move the struggle in the direction of the FBI. You talked about the police before. Did you have a particular view of the FBI while you were in law practice, which may have moved you once you got onto the bench? And, in particular, the Hoover FBI?

NG: I actually can't say that I ever had a case involving the FBI doing something wrong. I had no personal view of J. Edgar Hoover. I had no personal experience. You, of course, read about his excessiveness—the extent to which he was excessive in what he did.

JC: Excessive how? Like essentially "extorting" President Kennedy and his brother Robert, that if they didn't play ball with him he would expose President Kennedy as a philanderer?

NG: Right, and the surveillance of Martin Luther King …

JC: You're speaking about it in somewhat of a mellow tone, now. You mean you didn't have a more extreme view?

NG: It's hard to remember whatever my extreme view was then. But I'm a voracious reader. I read about it and knew about the accusations. But I don't have that indignation now. It certainly wasn't animating this decision.

JC: I'm not suggesting that; but I am suggesting that you might have had a view of him from having been a defense and civil rights lawyer—particularly given that Hoover was known for being opposed to the civil rights movement.

NG: I may have. I can't really remember now, but what I'm saying is that the enterprise for me was that you don't start off a case as if you've lived in a cave all your life. You don't start off any case like that. You know the lawyers. Boston is a small town. You know the issues. The enterprise is to examine what your proclivities are and make sure that there's not a one-to-one correlation with what the outcome is.

JC: But looking, say, at the Hoover or the FBI situation—you say part of the job is to analyze or introspect about whatever biases might be lurking. And suppose you do have a bias. Suppose you conclude "I think the FBI is [or was at the time] an antisocial organization." Of course, I'm expressing an extreme view. What do you do then? Do you recuse yourself?

NG: No. Your general view doesn't necessarily mean that you're going to take a position in this particular case. That's what I'm saying. You become a judge in your late 40's, early 50's, you have lots of general views. You're an informed citizen. The enterprise is to make sure that in the process of judging those general views don't dictate the outcome in a particular case.

JC: So, coming from your background you might have a view of the importance of, say, *Brady*[4] or *Giglio*,[5] in terms of how fundamental they are. That it doesn't really matter whether the defendant is guilty or not. Whereas some of your colleagues on the bench who may have been former prosecutors have a view that those doctrines are pretty much obstacles to a guilty person being convicted.

But that background that you have does bring you to a place in deciding a case that it would not bring your colleagues, doesn't it?

NG: But that's a bad example in a way. Because that's about process and about rights and constitutional issues. Are you saying that I cared deeply about rights and I had learned as a criminal defense lawyer to care about rights and less about whether the guy was guilty? There were certainly times I represented guilty people. And I was determined to give the defendant the best advocacy he could possibly have. That translated on the bench for me to, yeah, "I want to make sure that before someone's liberty is taken away from him, every constitutional right is respected."

So in that situation, if a prosecutor comes to the bench and says these rights are not important, the defendants are probably guilty, they're wrong. They're just flat out wrong. I didn't necessarily care who was in the case in front of me as long as the rights were respected. That's a position, it seems to me, that every American judge should take. That's not a liberal/conservative divide—that's a position that *every* judge should take. Your example—questioning whether my substantive impressions about Hoover impacted a case—isn't a process issue. It's an outcome issue. That's different.

JC: What you're saying is that you didn't yell out three cheers when that case was rolled out to you? You didn't feel, even in some subliminal way, that you wanted to settle scores for the past abuses by the FBI?

NG: No, not at all. I used to kid around, and I did it in my speeches too, I had an "oy" footnote. There were decisions that I wrote in which I would say "The First Circuit obliges me to do this." Or, "The law obliges

---

4. Brady v. Maryland, 373 U.S. 83 (1963).
5. Giglio v. U.S., 405 U.S. 150 (1972).

me to do this." And then I would have a footnote: "Oy. Is this ridiculous?" In other words, I could keep in the same brain the notion of what the outcome *had to be* because of law with which I fundamentally disagreed, but at the same time I recognized that I disagreed. What I wouldn't do would be to pretend that I had had a lobotomy and that I somehow believed in a mandatory sentence of 25 years, or I somehow believed in this outcome. So the struggle that I describe is actually in my work.

JC: Do you get the sense—again, this is a generality—that other judges aren't as capable of doing what you did?

NG: Capable is not the right word.

JC: You're really a law professor, after all. You keep challenging my words! "Willingness"?

NG: "Willingness" is the issue. Because to some degree it means that you have to be a critic of what you're doing. And that's not an easy thing to do. In writing about judging—by the way, I have records from every single case I decided, and I had bellyaches about many of them. The people I think I sentenced to too much time. The times when I would have balanced things differently. The instances in which the law has changed, and I wish I could go back now and re-do it. I have all of that in my memory.

JC: So with respect to other judges whom I've interviewed, I basically told them what case of theirs I wanted to discuss with them. Here, *you* said to me that the *Limone* case is the one you wanted to discuss.

NG: Actually, it was only because Boston is a small town. *Limone*, however, was very high profile, and would have national resonance. That's why I selected it. I could have selected others. There are two volumes here. When I left the bench, I asked my law clerks to each pick two cases which I would have called "intergalactic decisions." And in this volume, for example, there is a sentencing case where I refused to enhance the sentence of a black defendant who had a criminal history based almost entirely on "driving while black." When I read his criminal record and I saw it was "driving after your license was suspended"—30 days, in a white suburb of Boston. Then a second offense of "driving after your license was suspended"—60 days in another white suburb of Boston. Finally, a third offense, "driving after your license was suspended"—90 days.

The lawyers did not argue that this was "driving while black." But I read everything and I read the underlying documents. There were arrests without an accompanying traffic violation, like speeding. He was stopped simply for driving with a suspended license. This was the only charge. What, apart from his race, had attracted the police attention? And I knew, and I had been teaching sentencing at Yale for numbers of years, that I was saying something of significance: "Don't send this man away for more time based on convictions that are problematic in a host of ways." That was an "intergalactic" decision. It led to the Sentencing Commission to look at the racial impact of traffic stops.

All of this is a long way of saying that I had other decisions to bring to your attention. I selected *Limone* because it was a national decision.

JC: Once you started to learn the facts in *Limone*, did you think you wanted to use the decision for some purpose?

NG: It's a sound decision. It's based on the facts. It's based on a unique period in law enforcement history. It's not like I saw this as "It's going to advance the law on malicious prosecution." I love digging into complex things; that, I think, is what distinguishes a good judge from a bad judge. I get a complicated constitutional or fact question and I go, "Whoopie!" And there are surely judges on the bench who would go "Damn, now I can't move this case along. It's going to take me time to decide it."

So what I saw in this case was like an archaeological dig. Very limited testimony, but boxes and boxes of materials. To give you one example of where my experience mattered—the issue was whether or not the murder case against Limone and the others was independent of the FBI's investigation—whether the state had exercised independent judgment.

And a prosecutor who had been a prosecutor in the state case named Jack Zalkind, whom I knew years and years ago, took the stand. He testified, consistent with the plaintiffs' view, that he did not know that Barbosa was an FBI informant, and all the things that the FBI knew. But at the same time he wanted to show that he had exercised independent judgment. And he testified that this was like his first case as a D.A. He had a list of things that he was going to do, and the list came into evidence. My law clerk, who had never practiced, said "Judge, this really looks like he did a lot of investigation." I looked at the list. "Get the names and addresses of witnesses.

Get their criminal record." In other words, it was a to-do list that someone would do at the outset of a case. It was essentially nothing. It wasn't a significant investigative blueprint. It was at a level of superficiality that made it easy for me to say that the state investigation was a product of federal pressure. My law clerk didn't have that experience! I looked at that and said, "It's nothing." I was the fact finder. It was reasonable for me to put his testimony in the context of my understanding of the criminal justice process.

JC: But judge, you wrote a 250-page opinion which concluded with that famous quote from Brandeis's opinion in *Olmstead*,[6] basically saying that the law needs to be upheld by the people who enforce the law, who are righteous in their application of it, and how pernicious events, such as what happened in *Limone*, can be so horrible for society.

It sounded to me, when I read it, that you really wanted to "make a statement"—not just impose a judgment against the United States to the tune of $100,000,000. That you really wanted to say something much broader than that. Am I wrong?

NG: By the time that I had gone through everything, I *did* want to make a statement. That wasn't where I started. But it's where I ended.

I was indignant about what I saw. I was really horrified by what I saw. That's not where I started—whatever I thought about Hoover, I didn't start off saying "Oh, they must have done something wrong." I was horrified that the men involved, the plaintiffs in this case, were in their 80's, that they had been jailed for so long as a result of the defendant's actions.

JC: Limone was actually in jail in another case, wasn't he, at the time of his conviction that led him to a death penalty?

NG: I actually don't remember that. But the other three, Salvati in particular—there was no hint of any mob connection at all. In fact, it was Salvati and the people who worked for Salvati that ultimately opened up the case. Because of my concerns about the ages of the plaintiffs, I announced that I was going to have the decision ready by such and such date.

JC: And you say in your opinion that it took longer . . .

NG: Yes. But once I realized what I was going to do, I didn't want these men to be dead before the decision was issued. So I announced about a

---

6. Olmstead v. U.S., 277 U.S. 438 (1928).

week or two beforehand that I would have a decision on this date. I literally stayed up all night. This was like when I was a young lawyer, only I was in my 60's. Staying up all night wasn't easy. I think my entire staff stayed up all night. And on the day that the decision came down, I actually wanted to do what the Supreme Court sometimes does, which is to announce it in open court. And I did that.

So if your question is: Was I indignant? My God, was I indignant. I was horrified at what I read. But it was an indignation that came at the end of the process, after I had gone through everything. Not at the beginning. I didn't start off that way.

JC: Do you think you would have been less indignant if you didn't have the history that you did as a criminal/civil rights lawyer?

NG: Not in this case, actually.

JC: Do you think you would have been as indignant if you weren't a woman?

NG: [Laughter.] Not in this case, no. In other cases, maybe. But not in this case. The other thing is that maybe the judges that you've been interviewing have this self-confidence to be indignant. In other words, after I had looked at every box and stayed up all night—my law clerks didn't filter the evidence—I had to read everything and I would be in my office late into the night. After I did that, I would literally say, "Oh, my God. Wow. This can't be." But I had the confidence to be indignant, because I knew I had looked at everything.

JC: In being indignant, and writing a 250-page opinion that nailed the thing shut, what were you trying to accomplish, beyond what you would have accomplished if you wrote a 20-page opinion?

NG: One of the other things that I came to the bench with was an acute sense of the importance of the public's opinions. An acute sense that the public had to know, had to understand what went on in court. Part of that was defensive. I wrote long decisions sometimes because I worried that people would say "Gertner, of course; she had never been a prosecutor." That critique would have been wrong. My background did not determine the outcome. My work did. I worked tremendously hard, and took the time to engage with each and every case, each and every issue. I regularly wrote long decisions for the simple reason that if I could not justify my decision on the page, to the public, I simply could not do it. Writing was the check I imposed on myself.

JC: What does that mean, "Gertner, of course"?

NG: In other words, that people would say that, because I had been a defense and civil rights lawyer—that's in the nature of your questions—"That's why she did it." And I wanted to make sure that everyone would understand what I looked at, what I thought and what the analysis was. They would read the decision and it would fully explain the outcome. In fact, in every case the first four or five pages was a press release. Written simply, written in English, which I knew the press would pick up.

In *Limone*, I wrote 250 pages because I thought it was a big deal to come to these conclusions against the FBI. I thought that these conclusions needed to be justified in chapter and verse. I thought that people needed to know precisely what I had seen in order to give legitimacy to the opinion.

JC: Were you concerned that the days of Hoover could be reinvented or reestablished, and that's partly why you wanted to do it?

NG: I didn't have that concern then. I have to admit I have concern now.

JC: Because of the NSA . . .

NG: That's right. The NSA revelations reflect what happens when you say "getting the bad guys" justifies anything. That's really what *Limone* was about. Getting La Cosa Nostra was more important than almost anything, and the defendants were prepared to sacrifice all sorts of things—like constitutional rights—for that.

JC: How long did it take you to write the opinion?

NG: I don't know. I write fast. And the other thing is that I love writing. The advantage I have being a judge—which I don't have as a professor—every piece of junk you write you could publish as a judge. You press a button it goes to West Publishing. Now I've got to get it peer reviewed. It's really a terrible thing [laughs.]

JC: During the time frame when you were getting troubled by what was before you in court, in going through the boxes and analyzing them, did you, beside talking to your law clerks, who would typically be inexperienced in life, did you talk to anybody else?

NG: No. In fact there's a funny story about that. My husband was then the legal director of the ACLU. When I became a judge—I had gone to law school with Hillary Clinton and I went to visit her after my hearing with my family and she said "How does it feel?" to my husband, "Are you looking forward to her being a judge?" My husband John said: "Actually, I'm sort of sad, because we've spent 24 years talking about cases together, and now she won't be able to talk about her work." And Hillary said, "I wouldn't worry about that if I were you." But we—John and I—actually were very scrupulous about that.

JC: You wouldn't talk to your husband about the case?

NG: No. He might know I was working on a particular case—after all, I was in chambers until two in the morning. But he wouldn't know the details.

JC: But would he know that you were going to pretty much blow away the FBI, at least in terms of the mafia program, didn't he?

NG: No.

JC: I believe you of course, but it's really hard to believe.

NG: It's true. I felt strongly that it was wrong for him to be my third or fourth law clerk.

JC: Because he was a legal director of the ACLU?

NG: That's part of it. He knew what I was doing. There's an enormous amount of cognitive dissonance that I would have experienced if I had shared information with him. You can't go out on the bench and wear the robes and have *ex parte* communications with someone who knows the law of malicious prosecution, etc. without having a bellyache, without experiencing cognitive dissonance.

JC: Would you have talked to your colleagues on the bench about that?

NG: I could have, yes. We're a very close court in the sense that we have lunch together once a week and have court meetings once a month. But we rarely shared discussions about cases while they were going on. And I didn't share this case in particular because virtually every judge had—I'm going to call them Bulger cases. Judge Wolf had been enormously courageous with the first and then there were civil cases on various aspects of

Bulger's cooperation with the FBI. So, I actually didn't talk to anyone about it.

JC: You refer to Judge Wolf as issuing a "courageous" opinion, or being courageous in issuing that opinion. Why courageous? Isn't that what judges are supposed to do?

NG: First of all, I agree with you. Courageous may not be the right word.

JC: But it's the word you used.

NG: Then I'll stick by it. He had a criminal case involving someone who's supposedly a member of the mob. There had been rumors around the city for years that Bulger had some kind of protection from the authorities. The defense lawyers in the case kept calling for discovery about the FBI's relationship with Bulger.

This is actually an example of where experience comes in. Judge Wolf didn't dismiss those rumors off hand, as many other judges would have done. He, maybe because of his experience as a prosecutor, could understand the way that prosecutorial pressures could distort judgment. He had been a prosecutor; he'd never been a defense lawyer. So when the issue came up, he said "Yes, I'll give you that discovery." And the hearings that he held over a period of years is what finally exposed this program.

It was courage in the sense that it could have put at risk the prosecution of someone who was widely believed to be a member of the mob. It's saying "I'm going to open this box and wherever it goes I'm going to take it." So it took a certain amount of courage.

But it was also engagement with the issue. It was "Let me look carefully at this," kind of courage. It's interesting and I have been critical of judges who have described some of my decisions as courageous. When you have life tenure, why should you care about the reactions to your decisions? But it certainly took guts for Judge Wolf. For one thing it upended his docket. He spent month after month on this, at a time when we had enormous pressure to move cases. So he was prepared to take criticism from lawyers, from Washington. His docket was very slow. The press, actually, didn't criticize him. Because the rumors about Bulger had been swirling for a long time.

JC: Do you think your decision in the *Limone* case, awarding $100 million, and actually saying in your opinion that the wrongdoing went all the way up to J. Edgar Hoover, was that a courageous opinion?

NG: No. The only reason I say that it wasn't was because I think that the courage was Judge Wolf's and not mine. I thought that what I did was to look at the discovery—the information that had been produced. He was the one who opened up the book.

JC: But, if I'm correct, Judge Wolf isn't the judge who said that J. Edgar Hoover was involved in the wrongdoing. You did. If J. Edgar Hoover were still alive with his capacity to go after those who offended him, would that be a courageous opinion for a judge? Obviously you did it 30 years later.

NG: I never thought about that. I really never thought about the consequences. I have to admit that I didn't think of it in those terms. I became a judge notwithstanding a career of challenging everything. My book, *In Defense of Women: Memoirs of an Unrepentant Advocate*, begins with this funny story. A panel with me and Justice Sotomayor on it. Women students at Yale Law School wanted to know how to become a judge. And Justice Sotomayor, when she was on the Second Circuit said, "Well you go to this fine institution, you do very well, you work for the government, you work for a private firm, you're cautious about your opinions and then you become a judge." I got up and I said "How does one become a judge? Well. You represent the first lesbian feminist radical revolutionary accused of killing a police officer you could find. That would be your first case in prime time. You then do every abortion case in the Commonwealth of Massachusetts. You speak on the Boston Common. You burn things—I think I burned my Bar card once, because of some decision I didn't agree with—and then for the final *coup de grace*, you marry the legal director of the ACLU. And then you become a judge." I guess what I'm saying is that I did many things that were risky and challenging, legally risky, politically risky, career risky.

JC: But you're somewhat *sui generis*, aren't you? How many judges have come to the bench with those "black marks" against them?

NG: Right. Not a lot. In the "driving while black" case, a judge came up to me and said "That was a courageous decision." The word courage was very interesting. What did he mean by that? He did not mean that there would be formal retribution from any one; that would have been impossible.

What he meant was that I would be criticized in the press. I didn't give a damn if I was criticized in the press. I cared enough about the public's understanding of a decision so that I would try to justify and explain it in lengthy decisions. But once I did, and people disagreed, so be it.

JC: In *Limone*, was it necessary for you to say that the evidence went directly to Hoover? In the sense that you could have thereby justified the $100,000,000 judgment based on the fact that some of these defendants had literally sat on death row and had been in jail for 30 years or so?

NG: I really don't remember. I think that part of it was that there were actually wires between Washington and a local office in which the FBI agents were being praised, which created a motive for, or an incentive for, the local agents to do what they did. They were being praised for the prosecution of Limone and the others. They were being praised for taking down the Italian mob. So to some degree it was part of the story; that set of incentives that made my findings more legitimate.

JC: So you came up with the number $100 million, which is a nice round number. Thereafter, the judges of the Court of Appeals, in basically affirming most of your findings, said that not one of them would have awarded that kind of money—but they were sort of duty bound under case law to affirm what you had done. What did that mean to you?

NG: Two parts to that question. The affirmance of this case and the Court of Appeals in general. As to the affirmance of this case, I didn't care at all that they agreed or disagreed. In fact, I came to that number—it's a very difficult thing, as juries find, coming up with damages—because there was a body of law that had used $1 million per year of imprisonment as a measure of damages. Otherwise I had no stock in any particular outcome. I did it because there was a rationale for it. Not because I was trying to send a message.

As to the Court of Appeals in general, that is another book which I will write. I was happy to be affirmed in this case. I generally didn't care if I was reversed or affirmed except that I wasn't doing this—writing these opinions—for my health. In other words, I wrote decisions because they were right. And when I was reversed, I believed the Court of Appeals was wrong. It wasn't an ego thing. It wasn't a narcissistic thing. I just thought that they were wrong. And the First Circuit in particular, unlike the Second Circuit, spends a lot of its time *not* making decisions. In other words, so many decisions of the First Circuit are of this form: "The Third Circuit says this, the Second Circuit says this, we need not decide because this case meets the strictest standard." Which I think is ducking their responsibility.

JC: Whether or not you cared, did you take it as criticism that they said they wouldn't have themselves done what you did? In other words, did you think you were getting spanked?

NG: I didn't care. But sure, they did that all the time.

JC: To you, or in general?

NG: In my view the Second Circuit and the Ninth Circuit are enormously respectful of the district judges. Judge Weinstein may have been reversed but he gets reversed in decisions that are not perfunctory and disrespectful. Judge Rakoff will get reversed, but likewise in decisions that respect his engagement with the issue. The First Circuit will reverse in decisions which are perfunctory and disrespectful. And that made me crazy.

JC: Returning for a second to *Limone*, if you had been the government litigator in that case, and the case was wheeled out to a judge like you, would you have been concerned?

NG: No. Because I had a reputation at that point of being a hard worker and fair.

JC: Didn't you also have a reputation of being—to use a 1950's term— a "leftie"?

NG: Yeah; but I think the U.S. Attorneys would say that they loved trying cases in front of me. Even though they disagreed with me all the time. Because I let people try their case. So they knew they would get was a fair hearing. And also this case was so tied up in procedural technicalities that it was not a foregone conclusion at the beginning, that even if this had happened, that the law would permit recovery. There were many, many hurdles to climb. And they knew that I was a law judge—meaning that I was going to engage with the law and I was going to look at it carefully. So I think it meant to them that I was going to take everything very seriously, on both sides—and go where the chips fell. I think the answer to your question depends on whether the Government lawyers thought they had a good case or not.

JC: But they sort of knew, going in, that they didn't. Let's turn to something else for a second. You signed the brief on behalf of Judge Shira Scheindlin of the Southern District of New York.

NG: I organized it.

JC: And Judge Scheindlin, famously, among other things, told the New Yorker writer Jeffrey Toobin, that essentially she wasn't in the "hip pocket" (my phrase) of the government, whereas some of her colleagues, who had formerly been prosecutors in the U.S. Attorney's office were too deferential to the U.S. Attorney's office. Do you think that's a problem on the bench?

NG: Yes. But it's a more sophisticated analysis. It's not like you say "I was a U.S. Attorney, I want the U.S. Attorney to win in every case." It's a matter of experience. You were a fabulous U.S. Attorney. You were incredibly honest and careful, and you therefore, you assume that everybody else is. Your experience leads you to believe that "Gee, I never did anything like that. And these are good people. Why would anyone else." You can't even envision prosecutorial or police misconduct. You can't envision a problem.

JC: So it's the opposite side of what you were saying of having been a defense lawyer.

NG: Just as I had to struggle. I could envision a prosecutor cutting corners, but I knew that that didn't happen all the time, too. So when you get an accusation, your experience leads you to understand this as possible. If you hadn't had the experience of being on the ground that you don't even know it exists, you don't think it's possible.

Let me give you an example. I really practiced everywhere. Boston municipal court. Imagine, fancy Yale credentials, Boston Municipal Court. Oftentimes, it happened in criminal cases that guidelines would increase because of state convictions. And there was an interesting imbalance there. State convictions could have originated in a local court with a relatively informal process. Defense lawyers were going back and challenging the state convictions that were leading to these sentencing enhancements. I thought that was perfectly fair. These were community courts. It was not unusual for a defendant to be in jail for, say, 8 months, not get bail and then all of a sudden get a deal for "time served." At that point, he would plead to anything—an aggravated offense, rather than a lesser one, a felony rather than a misdemeanor. So I understood the pressures of the state court. One of the judges of my court refused to give lawyers time to challenge state convictions. He said "Convictions are not like a Las Vegas divorce that you can un-do so easily." It was a comment that reflected that he did not appreciate that the convictions were Las Vegas marriages; lawyers should have an opportunity to challenge them. He had never practiced in the state court. He didn't understand what a state court was like. Therefore, he couldn't envision this as a legitimate thing to do.

Your experience plays into your judging and if you've been a prosecutor and dealt only with federal law, never saw bad lawyers in state court, you're going to assume effective assistance of counsel. You're going to make assumptions about the good faith of the prosecutors, which may well be true. But you have to be prepared to consider the other.

JC: You think that every judge who gets on the district court should have experience as a prosecutor and a defense lawyer.

NG: I do.

JC: But you didn't.

NG: Not as a prosecutor.

JC: They should look at life from both sides.

NG: Yes, I suppose. But you can't ask for that. That's the way England functions, by the way, lawyers changing roles. What you can do is seek to nominate lawyers who have an understanding of what the system is like and struggled with it. I chair Senator Elizabeth Warren's committee to recommend to her who should be nominated to the next federal vacancy. She very much wants people with a broad range of experience, not just white and black and woman and man. These are important categories, but an equally significant question is have you done consumer work? Will you understand that a case that is only worth $10,000 may mean a lot to the union guy in front of you?

JC: Let's return to the "woman" issue again. I asked you before whether it might have had some influence in *Limone*. You sort of said no and looked at me somewhat querulously. Does it matter in deciding cases?

NG: Yes. If experience matters in deciding cases—if we're not robots, if legal issues don't rush over you out of context, then part of what I bring to the bench is that I'm a woman.

JC: How does it impact your decisions?

NG: I keep on using the word "envision." If I'm asked to read a complaint about an accusation of sexual harassment and I have never experienced sexual harassment—and in fact I think the world has fortunately changed for the better—then I might find that accusation implausible. I surely experienced sexual harassment in my youth. When I take off my robes and I go on vacation with my family, I'd run into people who would ask my husband what he did, and assume that the "little woman" was staying home. So the range of experiences that I could envision might be different from someone who had never experienced that.

JC: So if the case is assigned to a male colleague down the hall, the fact that you're a woman won't help at all. It does help in ensuring that differing groups of society are more equally represented on the court. That I understand. But in most cases that would appear before you—as a woman or a black or an Asian or a Jew or whatever demographic one comes from— it won't matter, unless that particular case . . .

NG: Aligns with the judge. For sure, advocates have to account for the range of experiences of the judge or the jury. In one of the last murder cases that I tried before becoming a judge, the defendant was accused of killing a white woman who lived across the street. I said to the jury "You want to understand this case. You want to solve it. You want to tie it up, all the loose ends. It's natural. But what you can't do is fill in the gaps in the evidence with your prejudice." You can't say I really don't have direct evidence; there is a gap in the evidence here or there, but the defendant is black and I can believe anything of him.

In effect, that was the advice that I gave myself in *Limone* as well as other cases. I understood where I had been before I was on the bench, my experiences, my predilections. I tried to identify where my background ended and the case began, where I was eliding my view of the world with my fact finding obligations. I could do this precisely because I knew whom I had been and where I came from, what I believed in and what the job demanded.

Chapter 5

Judge Alvin K. Hellerstein

There's no such thing as purity in judgment. Without facts and context, judgment becomes abstract—you lose out on the passion of judging. Justice does not require absolute purity, but a check on bias.
—Judge Alvin K. Hellerstein, September 30, 2013

Judge Alvin K. Hellerstein[1] was appointed to the Southern District of New York by President William J. Clinton in 1998 and, as of 2011, holds senior status. Judge Hellerstein is considered smart, tough, and direct—he is not afraid to share his thoughts about the cases and counsel before him.

The 10,000+ September 11 tort cases discussed here, which consumed his docket for more than a decade, are only some of the 9/11-related cases over which Judge Hellerstein presided. He addressed the wrongful death cases brought by the families of 95 people killed in the plane crashes, the insurance and other claims for compensation made by the owner of the Twin Towers, and many others.

In addition, he maintained a full docket of cases, which included Freedom of Information Act cases against the Department of Defense and CIA concerning captured enemy combatants, ruling for the release of the Abu Ghraib photographs but against the American Civil Liberties Union when it sought to force the CIA to release secret documents involving terror detainees, holding that national security should not

---

1. Judge Hellerstein and the author are friends of more than 25 years, having been law partners before Judge Hellerstein took the bench.

be at risk. In another, he rebuked federal prosecutors and law enforce-
ment, finding that they made a decision to tell "perhaps the truth, but
not the whole truth." And in an infamous case (at least to New Yorkers,
transplanted or otherwise), Judge Hellerstein resolved a three-year battle
between companies that each claimed the right to use the coveted name
"H&H Bagels." Notwithstanding that the case turned on the mundane—
the Lanham Act and Bankruptcy Code—Judge Hellerstein made sure
to expound and educate, tracing the bagel from its Eastern European
roots to the tenements of New York.

Judge Hellerstein graduated from Columbia College and Columbia Law
School, where he was an editor of the law review. Upon graduation in
1956, he clerked for Judge Edmund L. Palmieri in the Southern District of
New York. Judge Hellerstein next served as a First Lieutenant in the Judge
Advocate General Corps. From 1960 to 1998, he was in private practice
at Stroock & Stroock & Lavan LLP, where—before being appointed to
the bench—he cochaired its litigation department, where he, among other
things, represented defendants in complex securities cases. In addition to
his professional accomplishments, Judge Hellerstein has tirelessly supported
charitable activities, serving as president and then chair of the Board of
Jewish Education and on various committees of UJA-Federation. Judge
Hellerstein remains active in professional associations and publishes schol-
arly articles, including three concerning the 9/11 cases.

Notably, in his chambers, as was in his office when he practiced law,
hangs a framed calligraphy that says, in Hebrew, the Biblical call: "Justice,
Justice, Shalt Thou Pursue."

Judge Hellerstein sits in New York City.

Managing and Settling the 9/11 Tort Cases

We can all remember where we were on the otherwise sky blue morning of
September 11, 2001, when two planes crashed into the Twin Towers. That
day was devastating; the days and weeks following were a blur, particularly if you lived in New York City and watched what would come to be
known as "Ground Zero" burn well after the attacks. But most of us went

back to our lives—back to family, back to work, and back to the trivialities that make up our days.

But what of the more than 60,000 firefighters, police, medical workers, contractors, and volunteers who, over the course of some ten months, engaged in operations 24/7—first searching for survivors and, after a time, human remains—and who worked tirelessly to remove whatever was left of the Towers and clear the site?

It is difficult to conceive of the magnitude—ultimately, there were more than 11,000 plaintiffs who brought separate, but related, actions against the City of New York, the Port Authority, the Army Corps of Engineers, and the private contractors who supervised the work at Ground Zero. Those plaintiffs evidenced symptoms of more than 300 different diseases that they claimed were caused or exacerbated by the noble—yet hazardous—work they performed.

To ensure monies were available to help those who became ill—and to ensure that the defendants (including the City of New York) did not become bankrupt from the claims—Congress enacted legislation within days of the attack that created a no-fault Victim Compensation Fund, which would ultimately be available to a broad range of injured victims and bystanders who suffered health consequences as a result of the 9/11 attacks.

All of these cases, guided by the related case rule in the Southern District of New York, landed in the courtroom of Judge Alvin K. Hellerstein, a lifelong New Yorker whose courtroom, and office before that, sat a half-mile from the Twin Towers. It was possible—even likely—that Judge Hellerstein personally knew some who died in the disaster. Did he know the now-widows and widowers who came before him as plaintiffs? Had he worked—perhaps, dined—with any of the parties? Did he disclose his relationships and, if so, to what end?

Having been handed these cases, Judge Hellerstein had to first develop a matrix—with computer-generated statistical analyses—to address the claims and defenses in a way to ensure fairness to all parties. It would be impossible in this discussion to detail the ways in which he managed these cases, giving consideration to the plights of the plaintiffs as well as the contentions of the defendants. Indeed, the cases were so numerous, and the claims so diverse, that a special master was appointed with the primary task of organizing the claims so that there could be a reliable count of the plaintiffs involved and the specific harm they sustained, which were ultimately categorized by severity.

By all accounts, the defendants' counsel took a scorched-earth approach, litigating every aspect of the case and ultimately charging several hundred million in fees and expenses. By the time the case was ready for the first wave of staggered trials, 1,200 depositions had been taken and more than 100 motions were pending. With the prospect of trial, the parties reviewed their claims—the number of plaintiffs who suffered only minor injuries and those that sustained serious injury. Could those who were seriously hurt be fairly compensated without exceeding the likely available funds? Was the City of New York immune from suit, or was it an "employer" to some, so that different rules applied? Would the defendants have succeeded in *Daubert* hearings so that plaintiffs could not present expert testimony, thus losing their ability to receive compensation as a matter of law?[2]

Given the innumerable issues, the lawyers did what lawyers must often do—in 2010, before a single witness was called, they announced that they had settled: $575 million would be paid to the plaintiffs (with additional monies up to $657 million available under certain circumstances). Of that, counsel demanded approximately $200 million—the third of the recovery set forth in their retainer agreements. In response, Judge Hellerstein did what judges rarely do—he rejected the settlement even though no party in court stood up to oppose it. His action was applauded—in both the courtroom and the press. But what were his reasons? Was he concerned that counsel for plaintiffs—who had worked on a contingency and who borrowed millions to fund the lawsuits, including to pay the more than $3 million in court filing fees alone—were to receive too much of the pie? Was he concerned that the fund was withholding too much money for potential future claims, even though nine years had passed since the Towers fell? Or was the settlement insufficient because it simply did not give the plaintiffs enough money?

And in rejecting the settlement, Judge Hellerstein necessarily acknowledged that these cases were not "class" actions, which would have

---

2.   Daubert v. Merrell Dow Pharmaceuticals, 509 U.S. 579 (1993).

unequivocally subjected the terms to a fairness hearing. Did Judge Heller-stein inwardly—or even outwardly—question whether he had the authority to reject the terms? Was he concerned that a party, rather than accept his decision and go back to the settlement table, would appeal his ruling? Or did he conclude that, given that the attorneys represented so many plaintiffs, there was an inherent conflict—that they may have settled the cases of those severely hurt for less than they could have received at trial in an attempt to also settle the claims of those with minor injuries? Indeed, because of the sheer number of plaintiffs, was it the lawyers—and not the parties—who controlled the settlement? And did these factors allow him to resolve coun-sels' "conflict" by becoming the arbiter of what was "fair," notwithstanding that the settlement proposed was one made between parties to a litigation with the advice of competent counsel on one side, and plaintiffs' counsel alone on the other (subject to ratification by the represented plaintiffs)?

The parties did go back to the table and three months later arrived at a settlement for approximately $150 million more than initially proposed. Controversial and determined to the end, Judge Hellerstein cut plaintiffs' attorneys' fees to 25 percent—amounting to roughly $185 million in legal fees—and denied them the right to receive interest (more than $6 million) on the $30 million they borrowed to fund the suits.

Yes, despite the admirable work they performed and that, in Judge Hell-erstein's words, counsel "took on the cause" and "financed this cause at great, great expense," he determined that the settlement monies (or was it their work?) did not justify their fees. Did Judge Hellerstein consider the loans taken by plaintiffs' counsel to fund the case and the personal guar-antees they were required to give the lenders?

Did Judge Hellerstein—himself a litigator in private practice for 38 years prior to taking the bench—put aside what he personally knew about what it meant to be a litigator? Indeed, did he consider what he would have done differently had he been counsel for the plaintiffs? As defense counsel, would he have subscribed to a combative, take-no-prisoners plan of attack?

Was Judge Hellerstein concerned that, by rejecting the settlement, he would force parties to trial, even though it likely meant certain plaintiffs would receive nothing because it was probable they would not meet their *Daubert* proofs? Or did he roll the dice on their behalf, believing that if there was $575 million in settlement funds, there was indeed more? And did he see it as his job to play chicken simply because he alone thought the lawyers were getting too much money, and because aggressively "pursuing justice" was ultimately a responsibility that motivated him throughout the litigation?

And what did Judge Hellerstein think of the final settlement and how its terms would be disclosed to the plaintiffs (a percentage of whom had to approve the terms)? Having obtained a "fair" settlement—or as fair as he believed could be achieved—did Judge Hellerstein believe it was his job to meet with the plaintiffs to explain the terms to them? And did he advocate in favor of the settlement, believing it was the best plaintiffs could hope to gain?

The Dialogue

JC: In talking about the so-called 9/11 cases that you handled over the last ten years or so, we could discuss many different issues; but I wanted to concentrate on what led you to initially reject the settlement mutually proposed by both sides.

But before we go into that—I have wondered about this macro issue: Everyone in New York knew someone, directly or indirectly, who died on 9/11, or suffered serious injury or disease resulting from it. These chambers are literally in the shadow of the World Trade Center. Looking out this window on 9/11, you could have seen the billowing smoke. Like most New Yorkers, for two months afterwards, if you were downwind from the World Trade Center, you could still smell the horrific odor from that *ad hoc* putative cemetery as far away as five or six miles . . .

AKH: I could smell it every day when I entered this Courthouse.

JC: Despite the catastrophe that was almost adjacent to this Courthouse, you were called upon to sit on a case involving thousands of people who suffered in the aftermath of those 3,000 murders. If you were sitting, instead, in Kansas or Montana or Tennessee, you might have been able to be reasonably objective about what was pending before you. Could that possibly have been so for a judge where the facts were so proximate to you and your daily life?

AKH: I think that putting on the robes, or sitting at a desk like this, trains you to be objective. It trains you to be aware of your biases—given that we all have biases—to try to judge the case according to its merits and not according to your biases. In the cases I sat on, there was no "good" side or "bad side." I dealt with people who on both sides were innocents. The people who claimed to have suffered injury were suing the City or aviation companies or insurance companies who insured the City and the aviation companies, the private contractors and the like. None were bad individuals or entities in the conventional sense. Maybe some were negligent, but no one was bad. There were very few workplace injuries. So it's not a question of good guys against bad guys.

JC: But even with no good guys or bad guys, there were victims—maybe not all 10,000 plaintiffs . . .

AKH: Yes, some were seriously injured. Some were along for the ride.

JC: But knowing that some were indeed seriously injured, was it possible—despite your "objectivity" training—for you to be as objective as if you had lived elsewhere and hadn't encountered, both on the street and in the media, day after day, month after month, the post-9/11 suffering?

AKH: What I saw, smelled and heard, had nothing to do with the conditions of the plaintiffs. The plaintiffs might be entitled to recovery, but they had to prove their cases. Anticipating this interview, I tried to develop some of the things that I thought about. One recollection was my determination that the cases had to be aired—everyone had to be given a shot to prove his case. In that sense, I did have a bias to advance the merits. Second, I was particularly aware of a very heavy social responsibility. I was aware of a bias in society about plaintiffs' lawyers, about insurance companies, about people who might not have suffered injury but still sought a recovery. And I wanted to run this case, as best I could, in a way that the man on the street would find respectful of everyone, without letting anyone take advantage of anyone else. I wanted this process to be a credit to the courts and to the judicial system—to basically show that they worked. Indeed, I had a very close relationship to some people involved in the case.

JC: By "some people," you mean parties?

AKH: Yes. The earliest litigation had to do with the Special Victim Compensation Fund and the special master. One problem was trying to define just what the Fund was supposed to do. Some of the estates of those who died were people of extreme wealth who could make substantial recoveries if they sued. If they went into the Compensation Fund, they feared they wouldn't get their full due. And yet, the Fund was supposedly open to all. So they brought a lawsuit claiming that the Fund was not constructed lawfully. They wanted it changed to eliminate what they perceived to be the ceiling of recovery. Ultimately I held that there was no ceiling. But in this context, certain aspects of the case concerned me greatly as to bias.

First, I was reading affidavits and declarations of widows of people I actually knew. Indeed, Cantor Fitzgerald had been a client of mine, and I had litigated for them. Its principals were guests when I was inducted as a judge. I had worked with the people who died, and was compelled to read the affidavits of their widows. I had previously enjoyed breakfast at the Cantor Fitzgerald offices that were destroyed. And so I had an intimate knowledge of the parties.

I also wanted very much for the Fund to succeed because, to the extent it succeeded, it removed pressures in the cases before me and made more possible that there would be enough money for everyone entitled to recovery. This is because the Fund was funded by appropriations from Congress, and it had no ceiling. Ultimately, [Kenneth] Feinberg paid out over $6 billion. If that money had not been paid out by the Fund, it may have affected the ability of the carriers to pay out cases that were sustained against them. So I badly wanted that Fund to succeed. Third, I wanted to be sure that plaintiffs had the right to choose between them. That choice was not procured by pressure or by fraud. I wanted it open. So I tried to construct the whole thing as an open proceeding. With regard to the people and parties I knew, I knew people on both sides very well. So when I first became aware of this, I wrote a letter describing my conflicts, so that if people wanted to challenge me we could consider that . . .

JC: When you say you knew people on both sides, who on the defendants' side would you have known?

AKH: I gave Feinberg his first job.

JC: He was a party?

AKH: He was. It was *Collaio v. Feinberg*. Mark Muller and I had been friends for 20 years—he represented the aviation plaintiffs, many of them.

JC: Aren't you sort of making my point? Given the relationships that you had—relationships you wouldn't have had sitting in Omaha or Nashville or Montana—were you able, in your own mind, to do what you needed to do as "pure" judge, uninfluenced by the possibility of personal bias?

AKH: There's no such thing as purity in judgment. Without facts and context, judgment becomes abstract—you lose out on the passion of judging. Justice does not require absolute purity, but a check on bias. I'll go back to the Biblical signpost above your head: "Justice, Justice shalt thou pursue." Why does the Bible, which does not like to repeat a word, repeat "justice"? There are many interpretations, but the one I like best is that "Because justice is elusive it must be found. There must be a search for it. One must have a passion to find justice." To the extent that you treat this as just another aviation accident you lose the sense of the passion to do justice because there has been an outrage. That outrage must find its way into the sorting-out of the lawsuit.

JC: You mentioned before that you were aware going in that there was some bias against plaintiffs' lawyers. I assume you meant that they are in it "for the buck."

AKH: That's not what I meant.

JC: What did you mean?

AKH: I came to believe that one set of plaintiffs' lawyers had not screened their cases and were bringing cases to create a mass. In that way it would create leverage to help plaintiffs' side against defendants. And there were certain things that I found out in the course of presiding over the cases that fortified that view. But I would say that I myself didn't have a bias against these lawyers.

JC: No. I'm not saying that you had a bias against them, but that you felt that the public might have some bias against them.

AKH: The public is biased against trial lawyers. There have been various measures in Congress and various epithets used about trial lawyers. That's what I was referring to. I don't have any bias against lawyers—I was one, as you know, for 38 years before I became a judge.

JC: So of the roughly 10,000 plaintiffs in the combined cases . . .

AKH: More. There were 11,000 filed cases dealing with people claiming injury from working on the World Trade Center.

JC: Did you have a sense of what percentage of those were bogus claims?

AKH: "Bogus" is not a good way to put it. When enough discovery had come in to allow us to take a statistical sampling, we found that almost a third of the cases had no observable damage—that people who claimed damages could produce no medical tests to support their claims. And then we also found that about eight or nine percent of the cases, when pushed, resulted in plaintiffs failing to show up. They didn't show up for discovery, or were duplicate claims.

JC: When you didn't accept the term bogus, does that mean that you concluded there may have been actual injuries, but they weren't observable?

AKH: Yes. Compensable injury requires proof—you need some proof that you suffered an injury.

JC: When you say you're bothered that some of the plaintiffs' lawyers didn't screen their cases sufficiently, it's that they didn't screen the cases to determine which were compensable?

AKH: Yes. And accordingly they were doing their clients a disservice. Under New York law you have until a manifestation of injury to sue. It's possible that some individuals who had suits filed on their behalf did so because they had a cough or something like that, that would create a case with a small recovery. Or maybe no recovery.

JC: Was there anything that you could do to insure that the plaintiffs were legitimate plaintiffs in the sense that their injuries could be compensable?

AKH: Yes.

JC: What did you do?

AKH: We designed a discovery program requiring every plaintiff to respond with sworn answers to interrogatories designed to obtain disclosures—where they worked; when they worked; what kinds of safety devices were they given; what instructions were they given. Thus, everyone had to tell something about the essential facts of this case. If people didn't respond, I dismissed their cases—indicating to me that those whose cases were dismissed never really wanted to sue in the first place. Or at least many of them.

JC: How many cases got dismissed that way?

AKH: A thousand. Not all were dismissed. Rather, I was beginning to put them in a posture of dismissing them when the settlement came along. Because of the interest of the insurance company in taking care of every potential claimant, many of these cases were included. When they didn't show up the second time around, I dismissed them.

JC: If this case were a "class action," you would have had far greater supervisory power.

AKH: Yes and no. I would have been able to supervise a fairness hearing regarding fees and with the fairness and value of the overall settlement. I did that anyway. But there would have been specific provisions of law in Federal Rule 23 giving me this right. However, once a settlement is approved, typically the judge does not have oversight responsibilities. He could have, but he doesn't really have it in terms of the distribution of the money. That's left to the plaintiffs' lawyers. Sometimes there are different plaintiffs at different subclasses, and the judge has some power there. But typically there's very little oversight on the administration of a fund. By the way, I arranged the cases as aggregates of individual actions, I had supervisory power from beginning to end.

JC: There's a view that some have held that you arrogated—I don't use that word as an *ad hominem*—to yourself, powers that you really didn't have because you were displeased with the settlement proposed by both parties.

AKH: I don't agree with that word. I did gather to myself powers. There are two paradigms in settling civil actions. [Federal] Rule [of Civil Procedure] 23(e), the class action rule, accords the judge the duty to conduct a fairness hearing with regard to the settlement and fees. And Rule 41 allows dismissal at plaintiffs' request without a court order. If all parties settle, under Rule 41 there's no provision for a judge to supervise or review or sign off on the settlement. There's a practice in the Southern District of New York giving the judge that signature power but it's not necessary—it's a case that would be settled by the decision of the parties and lawyers alone, without the judge, particularly if the judge is not asked to do anything. So, I had to confront the situation where it was neither a class action nor individual action. And if I didn't "arrogate"—as you use the term—this power to review and supervise, there was great danger of inadequacies in these cases.

JC: With great respect to you, the plaintiffs and the defendants, both sides presumably well represented, wanted this resolution. Plaintiffs' counsel—capable lawyers, by most accounts—decided that the sum proposed was sufficient for their clients. Why did you feel the need to get involved?

AKH: When you settle a case for a client, who settles? Whose signature is critical . . . The client.

JC: Right.

AKH: Who has the right of approval?

JC: The client.

AKH: Who gives the instructions to the lawyer?

JC: The client.

AKH: In this case the agreement was between one party—the insurance company representing the City—and the lawyers for the plaintiffs, subject to ratification by ninety-five percent of their clients. Those that didn't ratify were basically opting to continue their lawsuits. That's a different paradigm.

JC: You're basically saying that these lawyers, in entering into this settlement, had a conflict with their own clients?

AKH: Potentially.

JC: Isn't that the case in every single individual case?

AKH: No.

JC: With a single plaintiff automobile accident, the lawyer thinks that if the case is settled for a million bucks his share will be $333,000. He wants that settlement rather than litigate a case that he might lose. The client wants to go for broke and demand $3,000,000 or go to trial. That lawyer too is conflicted, isn't he?

AKH: No. The paradigm there is the lawyer recommending the settlement to the client. But the client has the final decision. I'm confronted with that almost daily. Part of the judge's job is to try to accomplish settlements. Parties want to settle and the judge can facilitate the settlement. But it's always subject to the client's review. In many instances the lawyer will tell me "I wish I could settle but my client doesn't want to." In the case of these 9/11 cases—these aggregates—it didn't break that way. The money that was offered was not individual. It was for the group. There was an upside and a downside.

And the mode of settlement for class actions—Judge Weinstein has called these aggregates "quasi class actions"—I didn't use that. I mentioned it when I justified what I did. But the hallmark of what we're doing is "fairness." And fairness is very hard to measure if one lawyer represents a lot of clients. How do you measure fairness when the lawyer has to look to settle *en masse*? Are the really good cases being compromised in order to settle the weaker cases? Are the weaker cases getting more than they should be entitled to because of the defendant's desire to get releases from everyone? If a lawyer has been carrying the case for five or six years, borrowing at compound interest at rates going to 16 and 17 percent, is a lawyer independent when it comes to the opportunity to settle? Will he give the clients fair advice? Will he describe his potential conflict adequately? I think all these have to concern the judge and cause the judge to be more active in reviewing the case than the judge might be if it were one party against another.

JC: Let me be blunt in my next question.

AKH: As opposed to the previous questions?

JC: Even more so in this instance, my friend. Were you more bothered by the clients not getting enough of the pie, or by the lawyers getting too much of the pie?

AKH: Both. Because my experience with settlement is that defendants want to put up a certain sum and are indifferent to how it's divided.

JC: But the lawyers made a considerable investment in this case.

AKH: I was respectful that these lawyers had carried the case and brought it to the point where it could settle—that they had done a great job in doing that. They had proved their endurance, their zealotry, and that they were ready to take the case when other lawyers might not have been ready to.

JC: And they made a considerable investment of their own funds.

AKH: Yes, all that.

JC: The lawyers had made substantial investments of time and money for filing fees, experts and the like. Yet you were concerned that the plaintiffs weren't getting enough of the pie and the lawyers getting too much of it? Does that mean you're bothered generally with plaintiffs' lawyers in contingency cases?

AKH: No.

JC: In class action cases do you typically reduce the plaintiff lawyers' recovery?

AKH: Sometimes I add, sometimes I subtract.

JC: Sometimes you "add" to the plaintiffs' lawyers' recovery?

AKH: They ask for a certain amount, generally a liberal amount in relation to both percentage of recovery and in terms of what we call lodestar. So I typically don't give percentages of recoveries. I typically give the lodestar plus or minus a bonus or discount to reflect success, or lack of success, and quality of their work.

JC: Had you given thought in the 9/11 cases to, instead of rejecting the settlement outright, bringing in a monitor to assess whether the plaintiffs were satisfied with their recoveries—rather than, sort of *locus parentis*, deciding for yourself that it wasn't good enough?

AKH: How would I assess whether they got enough of the settlement? Compared to what? Compared to getting nothing? Compared to getting what they deserved? That's a difficult question.

You know why I believed the settlement was not enough? It's very hard to analyze a complicated settlement like this and say whether it's enough. You go to people experienced in settling personal injury cases, and settlements are all over the place. It's a function of the individual case. The extent of the injuries. The way the person has suffered. The ability to prove a case. Other considerations. It's very hard to do. So certain things affected me. One, the nature of the potential conflicts that I talked about. This was not a party driven settlement but rather lawyer driven, based on large categories of numbers that could not really be related to the merits of particular cases. Two, it drove from an analysis of the nature of the insurance recovery. Three, it reflected what I had experienced in the case.

So all the money for the settlement was coming from FEMA. FEMA had given the City a billion dollars to fund its defense and to pay the liabilities and litigation expenses of the City and its contractors. When the number was first agreed to by the lawyers, and I announced it to the assembled throng of plaintiffs and their lawyers, I commented that now the case is easy to settle. And the plaintiffs' lawyers said, "No, we need a lot more." And they went into intensive discovery. To find out the insurance situation for all the individual contractors caused six months of proceedings, I think. Lots of motion practice. So now they were settling for a fraction of that. So I asked myself, why was a billion dollars too little at one time and much too much now? And so I thought the plaintiffs settled for less than they might have gotten.

Secondly, and apropos of that, I thought there was a disparity in bargaining power. Even though the plaintiffs got all they could get, their lawyers didn't have the leverage, because the lawyers were overextended through borrowing. Third, the insurance company was not a continuing insurance company. It was a "single purpose" insurance company. Except for this case, they had no other purpose in life—so they were holding back much more money than I thought they needed to. That indicated to me that there was more that they should have been spending on this case. Those considerations, among others, led me to believe that the settlement was insufficient.

JC: While this was going on, given that you had been in practice for some 38 years, did you consider what you would have done differently were you the plaintiffs' lawyers or the defendants' lawyers?

AKH: I wouldn't have been a plaintiffs' lawyer in a case like this. But I did do some plaintiffs' cases. And, whether I'd be a plaintiff's lawyer or a defendant's lawyer, I would like to think that I would have handled the case in a more disciplined fashion than either of these sets of lawyers did.

JC: "Disciplined" meaning what?

AKH: As a defendant I wouldn't have spent the money they spent, at least I would like to think that. If I were the plaintiffs' lawyer I would have screened my cases and done much more to bring everyone along. But my experience probably isn't important here because I was not a products liability lawyer.

JC: Whether you were a products liability lawyer or not, you were a complex case litigator. You certainly would have had some ideas. As a more "disciplined" lawyer, you would have done something different. For example?

AKH: I think they were litigating too many issues. It's hard to understand all that goes on in a case and I'm not sure that's a sensible position for me to take. It may be more of a bias.

JC: As a plaintiffs' lawyer, wouldn't it have been extraordinarily difficult to tell a possible victim—a first responder, for example, who honestly

believed that he had contracted some horrible disease from the 9/11 dust—
"Look pal, I don't think you have a case because I don't see the medical
reports supporting your claim. Sorry, but I'm rejecting you as a client"?

AKH: That's not how the cases were taken on by the lawyers. They're
taken in union halls or firemen's associations or policemen's associations
and they're signed up. There's a book, "City of Dust," that discusses how
some of these cases were brought.

JC: Again, you say you were bothered by the fact that the lawyers
weren't more disciplined. I've also heard you to say that you felt that the
amount of litigation that was going on in the defense side caused unnecessary work on the plaintiffs' side.

AKH: Typically, the way to defend in a case like this or in a class action
is to wear out the plaintiffs' lawyers.

JC: Take too many depositions, and the like?

AKH: Yes.

JC: And since they're getting paid on an hourly basis, there's no investment on their side—whereas the plaintiffs' counsel would have to redouble
their efforts with no guarantee of compensation for their time.

AKH: It's an asymmetrical motivation. The plaintiffs' lawyers are thus
motivated to economize. And the defendants' lawyers are motivated to
increase their fees.

JC: What can a judge do to stop that?

AKH: I don't know. Try to control the case. Try to move the case in stages.
Try to get the people to account for the depositions they take to make sure
they have a firm idea of what they expect to get from those depositions.
And to make judgments according to practicality.

JC: Are you saying there's some flaw in the litigation process that
allows lawyers to do this kind of thing?

AKH: It's not a perfect process. I don't have any recommended solu-
tions. What I try to do is just to go from meeting to meeting to plan with
the lawyers what the next stages are and to try to exert whatever judicial
power I have to keep things in balance.

JC: Did you give them the sense during these meetings or court appear-
ances that you were disturbed that they were running up the clock?

AKH: Yes.

JC: And what did they say in response to that?

AKH: They didn't. These are my observations that I expressed to the lawyers.

JC: When you rejected the settlement . . .

AKH: I would say there was abuse on both sides.

JC: Well, the abuse on the plaintiffs' side wouldn't be running up the clock.

AKH: It was their unwillingness to make their cases clear—trying to obfuscate the good cases with the bad cases.

JC: You're basically saying that the settlement process leads to settling cases for . . .

AKH: It's the whole process. It starts with the pleading. And plaintiffs' lawyers try to make sure they can cover everything by their pleading so they're not giving precise notice. At pre-trial meetings, I tried to get more precision on the part of the plaintiffs' pleadings so that we can handle the case in a more intelligent way, but I couldn't get it.

JC: When you rejected the settlement the first time it was presented to you, did you do an analysis in deciding that you wanted to reject it, or were the numbers just so bothersome on their face that you said "I'm not going to accept this"?

AKH: I read the agreement. I considered what was being held back and that was much too much.

JC: Please explain "being held back."

AKH: In reserve by the insurance company, in case there would be later cases. I didn't think there would be later cases, or that they would amount to anything.

JC: And you thought that the legal fees were too high?

AKH: And I thought the plaintiffs' legal fees were too high and that if the plaintiffs' lawyers didn't have all those fees that the plaintiffs themselves would get more of that money.

JC: Did you consider telling them the number that you wanted to accept as a settlement?

AKH: No.

JC: Is there a reason?

AKH: Because the bargaining process was theirs, not mine.

JC: But weren't you getting involved in the bargaining process?

AKH: Uncomfortably so.

JC: Why didn't you take that extra step and say, for example, "I need another hundred million dollars for these plaintiffs"?

AKH: You know how negotiations go. If the judge says a hundred million dollars, the parties will try him at 50 million dollars or 60 million dollars. I left it open. The way it came out is that the insurance company put in an additional 50 million dollars and that money was going to the seriously injured. They enlarged the fields of those who would be entitled to seek recovery to include more cancer patients. They created a better process. The plaintiffs' lawyers, by reducing their fees from the 33–1/3 that they wanted to 25 percent, yielded another 50 million dollars into the pot. And they were able to negotiate the abatement of liens that amounted to maybe another 50 million dollars, or even more. So the ultimate settlement in its net effect was probably worth $150 million more than the first one. Plus, I think my active involvement in the case led to settlement with the Port Authority and other defendants that added another $75 million to the case.

JC: Needless to say, the 9/11 cases will have been viewed now and in history as the hallmark of your judicial career. Is it the most important thing you have done as a judge?

AKH: In the concept of administering a large number of cases and not letting it bog down my overall calendar—because I continued drawing the same number of cases as every other judge—I think it was a big achievement. In the sense of bringing justice and resolution to a large number of people, I think it was a big achievement. But you, Joel, have heard me talk about justice in smaller cases that gives me even more satisfaction.

JC: Since our readers wouldn't otherwise know that you and I are good friends, they would also not know that some years ago, while this case was proceeding in its heyday, I had the sense and worry—and maybe expressed it to you in these terms—that the overall case seemed to be grinding you down.

AKH: At times it did.

JC: Because of the legal work that you were being required to administer, or the pain that people had suffered that was before you on a daily basis, month after month, year after year?

AKH: No, not really.

JC: What was it?

AKH: It was that I felt that I didn't have a solution to the case. At various times I just didn't see a light at the end of the tunnel. I was feeling defeated by the sheer complexity and magnitude of the cases and, in that sense, I felt oftentimes depressed that I would not be equal to the task.

JC: Obviously that turned out not to be true.

AKH: I didn't know it then. It reminds me of a time as a trial lawyer where I really had delivered a good summation in a case and I won even though I had no right to win. One of my colleagues in the firm said, "You know Al, I'd like to read your summation." I said, "There's only one problem. There's no typed summation." I hadn't asked the court reporter to take it down. So, "Why didn't you ask the reporter to take it down?" I said "I didn't know before I began it that it would be so good." [laughter.] That may seem immodest, but that's the way I feel about this.

JC: If another tragedy like this occurred and you were assigned the case of this magnitude, what would you do differently?

AKH: Probably every step would be different. You read the judicial manual for complex litigation, you read some articles, you do other things. But basically this case was unparalleled. It had no precedent. There were several hundred different types of injuries to address. The magnitude of cases—eleven thousand. It defied easy resolution. There was jockeying among the different lawyers at the beginning. To get all this in one place and under some kind of management. It proved to be very difficult. I made a decision, first, that there would not be a class action. And the second major decision was that I would not surrender control to the lawyers. I needed to create a discovery program that could be automated, that could be subject to computer analysis, that would allow everybody equal footing to understand the cases, including the court. And under some kind of a schedule that would drive inexorably towards resolution at some reasonably prompt point. And that was very difficult because plaintiffs do not want to be definite and certain in their pleadings. They want to plead in a conclusory fashion. They often don't know enough about their own plaintiffs. They have too many to make this kind of analysis. They don't want to put themselves into a box and make it easier for the defendants to shoot at that box. So they try to be amorphous and to surround the defendants with huge numbers of cases to create uncertainty on their part. Defendants want to run their cases to take some of the élan out of the plaintiffs' lawyers and to grind down the case to make it difficult for the plaintiffs to recover. And these two motivations, these two tendencies were not jelling in a way that would allow me to grab hold of the case.

My two special masters, the professors, were appointed initially because I couldn't get accurate numbers of how many cases there actually were. There were wide differences between the plaintiffs' counts and the defendants' counts. And unless I knew the number of cases and what they were, I couldn't really grab hold of the cases. That was hard to do. Plaintiffs would bring cases to me, removed from the state supreme court, in batches of a hundred. I insisted that each plaintiff have his own index number. Otherwise I'd never get control. Otherwise I'd never get a sequence of cases. And that was done. And so gradually I got control of the case. And then the special masters were able to find a wonderful computer company that could work with us and I was trying to develop a core discovery program that was acceptable to gradation in terms of what a computer can analyze. We were able to achieve that. And as a result I was able to get a substantial amount of discovery disclosures in each and every case. Typically sampling takes place, the lawyers are asked to pick a couple of cases, and we'll try them. And we'll try some more cases until some number comes out and we get the valuation of the cases, and a few different kinds of scenarios and then there can be an overall settlement. I didn't feel this could work. There were too many injuries. There was too much complexity. And I didn't want to surrender control of the cases to the lawyers.

And so I developed a paradigm, and I think this could be a matrix for all these aggregate cases. So that everyone, lawyers and judge and special masters would have the same set of reliable data points. And they could then look at the case and consider similarities, patterns and derive values. And then go into a sampling of intensive discovery which would be a check on the reliability, because if the answers did not support the interrogatory answers then we'd know there was some problem. And we'd get very good information about each case and then make another sampling to select cases to go to trial. And that's how we laid it out. And in the context of that the settlement was reached.

JC: You went on a bit of a "road show" to "sell" the settlement to the plaintiffs, didn't you?

AKH: To "sell" is to express the view of some of my critics in the court.

JC: As I recall it, you did that over my personal advice to you. Did you find that any of the plaintiffs were unhappy that you rejected the original settlement?

AKH: None. When I announced in court that the settlement was not enough—that there was too much for the lawyers and not enough for the plaintiffs—I was embarrassed at the applause I got. The Daily News put me on its front Sunday page. There was one word on the front cover. It said, "Finally." There was an overwhelmingly favorable response. I told the parties that if they could come up with a settlement that I would find reasonable I would create a procedure by which we would go out to the people where they lived and explain the settlement to them so that they could make the decision for themselves.

And I would let people know what my views were. When the settlement came in, I approved it, I approved it as fair and reasonable, not perfect. It was not perfect because I didn't think that it included enough of the cancer cases. The cancer cases were hard to prove as to causation and since the settlement was not a compensation scheme but a settlement, the consensus view among the lawyers and others was that the settlement should not be just giving money to people who couldn't prove the likelihood that their sicknesses derived from their work on 9/11. I felt differently. I felt the converse also was true. You couldn't disprove it. When people went to work at the WTC site, they were healthy. Then they got sick. And in their minds the work was a contributing cause to their sickness and there should be some allowance for them in the settlement. But I never achieved that.

JC: Did you get criticism for the "road show"?

AKH: No. I spoke about it with some of my colleagues, and based on their early criticisms I adapted modified procedures and the procedures worked. Instead of my making the presentation I had a full complement of lawyers on the case with a court reporter and with court officers—we in effect extended the Southern District of New York into Staten Island and into Queens to reach most of the people. It was virtually the same as if it were in my courtroom, which obviously couldn't happen with the sheer numbers of plaintiffs involved. I invited the press and I had each side explain their views on the case. I regulated the procedure. I spoke also. Ken Feinberg spoke—he was the special master for appeals from determinations by the administrator of the settlement. And in effect we had the same kind of presentation that we would have had in the Southern District of New York, bringing it to where the people were.

JC: What was the core criticism by your colleagues?

AKH: They thought it was inappropriate for the judge to go out and advocate the settlement. And I thought there was some point to what they said—that there had to be a distinction between explaining the settlement and advocating the settlement. Nonetheless, I had a view and I was going to express it. I do think the procedure I created was enormously improved by the criticisms I received.

JC: But at the end of the day you did advocate, didn't you?

AKH: I presented my views. People asked me what I thought. I said I thought the settlement was not perfect, but reasonable. And people came and expressed their views and some people were regretful that they could not qualify and there was debate at some of the meetings. There were people who came up and spoke against it and that engendered debate. The debate was more by the people involved there than by me. I didn't debate.

JC: Last question. If another mass tort case were to be rolled out to Judge Hellerstein should the plaintiffs' lawyers, or defendants' lawyers, or both, be troubled by it being assigned to you?

AKH: I hope not. I hope not. I don't know if they criticize me as being fair or unfair, hard or not hard. Obstructive or not. In my own mind, I think I moved the cases towards a resolution that was fair. I think I was respectful of both sides, and I think both sides felt that they had a very good day in court. And a judge who can produce that, I think the judge is doing his work.

You know, an adversary procedure motivates people sometimes to go to excess. And when there's a check on excess and when people go into the median and substantial justice gets done, I think everyone is basically pleased. And I think the fact that over 99% of the eligible people approved the settlement—both those that were getting small amounts of money and those getting sizable amounts of money—is a very powerful approval. I don't know of any settlement that has achieved a 99% plus vote of approval. I don't know of anything in life that gets a 99% plus vote of approval.

And I guess that's the best reflection of what I did and frankly, what I'm very proud of having achieved.

Chapter 6

Judge David Hittner

The one thing we're taught as lawyers is that we need to be able to see the other side. You may disagree with the other side; but as lawyers, if you understand where the other folks are coming from, you can try to work toward the center. If you can't, then the judge has his or her role.
—Judge David Hittner, July 30, 2013

Judge David Hittner was nominated to the U.S. District Court for the Southern District of Texas in 1986 by President Ronald Reagan. He has a reputation as tough, creative, and no-nonsense.

In addition to ruling that the remaining residents of Allen Parkway Village had to immediately vacate or be arrested after a more than ten-year battle with Houston's Housing Authority (discussed in this interview), Judge Hittner granted a writ of habeas corpus to a defendant who was convicted of murder and sentenced to death while his attorney slept through key portions of the trial, repeating the Ninth Circuit's admonition that sleeping counsel is equivalent to having no counsel at all. (Remarkably, a panel of the Fifth Circuit reversed in a 2–1 opinion, but then affirmed the district court, en banc. The U.S. Supreme Court denied certiorari.) In his Enron matter, he rejected the plea deal reached for Lea Fastow, believing it insufficient.

Judge Hittner presided over the case of financier Robert Allen Stanford. Determining that he was competent to stand trial once doctors weaned him from his medications, Judge Hittner sentenced him to 110 years in prison after his conviction by a jury for running a Madoff-type Ponzi scheme. In another Ponzi scheme matter (a mere $7.8 million scam, far smaller than

Stanford's $7 billion deceptions), Judge Hittner sentenced former Houston lawyer Bill Davis to ten years, time in excess of the sentencing guidelines. In announcing the sentence, Judge Hittner read from victim statements where it became apparent that Davis traded on his friendships to support his criminal activity. He also presided over the case of Alydar, the injured racehorse who had been insured for some $30 million.

The U.S. Supreme Court's June 2013 decision striking key portions of the Voting Rights Act immediately came to Judge Hittner's attention when, the day after the Supreme Court ruled, he denied the stay he was asked to consider, rejecting claims that annexation of a Texas school district would violate the rights of minority voters. In so doing, he noted that Texas no longer needed to seek preclearance for a change affecting voting.

His years in Texas notwithstanding, Judge Hittner is a native New Yorker. Born in Schenectady, he received his B.S. from New York University and his law degree from NYU School of Law and was admitted to the New York bar. He joined the army in 1965, during which time he served as an infantry captain and paratrooper and was later assigned to Fort Polk, on the Louisiana–Texas border. Taking the Texas bar, he became a trial attorney until taking the Texas State District Court bench in 1978, where he served until appointed to the federal bench in 1986. Judge Hittner assumed senior status in 2004. A Boy Scout, Judge Hittner earned 81 merit badges and achieved the rank of Eagle Scout. He serves on the national council of the Boy Scouts of America.

Judge Hittner sits in Houston, Texas.

An Inner City Project's Demolition

Allen Parkway Village (APV), completed in 1944, was one of the oldest public housing projects in Houston, Texas. It had almost 1,000 apartments and was owned and operated by the Housing Authority of the City of Houston (HACH), a state agency established to provide low-income persons with safe and affordable housing. It received federal funds for the project through HUD—the U.S. Department of Housing and Urban Development. Forty years after its construction, HACH decided to demolish APV, deeming it to have become "obsolete," "physically deteriorated," and "located in a neighborhood which is blighted." The demolition application, as required, contained a plan to allow those living there to be relocated.

The decision to demolish APV was politically charged. Everyone was involved—organizations to protect the poor, state government, federal government, local politicians, architects, historical preservationists, and, of course, the residents. Indeed, before HUD acted on HACH's application to demolish APV, two U.S. Congressmen—Marvin Frost and Mickey Leland—passed an amendment to HUD's appropriations bill that provided that HUD funds could not be used to demolish, among other projects, APV.

The Resident Council and individual residents of APV sued—in what they characterized as a class action on behalf of residents of APV—to enforce the Frost–Leland Amendment to prevent both HUD and HACH from using federal funds to "prepare, revise and advance" the APV demolition application. The District Court, in the person of Judge Kenneth M. Hoyt Jr., granted a preliminary and then ultimately a permanent injunction. Among other things, Judge Hoyt prohibited HACH from spending any funds, if such spending "promotes, advances or explores" the demolition of APV, including using those funds to establish that "rehabilitation and renovation of part or all of HPV are useless."

HACH appealed and, on January 13, 1993, the Fifth Circuit Court of Appeals rang the initial death knell for the plaintiffs. They reversed Judge Hoyt's decision—without getting anywhere near the merits of whether Judge Hoyt was correct that Frost–Leland disallowed the use of federal funds for any demolition activity. Essentially finding that the plaintiffs did not have standing—there being no "private right of action" available to them—the court reversed and remanded the case to the District Court with instructions that the complaint be dismissed. This basically left the plaintiffs with no remedy as, according to the appellate court, they had no right to sue.

The above is what one would learn were he or she to simply read and consider the Fifth Circuit's opinion. The reader would not learn that APV was originally built as an all-white development; that in 1977 the director of HACH first proposed that APV be demolished; that development of the complex was viewed by local historians as having led to the decline of Houston's Fourth Ward; that public housing officials and private developers were in favor of demolishing the housing, while preservationists and residents were in favor of maintaining it; that, over the years, APV had turned into a virtually all-minority project; and that in the 1980s and 1990s the continued future of the Fourth Ward came under attack due to the plans to demolish APV and replace it with high-end housing and office buildings. Further, the Fifth Circuit opinion would not have told the reader that the matter was complicated when, in 1988, APV was listed on the National Register of Historic Places.

Nor did the Fifth Circuit opinion reflect—interestingly, but likely irrelevant to the case's disposition—that Judge Hoyt, appointed by Ronald Reagan, who had granted the injunction in favor of plaintiffs, was only the second African American federal judge to sit in Texas, or that when the case was returned to the District Court after the appellate court reversed, it was not sent to Judge Hoyt. As a matter of procedure, the case was assigned to another district judge, David Hittner, because Judge Hittner had before him a dormant—but earlier filed—companion case.

The Fifth Circuit decided the case with instructions to dismiss in February 1993, yet the remaining residents—dwindling in number but determined nonetheless—were not forced to move until more than three years later when Judge Hittner issued a permanent injunction directing the remaining squatters to evacuate the very day after his order, at penalty of being arrested by the U.S. Marshals. If Judge Hittner had in hand in 1993 a Fifth Circuit order essentially saying that the plaintiffs had reached the end of the road, what would account for the law's delay? Did Judge Hittner agree with Judge Hoyt's decision, which found that there was, indeed, merit to the plaintiffs' assertion that they were being evacuated without suitable alternative housing? Was he swayed by the pleas of the remaining residents who were going to lose their homes with no confidence that HACH would restore the property and let them return? Did anything change when HUD announced, in 1994, that no APV land would be sold for commercial development?

Why would Judge Hittner allow what HACH considered to be a "blight" on the community to continue? Was it a desire to appear to be benevolent? Was it simply an intrinsic inability to address the dire poverty of the squatters with which the Court was being directly confronted? Was it simply the "law's delay" occasioned by the back and forth of motion practice to bring a result to finality? Or did Judge Hittner use his position to help the parties reach an agreement that allowed HACH to tear down and rebuild the project while relocating the remaining residents?

And what of the residents who remained? Were they adequately represented by the plaintiffs' counsel? Were they persuaded to leave peacefully only because of the threat of arrest? And were they able to return to a renovated APV?

The Dialogue

JC: Judge, before we turn to the *Allen Parkway Village* case—I suppose that every judge comes to the bench with certain philosophies of life.

DH: What do you mean by that? You mean as far as a judicial philosophy?

JC: A personal philosophy of life. So it might be "Live and let live." Or not. Or "Give people the benefit of the doubt. " Or not. Or "We as a society have an obligation to help or protect the impoverished, the downtrodden, the underclass." Or not. Or maybe something else. Did you have a view coming on to the bench—or do you have a view coming on to the bench every day—that says that society has an obligation to help the downtrodden?

DH: Oh I think they do. I think that's what the Federal courts are for. If you're looking for a philosophy I've developed in both state court and Federal court, it's this: "If they're not hurting anybody, leave them alone." When it gets to hurting them financially or physically, that's when the court system will step in. If you boil it down to a basic philosophy— I may not agree with some things; but if it's not illegal and not hurting anybody, I'm reluctant to step in just to impose what I think is right. But if I have to, I will.

JC: So turning to the *Allen Parkway Village* case, did you know anything about Allen Parkway Village before the case was wheeled out to you?

DH: Not really. It was a huge, sort of drab looking apartment complex. I guess you'd call them almost like patio homes. It was all of these greyish brown buildings as you drove close to downtown Houston. Low cost housing, predominately minority. But beyond that, no—that's all I knew about it.

JC: Did you know that it was originally begun as largely a white low-income housing project?

DH: Not really. I may have learned that later on, but not initially. It's on one of our main street thoroughfares. It's kind of like a street that's part expressway, but it's a city street—and we were all aware of it and it took up a large area of the frontage road. That was the extent of the knowledge I had of it.

JC: Was there a view, maybe reported in the media, that the project had become pretty much a blight on the community?

DH: I wouldn't say a blight. It certainly was run down—unfortunately in many communities that's the case with public housing. It had seen its better days. But a blight on the community? I couldn't say that.

JC: "Run down" in the sense that local politicians were looking for a way to remedy it?

DH: They all wanted to rehabilitate it. I think that was the concern that the public and the city housing authority had. But again, it never came to me. No issue had ever come before me on Allen Parkway Village in my years on either the state or federal bench. The first time I had heard of it was in the litigation. So a lot of that may have been going on. A lot of city hall court watchers, or community activists were probably aware of it, but not me. Most of the community was not, unless one had real business at city hall and one was looking at the contracts that the city council had a vote on.

JC: I take it when you have a case in the public domain, you sometimes have conversations at community organizations, at family events, or things like that where people might offer their opinions to you about a particular controversy. Not trying to influence you, but just articulating their views.

DH: It rarely came up. Some high profile cases surely do, but Allen Parkway Village didn't. The only time it heated up was when I had to decide: "Do I order it torn down or not?" The hearing was very intense and there was much scrutiny. A lot of politicians from the community were monitoring it closely, some in the courtroom gallery.

JC: Did any politicians actually communicate formally with you as the judge concerning their views of it?

DH: Not at all. Mostly involved were city council members. There was one African-American congressperson in Houston but I never heard from their offices.

JC: As I understand it, when the case was initially assigned to you there was a companion case assigned to Judge Hoyt?

DH: That's correct.

JC: Why were the two cases not related to each other?

DH: For some reason Judge Hoyt's case heated up first, and mine was basically put on hold because a lot of the issues were going to be litigated before Judge Hoyt. When they were later consolidated, because mine had the lower number having been the first filed mine took off.

JC: When there are companion cases in your District but they're not assigned to just one judge, as here, do you typically talk with the judge to whom the related case is assigned?

DH: Sometimes, but not usually.

JC: Do you recall whether you did it in this instance?

DH: I did not.

JC: Is that because you typically don't talk to Judge Hoyt about pending cases or just . . .

DH: It's rare that I ever talk to any other judge about a pending case—perhaps I might congratulate a judge after they've done well, or I think they've done well. Or if it's a case that's somewhat similar. I might ask something like, "What do you think of the lawyers?" And things like that. But generally we don't. We have a very cordial court. In many Federal courts in the country, sometimes there's a lot going on behind the scenes. Some judges don't get along with each other. In Houston, we all come from different political spectrums, but we're all cordial with each other.

JC: But in this case, given that they were companion cases about a controversial issue in the community, why wouldn't you talk to another judge, if you respect him or her, to solicit their views?

DH: You just don't. Rarely does anybody call me when they have something I decided on remand. If I recused myself, I might want them to know the reason, so that they don't think I'm just dumping the case. I might call them off the record and give them a reason why I got off the case. My case manager may call another judge's case manager and just say, "What's behind the scene?" But generally judges don't go one on one.

JC: Maybe I'm beating a dead horse, but why wouldn't you do that? If another judge sitting on your court is someone whose opinions you respect, why not? I can walk down the hall and talk to any number of my colleagues in whom I have confidence to gain the benefit of their wisdom. Why wouldn't you talk to another judge in whom you do have confidence?

DH: Well, you're independent fact finders also. In this case it was reversed and sent back. You don't want to create a mindset one way or another before you take a look at it. At least in my operation, it is very often staff to staff, if at all, rather than judge to judge.

For instance, in a bench trial, I'll very often not get into what the settlement offers were back and forth, because I don't want to know that. They want to talk about that and have a judge be an arbiter, very often I'll say, "Well how about my magistrate judge, or even another district judge?"

JC: So while your case was *de facto* on hold, and Judge Hoyt was deciding his case, he issued a preliminary and then a permanent injunction with respect to the demolition project—deciding that no money from HUD could be used for the demolition project. Were you following that proceeding?

DH: No.

JC: Did you even know about his decision?

DH: I knew about it. I knew he decided it, and I knew that it got reversed. Then when it started heating up and the parties made a motion to consolidate I went ahead. It sounded like an interesting case.

JC: When you first read about Judge Hoyt's decision and you knew he had granted an injunction, did you have some view on your own about what he had done?

DH: No.

JC: Even though you had a companion case?

DH: Believe it or not, my case wasn't hot. It wasn't in front of me and it only got my attention when it was ready to go in my court. That's the honest position. No, I didn't follow it. I read it in the newspaper that he granted the injunction. I just went on. Not oblivious—but sometimes you don't know what case may be on your docket until it starts heating up; until somebody's making noise.

It's like some prisoner that has been in jail without a hearing for a while. We try to keep track of it but only if we get a letter from the prisoner or if his lawyer comes in does it come to the front burner. It just was not on the front burner.

JC: So, then, your philosophy is: If nobody—on either side, plaintiff or defendant—is pushing a case before you (other than a criminal case in which speedy trial or other Sixth Amendment issues are implicated), you'll just let the parties decide on their own to basically hold the case in abeyance?

DH: It does automatically come up every once in a while, due to our initial scheduling order or with what we call the "three-year rule." In other words a case on your docket for three years with no action. We also have a "six-month" rule on pending motions, and we're very conscious of that. So the only time it would bubble up would be the three-year rule, and it did not get to that because by that time I jumped in.

JC: So the Fifth Circuit reversed Judge Hoyt. As you undoubtedly recall, the Circuit didn't reverse him on the merits. It reversed him on whether the plaintiffs had standing to address the issue. Did you, *at that time*, look to see what Judge Hoyt had done, now that the case has basically been consolidated into your courtroom?

DH: I saw what they had in mind, and just made sure I didn't step into the same problems he encountered in the next go-round. The plaintiffs before me were, indeed, aggrieved parties—they were some of the residents.

JC: Is there anything that Judge Hoyt had done in granting the preliminary injunction on the merits, that influenced your thinking one way or another? Perhaps, for example, a view that Judge Hoyt was on point. Or that his decision was all wet. Or did you agree and disagree in some ways?

DH: No. For me, the plaintiffs were coming in brand new. My policy would be, "Tell me what you need." And to the other side, "Why not?"

JC: That's surprising to hear. Another judge of equivalent jurisdiction makes a finding and creates a strong remedy such as an injunction. And you say, "Not interested. I'm a *tabula rasa*."

DH: Remember, he got reversed.

JC: But Judge Hoyt didn't get reversed on the merits. He got reversed on the standing issue.

DH: That's correct. So now it came back to me with the folks who allegedly had standing, and that was in my court. So we pooled whatever was left from his into mine and now I took it with the impediment to the case removed, according to the Fifth Circuit's initial decision.

JC: So now you are presented with a case where there is standing, correct?

DH: Yes. And nobody raised that again, if I remember correctly. Yes, we have "standing," but we need to get this done. We need to get it torn down.

JC: So what was your view of the arguments made by the plaintiffs that it shouldn't be torn down? After all, there were people who lived there, whether you call them "squatters" or not. They feel at the time that, if evicted, they were not going to be accorded equivalent housing. What did you think of that argument?

DH: I didn't buy it.

JC: Why?

DH: All I knew was that the government proved that it was dilapidated, and that they touched all the bases. We had all the *amici* in. We had the architectural people. We had the historical people. We had the African-American groups. We had the Hispanic groups. And they all agreed. So it was an agreed judgment.

They all said, "How did you get it done?" I get that question all the time. I said "Believe it or not it was an agreed judgment." That's why a few of the buildings, even today, are still standing—so you have a few of the original shells of the buildings there. Everything else is brand new public housing. Two story houses. Downstairs and upstairs apartments. Now I haven't been in there in many years. You can see a few of the original structures at the edge of the project.

JC: How did you go about getting them to agree?

DH: I talked to them. I cajoled them. I then checked to see that every legal blockage had been lifted. They'd addressed them all. The environmental studies had been done. The historical commission signed off on it. The architectural people, for the history of architecture in our city, signed off on it. But the bottom line is—especially important with the minority groups representing the residents there—when these groups also signed off on it, I said that I'll go along with it.

JC: When you say you cajoled, how did you cajole?

DH: I just said, "You need to settle this thing. If you need me to jump into it, fine, but I prefer that you do it on your own." I got them back in from time to time, for status conferences. They started looking at it and I kept up the heat as the judge. I did not refer it to my magistrate. I did it all. And little by little they reached an agreement.

I had another case that took me four or five years, to finally get a settlement. I'm not averse to ruling. But there was some heat in the community which is always a potential problem. I didn't want anything breaking down. So I said, "You keep doing it, you keep doing it." I had good lawyers before me and eventually they all agreed. And then I issued the demolition order— by agreement.

The problem was that about a dozen families wouldn't move out, even in light of the order. Most cleared out. But these others said no, notwithstanding that everybody, that is, all of the legal entities that had agreed, including the minority organizations. Then I simply said, "I have a court order here. It may be by agreement, but it's still an order of the court."

JC: What did you do with the squatters who wouldn't leave?

DH: That's where the show of force had to come in.

JC: Before you get to the show of force, did you personally go out to the project?

DH: No, I didn't go out to the property.

JC: Couldn't that have shown them a degree of concern or sensitivity to them?

DH: It might be; but at that point, very frankly, we had an agreed judgment. There were provisions to take care of these folks, and it just was a matter of law. I issued the order and I was going to back it up.

JC: But being the devil's advocate, it seems that while you had all of the lawyers on board, those lawyers, apparently, weren't speaking for those 12 families.

DH: Apparently not.

JC: So it was your sense, given that you had all the *lawyers* on board, they were speaking for everyone?

DH: Not only the lawyers, but the community organizations too. It was just the individual residents, that notwithstanding all of this, touching all the legal bases, and up to a point, when you do something like this, it's also a matter of equity. You're sitting both as a court of law and a court of equity. The question is do I go out to the site, and I just did not. In other words it could have been done like that. I did the best I could. I'd been working with it for three of four years. Good lawyers. Many members of the community understood it and they were ready to vacate and then, eventually, move back in.

I understand the recalcitrance, because it was basically down to turning over your home and moving somewhere else, even temporarily. But that was a judicial decision. Once it was made it was going through, period. But no, I didn't go out to the premises. I'm not sure that many judges, if any, would do it.

JC: Do you think it's dangerous for a judge to do that? I don't mean physically dangerous. I mean dangerous in terms of use of judicial power to go out there—that it might be intimidating to the community . . .

DH: No I don't think it would be that. It was just not appropriate, I thought. Actually, it didn't cross my mind, and nobody brought it up, including the community, asking "Well, will the judge come out here and look at it?" I very rarely go out to a site. The closest I came was a huge fight about an oil pipe line and we actually had a section of the pipeline brought across the street from the courthouse and I went down with the whole jury to view this huge pipe. I remember that was one time we went out, but usually we don't.

JC: Would you give any thought—I take it you did not in this instance—to talking to local representatives to encourage them to get the remaining folks on board so that you would not have to show force?

DH: No, I believe that's not a judge's prerogative, to invite non-judicial intervention. Eventually, that's what independently happened and resulted in a last-minute acquiescence.

JC: Explain that, please.

DH: That show of force was there with the marshals, the police and the EMTs with the ambulances, the constables and the sheriff's department. It was a lot of folks out there including a canine unit. Not to go after anyone, but just as precaution. A number of the minority city councilmen then went in and talked to them, and that was it. They came out. Therefore, the officers didn't execute the eviction. I didn't know it until a long time after that, that if you're arrested you cannot get public housing. There's something like that in the law. I don't know if the city councilmen mentioned that, but they were a significant assistance and the families finally came out and everything receded. As soon as they left the officers put the fence up and they started demolition and reconstruction.

JC: Do you know what ultimately happened with those families, in terms of obtaining housing?

DH: I don't. They were offered to come back in and many did. I think they also arranged some interim housing for that particular group. But initially they just wouldn't come out. There was a gentleman, Mr. Johnson, who was the longtime spokesperson for that group of residents. I think he was holding back until the last minute. When the city councilmen went in, they visited with him. At that point the few remaining families moved out.

JC: You managed to accomplish an agreed-upon judgment at some point. Did you conclude before you gained that, that if there was no agreed-upon judgment that you would have simply removed all these families?

DH: I don't think you could get any judge to say what he or she *would have* done. Let's put it this way: I'm glad it was taken out of my hands to make the decision for these folks to be vacated. But if I had to, I would have. I believe every "T" was crossed, and every "I" was dotted legally. At that point they had had plenty of time. It had gone on for years and it was time to let the authorities start the demolition.

JC: You say you were glad you accomplished the settlement. Are you glad whenever you accomplish a settlement?

DH: Absolutely. Let's put it this way: if people want to settle and I have no problem signing off. Sometimes, however, you have to look carefully at what the balance of power is. This is of lesser concern in civil cases. I have turned down some plea agreements in criminal cases. I turned one down in an Enron case.

JC: Because it was too lenient?

DH: Yes, the defense and government had agreed to a term of imprisonment subject to my approval, and I didn't agree to it—the term was too lenient.

JC: Was that Lea Fastow?

DH: Mrs. Fastow. It had to go all the way through the pre-trial investigation proceedings and then presented to me at sentencing. Only one other time did I refuse to accept a guilty plea, only once.

JC: You distinguish the criminal situation from civil cases. Are you saying if the parties are in agreement in a civil case you will endorse it?

DH: Generally so.

JC: Can you think of any examples where you wouldn't because perhaps the plaintiffs weren't adequately represented?

DH: I was going to say, represented, or *pro se*. You've got to look real carefully about that. Assuming a *pro se* litigant's case remains viable and he or she has done the research, and the other lawyer is very able. The power may be very imbalanced there and then they present a settlement agreement. Well then at that point I can't practice law. I've told a lot of *pro se* litigants when they try their own case, "Look, I can't help you in trial because I can't practice law." Ordinarily I do not get involved in an adversarial position. We have an adversary system and I'm not getting mixed up in that as the third party. However, I don't believe we're just an umpire. Some people say a judge is an umpire, but occasionally, a federal judge may become quite active in a case.

JC: Sort of like the Chief Justice of the Supreme Court, John Roberts, said during his confirmation hearing that he sees himself as an umpire calling balls and strikes?

DH: Well that's right. That's what *he* says.

JC: Let me bring you back for a moment to the *Allen Parkway* case.

DH: Absolutely.

JC: You present clearly as a no-nonsense judge. You get this case on remand from the Fifth Circuit in 1993 and the demolition doesn't occur until 1996. So you have it for three years before you finally put this package together.

DH: Exactly.

JC: Why did it take so long? You look like the kind of judge who gets something done in a hurry if he wants to.

DH: Because on this kind of a very sensitive subject you don't want to . . .

JC: Shove it down their throats?

DH: That's right. You don't want to shove it down their throats. The way I saw it, if I give them enough time, reasonable people—and you may need some reasonable people coming in from the outside, to bring the folks to realize it. Because the other alternative was what I almost had to do, and that's the last thing you want to do.

JC: Is that the last thing you wanted to do because you don't want to appear in the press to be a bad guy? Or because you thought somehow you'll get them cajoled over time?

DH: Most federal judges are aware of the role of a free press but you can't be concerned with, or control, their coverage. There was no real necessity for speed.

JC: There was a necessity, wasn't there, in the sense that the government wanted to tear it down?

DH: True—but still, these were people's homes. That's the other side. So if you can work it out by agreement, it's far better. The first big case I had in Houston was a right to life case—it was the pro-choice versus pro-life advocates. One group was coming into the schools to lecture to the kids. The others were out on the sidewalk with all these signs up. I said it would be best if we can get these folks to agree, somehow. I saw, right at the beginning, that one group had access and the other didn't. But if you start ruling one way or the other real quickly, it won't work. They negotiated for about two years behind the scenes, with everything on hold. They finally agreed that both sides would have access, and under what conditions. Fortunately I had good lawyers on both sides, even though they were diametrically opposite in their philosophy. As lawyers and advocates they were able to work together. The one thing we're taught as lawyers is that we need to be able to see the other side. You may disagree with the other side; but as lawyers, if you understand where the other folks are coming from, you can try to work toward the center. If you can't, then the judge has his or her role. Then it turns into a fire where you only have smoke right now. So, let's see if we can tamp it down before the judge has to intervene.

JC: In tamping it down did you use "shuttle diplomacy" between the various sides? For example, "I need this from you. I can get the other guy to give me this if you do this."

DH: No, that's a mediator. That's becoming an advocate or a mediator. I don't do mediation. But they had good lawyers on both sides, and they were able to do that. In the APV case there also were lawyers for all of the architectural groups, the historical groups, and they had to come in and be convinced that some of the area would be preserved and under what conditions. And later on as you see, there was a cemetery—going back many years. It was known as Freedmen's Town. That whole Allen Parkway area was an historic African-American site. You had to take into account all those considerations. So I said "Look, I have to wait." It's the same thing I did in the *Stanford* case. I had to wait eight months for him to be certified as competent to stand trial. You can't be antsy. Let them know you're there. If they want more time—sometimes you give it to them, sometimes not.

I was told during the first month in state court, in learning how to be a judge, that: "You give somebody a trial date and then don't budge off that trial date unless an attorney is ill or in another court trying a case." If you get that reputation, they'll either settle in a civil case or they'll plead out in a criminal case, if possible. Or then you go to trial. But if you don't have that definite date and have a reputation for easily granting continuances, then they're going to run all over you and everything will be continued. In a case like Allen Parkway, they knew I would try it. They knew I wasn't going to avoid ruling.

JC: You think that's important that they knew it?

DH: I really do.

JC: The lawyers knew that. But did the remaining squatters?

DH: I have no idea. Probably not. It's emotional. You're taking their homes away from them. You always have to see it from their point of view.

JC: Did you bring them to court? Did they know exactly what was going on?

DH: They had representatives there.

JC: But when there's an emotional thing such as this?

DH: No I don't bring them in.

JC: Were they coming in on their own?

DH: Some were. I think Mr. Johnson—the most strident of them—was there for all of the hearings.

JC: Did you consider bringing them into court—since you didn't find it appropriate to go out to the site—so that they would realize that you were a caring judge who was concerned about the fact that they were being asked to leave their homes?

DH: No.

JC: Would that be wrong for a judge?

DH: I wouldn't say wrong. It's just not the way I operate. Beyond that, I knew the community was out there, every time I had a hearing. Sometimes I had to borrow the bigger courtroom—and you could see these residents there. They were in there listening. They would hear me say, "Look I could order it torn down immediately. I could order the marshals in. But I want you to continue to work on this to see if you can reach an accommodation." The question is, "Do you use a velvet glove or do you use a hammer?" Sometimes you need both. And unfortunately it came to the point where with just a few families eventually, and I had to use—at least demonstrate—a show of force. Hopefully nothing was going to come of that, and thankfully it did not.

JC: Were any lawyers opposing the tear-down order?

DH: Not that I recall. Because any one who had piece of the case, had their own attorneys who worked on the settlement. They could bring their people to court whenever they wanted, to observe all of the hearings.

JC: So, no one was asking for a stay of the demolition order?

DH: Only a few individual residents were, but not the official parties. I understood the residents' situation.

JC: But there was no legal action to stay?

DH: No sir. This was an agreed judgment on this major community matter. To this day many people don't realize it was actually an agreed judgment.

JC: Let me ask you this. Did you consider imposing a *sua sponte* stay, basically to take the weight off yourself? In other words, let the Circuit decide that it wasn't going to grant a stay.

DH: No. I make a decision. I fully respect the appeals court. I really do. But I have to make my decisions.

JC: What newspaper in Houston do you respect the most?

DH: The only big daily left is the Houston Chronicle.

JC: So if the Houston Chronicle—which presumably you read every day—were to publish an editorial saying that "Judge Hittner is going off the rails here. He's being too harsh with these squatters. Let those people have their day in an appeals court." And you saw that they published that editorial before the demolition was going to occur. What would you have done with that?

DH: I can't say what I would have done, but I say what I wouldn't have done. I wouldn't be swayed by what the press said in that situation. I knew it, I lived it, I was there and I simply knew the law of the case. I know you've talked to many Federal judges for this book, but I'm not driven by the press at all. I can't be. That's why the Constitution gives us lifetime appointments. They give us lifetime appointments to do the best we can. And if what I was doing was that bad, they could have applied for an emergency stay from Circuit.

JC: How long have you been on the bench, state and Federal?

DH: Thirty five years.

JC: In those 35 years, have you ever read a story or an opinion column about something you had done or were contemplating in a case where you said to yourself, "You know, maybe they're right, and I ought to re-think this?" In other words, were you ever influenced in your judicial thinking by an editorial or news report?

I should note that there's a long pause.

DH: No.

JC: What does that say, by the way? That you have so much confidence in your views that a newspaper could never influence you?

DH: That's not what I'm saying. But one can't be a Federal trial judge and be driven by the press. You do what you think is right. With your background, your education, the statutes, and the case law. You just do the best you can. At that point if you're wrong, it's not for the press to decide. That's what appeals courts are for—that's the way our system works. And it works very well.

Chapter 7

Judge John E. Jones III

[A]n "activist judge" is a judge with whom you disagree. Most of us who have been in the business for a while get the point that the judiciary is misunderstood on some of the points we've talked about—including that somebody's political orientation or prior political affiliation predicts how they're going to decide a case.
—Judge John E. Jones III, August 12, 2013

Judge John E. Jones III was appointed to the District Court bench for the Middle District of Pennsylvania in 2002 by President George W. Bush, at the urging of Governor Tom Ridge, Senator Rick Santorum, and Senator Arlen Specter. Notwithstanding his "conservative" credentials, his actions both prior to taking the bench and since suggest that it might be a mistake to predict any ruling based on his political affiliation. Indeed, in a speech to the Anti-Defamation League in 2006, he was unequivocal that his duty is to the Constitution and not any special interest groups.

Conservatives cheered when, as chair of the Pennsylvania Liquor Control Board, Jones banned Bad Frog beer because its label (a frog with a raised middle finger) was in bad taste. Since taking the bench, Judge Jones struck down portions of Shippensburg University's speech code as it violated the right to free speech guaranteed by the First Amendment. Yet in another First Amendment case, he determined that the U.S. Department of Agriculture's statute assessing milk producers in order to fund advertising did not infringe on the producers' free speech (this decision was affirmed by the U.S. Supreme Court). In a matter involving the Rigas family and *their alleged scheme to defraud shareholders and creditors of their Adelphia Communications Corp. in amounts in excess of $200 million, Judge Jones refused to dismiss indictments on double jeopardy or collateral estoppel grounds, finding that a prior New York action was not dispositive as—even though the overall conduct may have been the same—the objectives of the charged crimes were separate and discrete.*

None of his cases, however, prepared him for the outcry of public opinion and criticism the Kitzmiller v. Dover *case would bring. After he rendered his decision, conservative pundits accused him of butchering their rights, while* Time *magazine named him one of the Time 100 most influential people in the world. He often speaks publicly about his experience in the case in an attempt to inform and educate—it is important to Judge Jones that the public understand the judicial process and all that it entails. His service on the Pennsylvania Commission on Judicial Independence—which raises public awareness of the importance of a strong, independent judiciary—allows him to further that goal.*

If one were to question whether Kitzmiller *was an anomaly for Judge Jones, he recently struck down as unconstitutional those portions of Pennsylvania's statute that limited marriage to opposite-sex couples, describing the plaintiff gay and lesbian couples as "courageous." After tracing the history of homosexual discrimination, Judge Jones wrote that "in future generations the label* same-sex marriage *will be abandoned, to be replaced simply by* marriage. *We are a better people than what these laws represent, and it is time to discard them into the ash heap of history."*

Considered inquisitive, intellectual, and funny, Judge Jones was born and raised in Pennsylvania. He graduated from Dickinson College and the Dickinson School of Law at Pennsylvania State University, where he currently teaches. He began his legal career as a law clerk to Judge Guy A. Bowe in Pennsylvania and thereafter entered private practice. In 1992, he unsuccessfully ran for Congress on the Republican ticket. In 1994, he became a member of the transition team for his friend and mentor, Governor-elect Tom Ridge. Judge Jones was then nominated by Governor Ridge to chair the Pennsylvania Liquor Control Board, where he served for seven years before being appointed to the District Court. In 2013, Judge Jones was appointed by Chief Justice John Roberts to serve on the Committee on

Judicial Security, which addresses the rising number of threats made against federal judges and their families.

Judge Jones currently sits in Harrisburg, Pennsylvania.

Intelligent Design

Beginning in 1925 with the *Scopes* "monkey" trial, religionists and secularists in America have battled over the propriety of teaching Darwin's theory of evolution in schools. To the cognoscenti, the *Scopes* trial was actually a collusive criminal trial, designed to put the floundering city of Dayton, Tennessee, on the map by making the trial a cause célèbre, pitting legal giants William Jennings Bryan and Clarence Darrow against each other over the teaching of evolution in public schools. For the rest of us, *Scopes* was simply the first battle in the war between the religious right and those who don't take the Bible with such literalness, particularly over the proper meaning of "creation."

Fundamentalism, which began in the 19th century, led religiously motivated groups to lobby legislatures to prohibit the teaching of evolution. A law in Arkansas did just that until, in 1968, in *Epperson v. Arkansas*, the U.S. Supreme Court determined the law was unconstitutional. The courts later also struck down "balanced treatment" statutes that required those who taught evolution to devote equal time to the Bible's view of creation. They did so on the basis of the Establishment Clause of the First Amendment— "Congress shall make no law respecting an establishment of religion." In other words, states could not sponsor the teaching of religious doctrine in public schools.

But these rulings did not end the dispute. Fundamentalists began using language that sounded scientific—such as "creation-science" or "scientific creationism"—as alternatives. In 1987, in *Edwards v. Aguillard*, the U.S. Supreme Court struck down a Louisiana law that required teachers of "evolution-science" to also teach "creation-science." While the proponents argued that creation-science was "educationally valuable scientific data" that had been censored from the classroom, the Court found that it was nothing more than religious doctrine.

And yet the battle still did not end. Now, in the 21st century, the "Creator" described in "creationism" effectively became the "Designer." We no longer have "creation-science," we have Intelligent Design (ID). And the proponents of teaching ID as an alternative to evolution became more inventive at creating, or at least trying to create, a loophole in the Constitution's largely restrictive legal landscape over the issue of state-sponsored teaching of religious tenets.

In 2004, the school board in Dover, Pennsylvania, a rural township in York County, by a 6–3 vote, devised a thinly veiled vehicle—one that did not speak of a specific supreme being—so that the Bible's view of creation would be acknowledged alongside evolution. In a press release sent to every home in Dover (regardless of whether a student lived there), the board noted that Pennsylvania students were required to learn about Darwin's theory of evolution and eventually had to take a standardized test of which evolution is a part. However, grasping at the word "theory," the Dover School Board determined that "Intelligent Design is an explanation of the origin of life that differs from Darwin's view" and announced its decision to make available a reference book so that interested students could properly understand ID.

The Dover School Board thus required science teachers (or principals if the teachers refused, as they did) to read the following statement to students in conjunction with their teaching the "theory" of evolution:

The Pennsylvania Academic Standards require students to learn about Darwin's Theory of Evolution and eventually to take a standardized test of which evolution is a part. Because Darwin's Theory is a theory, it continues to be tested as new evidence is discovered. The Theory is not a fact. Gaps in the Theory exist for which there is no evidence. A theory is defined as a well-tested explanation that unifies a broad range of observations. Intelligent Design is an explanation of the origin of life that differs from Darwin's view. The reference book, *Of Pandas and People*, is available for students who might be interested in gaining an understanding of what Intelligent Design actually involves. With respect to any theory, students are encouraged to keep an open mind. The school leaves the discussion of the Origins of Life to individual students and their families. As a Standards-driven district, class instruction focuses upon preparing students to achieve proficiency on Standards-based assessments.

A number of Dover School District parents brought suit in *Kitzmiller v. Dover*, claiming that this protocol was designed to try to circumvent the Establishment Clause of the First Amendment. Since the U.S. Supreme Court had long ago prohibited the teaching of creationism, in whatever form fundamentalists then devised, the plaintiffs in *Kitzmiller* argued that the teachings of ID were no different.

By random selection, the case was assigned to Judge John E. Jones III, a practicing Lutheran who had been named to the court by President George W. Bush and who was—it was believed—a "conservative" Republican. Judge Jones's nomination was supported by Governor Tom Ridge as well as Senators Rick Santorum and Arlen Specter. His conservative credentials solidly in place, the proponents of ID were undoubtedly confident that they had the right judge for their fight.

The case became a minefield; Dover neighbors who had once been friends could no longer communicate. The local papers published more than 200 letters and 60 op-ed pieces. The national press did its job—articles and editorials appeared throughout the country, and everyone had an opinion about whether ID was merely another term for creationism and whether it should be taught in school. News programs and pundits weighed in.

But this was not the first time since *Edwards* that proponents of ID sought to ensure that students learned that evolution was merely a "theory" and that ID was a viable alternative. Why did the press cover the *Dover* case with such vigor and all but ignore other attempts to build ID into a school curriculum? Was it because Judge Jones was a Republican whose nomination was supported by Senator Santorum, a leading member of the conservative right? Did the proponents of ID—confident they had a winning suit with Judge Jones in place—use conservative media outlets to get their message to the public, hoping that it would influence Judge Jones?

Moreover, why did Judge Jones render his 139-page decision even after new Dover School Board members had been elected and reversed the decision to require statements about ID as an alternate "theory" of how life began? Did the parties demand that he do so, each so sure that its own position was correct? Was Judge Jones concerned that, even though the issue was then moot, it would arise again with the next school board election? Or was it that Judge Jones was angry, having invested in a six-week trial where he found that the Dover School Board members "outright lied" under oath—in one instance to deter the plaintiffs from making what would have likely been a successful motion for an order preliminarily enjoining the board from requiring that the ID statement be read to students? Or was it that the testimony was clear—"not a close call"—that the board's claim that it had a secular purpose in introducing ID was nothing more than a "sham"? And did the decision in some way reflect Judge Jones's own subliminal, religious views that perhaps he brought to the bench when he heard and decided the case?

Still, equally important, what should one make of the fact that Judge Jones's role in the process of dealing with the controversy over Intelligent Design and the schools didn't end when he decided the case and no appeal followed? Conservative activist Phyllis Schlafly, conservative talk show host Bill O'Reilly, conservative pundit and author Ann Coulter, and others attacked Judge Jones for being an "activist" and a "fascist"—a judge who "stabbed the evangelicals who got him onto the federal bench right in the back," taking away "our" rights. And doing so, as Fox TV pundits Bill O'Reilly and (retired) Judge Andrew Napolitano bitterly complained, just before Christmas.

Notwithstanding the provocation, though, why did Judge Jones not do as most judges do when they are attacked for a decision unpopular in some circles: stop reading certain newspapers or simply change the channel? Why has Judge Jones been so vocal in giving speeches, submitting to interviews, and writing on his experiences that derived from the *Kitzmiller* case? Is that the proper role of a judge, even if the case is over? It almost appears, although it hasn't happened, that Judge Jones was using the controversy as a platform to run for office, as he once contemplated prior to being appointed to the bench. Was he?

The Dialogue

JC: So, Judge Jones, this book is about what judges bring to the bench in deciding cases—from their studies, their experiences, their personal beliefs, their philosophies. So why beat around the bush? The day before the *Dover* case was assigned to you, were you a churchgoer?

JEJ: Yes.

JC: Did you believe in God?

JEJ: Yes.

JC: Given your belief in God, what is the status of the Bible in your religious life?

JEJ: I guess I'd describe myself as a person of faith. And that's been a constant in my life. As I've joked with people, if I told you that I attended church every Sunday, I'd be telling you a lie. But I have attended church regularly throughout my life. I believe that there's a higher power. And as with most people, I believe religion is a source of comfort to me in what I do, day after day.

JC: Does your belief in God impact your belief in the Book of Genesis?

JEJ: I think that an enlightened view of the Bible—and, in particular, the Book of Genesis—is that there are allegorical aspects to the Bible's teachings. And it might be erroneous to accept every statement in either Genesis or the Bible at large in a literal way. To accept the Bible with that enlightened view is, in my judgment, likely a more consistent view than accepting the somewhat supernatural or allegorical aspects as literally true.

JC: So when the Bible says that the world was created in six days and that man was created by God molding him from the dust of the earth, you believe that that's an allegory?

JEJ: I'm not sure that my answer will be particularly helpful to you on that point. I can tell you—if we look at it in a more overarching vein—that was not part of my calculus in deciding the *Dover* case. Again, I think it's fair to assume that some of the time lines are contracted for the purpose of the Scriptures. And I think that it's generally an enlightened and safe assumption. But that said, it's quite clear that there are sincere and good people who would disagree with me on that point. That there's a disagreement on that point is not the fulcrum on which *Dover* was decided. In other words, happily, the resolution of that case didn't turn on my interpretation of Scripture.

JC: I guess you're saying that the time line may be off in the sense that a "day" in the Bible's term isn't the same as a day in contemporary terms, correct?

JEJ: Correct.

JC: But on the key issue in Creationism, *i.e.*—that man was created from dust and didn't evolve from apes—I imagine that you see the Bible's account as allegorical?

JEJ: Well, whether I do or not is not the issue, and let me go further. What was repeatedly misapprehended about the *Dover* case was that it had to do with the origin of man. It did not. And so again, happily for me, that's not an area that I had to address. Nor should I have addressed it in resolving the case. Nor, although it was characterized this way, was evolution itself necessarily on trial.

What was on trial—the somewhat seminal question in the case—was this concept known as Intelligent Design. And whether at the end of the day it was a successor to or the progeny of Creationism—Creationism having been defined and labeled by precedential court decisions. So if you cabin the inquiry into that, then some of these perhaps mind numbing but interesting questions about the origin of man—science versus the Scriptural account—that analysis is fun to discuss perhaps. But it is not essential to the resolution of the question I had before me.

JC: Well, do you think it would be possible for a judge who believes in Creationism—who believes, as the Bible describes it, that man was literally created from dust, rather than having evolved from apes—to have been capable of deciding this case in an unbiased, non-prejudged, way?

JEJ: I think, Joel, relating to my prior answer, that the origin of man was not the issue. But let me twist your question somewhat. If a judge, for example, adhered to a belief that the earth was six thousand years old, that could have been problematic in terms of resolving the case. I'm not sure that the judge's interpretation of the origin of man and—of course, it would depend on his view and interpretation—would be quite as problematic. But there are other issues.

Or if a judge, for example, came with a preconceived notion that rejects evolution or evolutionary theory. Again, evolution itself was not so much on trial, although there was certainly evidence in support of evolution that was presented by way of showing the flaws and the religious nature of Intelligent Design. My guess is that a *per se* rejection of evolution by a judge would have been enough to have caused that judge to recuse him or herself in the case. Or should have been.

JC: So you believe if a judge did not believe in evolution—thought it was completely unscientific—that it would be difficult . . .

JEJ: My guess is that that might color that judge's determination as to Intelligent Design. Again, to expand a bit, I was taught evolution in high school, as most students were. I was a political science major in college. I didn't take biology in college, so I hadn't visited the concept of evolution for decades when *Dover* arrived on my docket. So I needed a primer on evolution and, believe me, I received one.

The very first witness was a very prominent professor from Brown, Ken Miller. And one of the wonderful aspects of the case was that the attorneys knew their judge. They knew they didn't have a biologist, so they gave me a good foundation to start the case, and a refresher course on evolution. I never had any reason in my life to doubt evolutionary theory, but I was not particularly invested in its nuances when the trial began. As I've often said since the trial, I had never heard of Intelligent Design, so I had no pre-conceived notions about it either.

JC: How do you differentiate in your own mind between Creationism and Intelligent Design?

JEJ: Intelligent Design can be cast different ways by different observers. But at the end of the day, as its name implies, Intelligent Design proffers that there is a "designer," that there is some supernatural force; that organisms are so exquisitely perfect, so irreducibly complex, that they had to be the work of a designer. Time and again during the trial, the proponents of Intelligent Design, when pressed, would say that while they didn't know who the intelligent designer was, the fair assumption was that the intelligent designer was God. And so to that extent my ultimate finding was that it dovetailed extensively with Creationism, and was really the successor to the concept, for example, of creation science, which had been rejected in prior court decisions.

JC: Is Intelligent Design inconsistent with your own view of the role of God in the universe?

JEJ: I'm not sure that I've ever thought that out, and I'm not sure that I have a good answer for you on that point. What I can tell you is what I found—which is that Intelligent Design is at bottom, in my view, a religious precept that violates the Establishment Clause.

JC: You said before that your personal belief system and view of the Book of Genesis did not impact your decision. How does a judge, in deciding a case, put aside his or her learning and belief system, particularly when deciding a controversial case such as this one?

JEJ: Well, I think we're all too human, and as you delve into a case either at its inception or at any point along the way, you have to ask yourself this, particularly in a case like this that was a bench trial: can you apply the requisite intellectual honesty to a case, or are you being pulled in one direction or another despite your oath and despite the objectivity that you're duty-bound to bring to a case? And if you feel that pull, or you believe you've lost that objectivity, then it's your duty to recuse and get out. I never felt that in this particular case.

I guess that for most of us on the bench—having practiced law myself for 22 years and having been on the bench for a few years by the time this case reached me—I am conditioned reasonably well to call them as I see them, and as according to the law. I can't think of a time since I've been on the bench that I recused because of a strong personal belief about the essence of the particular dispute. My recusals have been because of knowledge of a party or because of relationships or stock ownership or other things. There are technical reasons to recuse.

JC: When the Dover School District first enacted the resolution in issue, did you know about it then?

JEJ: No, it's a very big judicial district. And the Dover School District is 80 miles from my home, so I would not have read about it. It was, as it turned out, a very hot, significant local issue in York County, which is south of Harrisburg. The first I knew of any aspect of the case was when the suit was filed in December of 2004. I was on my way home from this courthouse and I turned on a local radio station for a traffic report, and heard the news at the top of the hour that the suit had been filed and that there had been a press conference in the rotunda of the state capitol building to announce it. I remember thinking to myself—because I knew it had been filed in my court—"Well, I wonder who's going to get that." There are six active judges on the court and I was eligible to get it. But it's an algorithm that's used as most courts do, and distributed amongst the active and seniors. So there was no way of knowing whether I would get the case or not, and I never found out until the following morning that the case had been assigned to me. The radio report was the first I knew of the dispute.

JC: When you heard that radio report, did you want the case?

JEJ: I'll put it this way. I think that all of us who hold these positions take them so that we have the opportunity to resolve significant questions. If you spend a long enough time on the court you get your share of big cases. I wasn't unhappy that I had it because I thought it would be a challenge. That said, as you know, most disputes that reach us resolve by settlement. So the mere fact that the case had landed on my docket did not necessarily portend that it would become the mega trial that it ultimately became. I couldn't know that at the . . .

JC: As we say in our trade, Judge, "There's a question pending." Did you want the case?

JEJ: Sure, and I think any of my colleagues worth his salt would tell you that such a case is a great challenge. And frankly, we shouldn't be on the Federal Courts if we don't want cases like that on our docket.

JC: So when you first read the complaint and saw the Dover District resolution—meaning long before motion practice or taking testimony—did you have a view then that what the Dover District was doing was essentially endorsing a religion?

JEJ: Not at all. I was, frankly, more worried about scheduling. In fact, I did something that I don't normally do—I pulled the plug on a telephonic case management conference and decided that I would do scheduling in person. I was far more concerned about logistics. Lawyers seemed to be parachuting out of the sky to get involved in the case, and so at the beginning my concern had little to do with the merits. It was how I was going to manage it. For example, whether there was going to be a preliminary injunction hearing, which there was not, whether they would want to do discovery before the preliminary injunction hearing, and the like. Those were the things that were on my mind at that point.

JC: Before the trial began, did you start having a sense that there was a legitimate claim that this was an endorsement of religion?

JEJ: Oh sure. It was hard not to see that as things unfolded. But again, I was not privy, for example, to the deposition testimony. The discovery was pretty orderly, so I didn't have to wade in much on discovery disputes. Some pretrial sparring about motions to intervene, for example, gave me a window into some aspects of the dispute. But understand, other than what was in the complaint, the motion practice was not particularly spirited. No motion to dismiss. No preliminary injunction hearing. So I didn't have a lot of exposure to the merits.

JC: But in the back of your mind, as an intelligent person (whether designed or not, by God) you're getting the gist of what the Dover Board had done long before you had to . . .

JEJ: I had the allegations in the complaint. If you took the allegations at face value, and if you assume that they were true, which I did not . . .

JC: Why didn't you assume that they were true?

JEJ: Because it's inappropriate for me to assume that they're true. They are statements in the complaint. We all know that the plaintiffs had to stand and deliver.

JC: Yes, they're statements in a complaint, but they're black and white. You know exactly what the Dover Board wants to do. And just looking at what they want to do, don't you conclude that they are asking students to consider a view of creation that is different from evolution?

JEJ: Understand that I didn't know what Intelligent Design was. I had no clue. And it had been so long since I'd been exposed to the theory of evolution itself. I wasn't a clean slate, but I was a "cleaner" slate; and happily counsel recognized that, and I was open for business at the time of the trial. I wanted to hear what everybody had to say on that point. Prejudging in any respect assumes, for example, that I knew what Intelligent Design was. I did not. And I'm fully confident that through the course of 20-plus days of testimony over six weeks, we gave Intelligent Design the opportunity to stand and deliver and say what in fact it was or what it purported to be from the defendants' standpoint—which is a scientifically accepted non-religious alternative to evolution.

JC: Before the first day of trial did you believe, or do you believe now, in Darwin's *theory* of evolution as scientific? I know they've grabbed onto the word "theory." Do you believe in evolution as scientific?

JEJ: That casts the question the wrong way. Do I believe in evolution? Because that assumes that evolution is almost tantamount, I've come to believe, to a religion in and of itself. I believe that the scientific evidence, having heard it, demonstrably shows the vitality of evolution theory. To be sure, I believe that not every principle espoused by Charles Darwin turned out to be correct. There are certainly some flaws in Darwin's theory. He didn't understand the human genome. Nor genetics. Nor so many of the things discovered through scientific research after he posited evolutionary theory. But I think that demonstrably, almost unimpeachably, through the years, it's been established that evolution is good science. So it's not necessarily a question of whether one believes in evolution, as if it's a sort of a religious principle. I often think that's miscast. I think it's "Do you find that it's good science?" I think that it is at the end of the day.

JC: Were the shortcomings of Darwin's theory of evolution something you learned sitting on the bench or in the parties' submissions? Or did you go out and try to amass more knowledge than you remembered from your high school studies?

JEJ: No, I certainly didn't do that. And I'm not a French court where I conduct my own examination, nor should I be. Everything I needed to resolve the dispute I received within the corners of my courtroom. As I said to you earlier, I never had any reason to question evolution extensively. I learned it. The nuances of evolution had long since left me by the time that the trial started. I suspect that in the decades between when I studied evolution as a junior high school student and the time that Ken Miller testified in my courtroom, there were myriad discoveries that enhanced the vitality of evolution. I heard about all of those when I was in trial from a full and comprehensive record. As I said, evolution wasn't on trial so much, although it certainly appeared that way. But it was necessarily contrasting evolution with Intelligent Design. The trial was for the purpose of having me decide whether the teaching of Intelligent Design violated the Establishment Clause.

JC: Before you decided the case, did the media try to influence the outcome, perhaps reporting about your having been a political figure before becoming a judge?

JEJ: It was interesting. No, I don't think that they did, to answer your question succinctly. But more broadly, one of the great take-aways for me in the case was how we type-cast judges in America. It was so often written that I was a "Bush-Appointed Federal Judge," that that's what I came to think my name was: "Bush-Appointed Federal Judge." And then, as the press does and Americans do, they equate Republican with conservative and Democrat with liberal. Time and again I was described as a conservative, church-going Republican judge. And I often wondered about that. And I'm not sure how I had the conservative mantle hung on me, other than the fact that I was a Republican.

JC: Who recommended you to the . . .

JEJ: Both senators did. I think I was a consensus pick for the court from both Senator Specter and Senator Santorum. Certainly if you take Senator Santorum, you can assume conservative. Not so with Senator Specter, who was just as supportive, if not more so in many ways, although Senator Santorum was certainly a booster. But I wasn't *litmussed* for conservative versus liberal. I freely concede my Republican affiliation at that point. But that's beside the point.

In answer to your question, what I was driving at was that this was newsworthy for the press and for the punditry, and the blogosphere was not as pronounced then. Happily, I guess, there was no Twitter back then. So you didn't quite see the on-line media as pronounced as today. But some people did make a prediction based on my background that I would rule a certain way in the case, and I suppose that would have been in favor of the defendants.

Related to my oath and my responsibility to rule on the evidence, there was a profile of me done in the New York Times in December 2005 before I released the decision. It was by Laurie Goodstein, who is an excellent writer for the Times. She came and visited me. And I could tell, though, whether Laurie would admit it or not, that she was looking for an angle. She questioned a lot of my friends, and she asked me in particular for some Democrat references. Friends of mine who were not of the same party. And I carefully explained to her that I don't pick my friends by their party affiliation. And she went out and did a pretty good investigative job. But she couldn't get what I think she might have wanted, which is a sort of Jones as doctrinaire, Jones as arch-conservative. And the article that she ultimately wrote was a very nice piece, but it was clear from Republicans and Democrats alike that she talked to who said that "He'll call this case as he sees it because that's the way he addresses everything." And that article sort of debunked some of the suppositions that I was some conservative firebrand who would only rule a certain way.

JC: Do you think that a skilled courtroom observer could have detected from any questions you were asking at the trial which way you were leaning?

JEJ: I'm sure they wouldn't have. The most questions I ever asked in the trial were of a fellow named [Alan] Bonsell who had been present at the school board. He piqued my ire because I felt that he had lied under oath.

JC: How?

JEJ: He had been deposed in early 2005. At issue was a textbook allegedly donated to the school. The text was "Of Pandas and People"—it was sort of the basal text for Intelligent Design. Obviously the defendants feared that if the actual source of the money for the text had been revealed, it would injure their case because the way the text was purchased was with a hat passed around a church. Money was donated by the church, and then run through Bonsell's father's checking account.

When Bonsell was asked about this—way before the plaintiffs decided whether or not they would seek a preliminary injunction—Bonsell testified that he simply did not know where the funds came from or who the book donors were. He got caught, and at trial he was forced to admit that he knew very well that his father had solicited the donations in church and had washed the money through his checking account. That may have been enough to get a preliminary injunction way back when. I think he deliberately obscured that months before. And here we were in the middle of trial with that testimony. So I asked him some fairly pointed questions about what he knew and when he knew it. But other questions from me were very rare. I didn't ask a lot of questions from the bench. I think there were some structural questions but they wouldn't have tipped one off to my thinking one way or the other.

JC: You said earlier that when you first get a case you don't know whether it will get resolved through a settlement. Did you try—by yourself or by using a magistrate judge—to find common ground for the litigants?

JEJ: Not myself, because in a bench trial like that, I wouldn't. It wouldn't be appropriate. And to the best of my knowledge, I never suggested that they go to a magistrate judge. It was as clear as any case I've ever had that it was heading inexorably towards trial. If I see a little daylight typically I'm the first one to send a case to a mediator or a magistrate judge to mediate it. But when I had the first scheduling conference in January 2005—I'd been around long enough—the body language and demeanor of the lawyers indicated to me that this was deadly serious, and that both sides were invested and headed toward a collision course, and that there was no room for resolution.

JC: If they were more amenable to settling, did you see any language that the District resolution could have used to modify the offending language?

JEJ: Frankly, Joel, I never thought of it. I'd have to puzzle over that. I'd be wading into the extreme hypothetical at this point. I just don't know.

JC: Let me ask you this. It seems to me from reading the literature about the case, that you probably knew before you took the bench, or certainly before you decided the case, that the Dover Board members that issued the resolution were or would be out of power and that the newly composed board was going to abandon (if that's the right word) the resolution. Why, under those circumstances, wasn't the litigation subject to a mootness argument?

JEJ: Nobody made the mootness argument.

JC: Why didn't you advance it *sua sponte*?

JEJ: Well I thought about that—but both sides, quite clearly by their submissions, wanted me to decide the case. Those submissions having come in, in part, after the school board election. I think that the possibility that the circumstances would be replicated, perhaps through another change effected at the ballot box, was sufficient reason for me to decide the case. I did give consideration to a *sua sponte* mootness determination; but at the end of the day I thought that that was not the appropriate way to go.

JC: What I'm saying, Judge, is that judges, as a matter of judicial policy, typically want institutionally to avoid deciding cases that they don't have to decide.

JEJ: Sure.

JC: And, to be blunt, it seems that you actively wanted to decide this case—somewhat unusual, at least in my experience.

JEJ: I don't know that I actively wanted to decide the case. That might be a stretch. I think that you start with the principle that neither side suggested mootness because of the school board's election. I think they were both eager for a determination to guide future members of the school board who might be so inclined. So there was the propensity that the dispute would replicate. Frankly—and this is not the be-all and end-all—having invested so much of the prior year litigating the case and having sat through twenty days plus of mind numbing testimony, I thought it was appropriate to resolve the controversy. As in all decisions, reasonable people will differ perhaps on whether I should have *sua sponte* requested submissions on the issue of mootness.

JC: Has that been raised before this conversation?

JEJ: No, actually not. It's been mentioned, but it has not been a significant point by any of the commentators. And I think it's because of the possibility that it could replicate in the future. Remember, too, that there was a significant counsel fees issue because this case was filed as a 1983 action—so not so easy to just abandon ship at that point. There was a very real issue about fees and costs having been invested in the case. Ultimately that was settled by the parties, but I couldn't have known that then.

JC: Phyllis Schlafly, among others, was quite critical of you because, her words, "The evangelicals had put you on the bench and you were stabbing them in the back." Did she have any basis to believe that the evangelicals had something, or much, to do with you becoming a district judge?

JEJ: The last time I checked, the United States Senate voted me onto the bench.

JC: True, but Senator Santorum is . . .

JEJ: Well, last time I checked Senator Santorum had been a member of the United States Senate, and was happy to suggest my name to the President of the United States, who made his own determination about my *bona fides*. So I thought that was a grossly hyperbolic and unfortunate statement by Mrs. Schlafly who's been around a long time, and ought to know better about those things. I took her comment as a cheap shot.

JC: Your bio suggests that you're a member of the Pennsylvania Commission on Judicial Independence. What is that?

JEJ: The Pennsylvania Supreme Court ironically enough, as the litigation was going on and completely apart from it, decided to form a judicial independence commission. It had to do with public initiatives to make people understand better how judges go about their work and decide cases. It particularly sprang from some retention fights that happened in Pennsylvania, where there had been controversies because of how some judges decided particular cases. It was determined by the Pennsylvania Supreme Court that they wanted a mix of lay persons, state judges, academics and some federal judges. So I was actually named to that in 2005.

JC: Did that have any influence in terms of your thinking in the *Dover* case?

JEJ: I think I might have influenced their thinking. [laughter.] I'm not sure it influenced my thinking. I received an education sitting through this case and I hope that I've been helpful or enlightening to them in terms of a judge's experience. I didn't have that skill set when they named me to the Commission. I hadn't decided the case—but if the case has done nothing else for me—and it's done a lot for me, I suppose—it's given me a passion for speaking out about judicial independence issues.

I think that the phrase "judicial independence" is somewhat unfortunate, because the independence part of it somewhat implies that judges are untethered, and that we don't rule according to precedent and do all the things that judges are supposed to do. But as Sandra Day O'Connor invokes so frequently, an "activist judge" is a judge with whom you disagree. Most of us who have been in the business for a while get the point that the judiciary is misunderstood on some of the points we've talked about—including that somebody's political orientation or prior political affiliation predicts how they're going to decide a case.

JC: I'm glad you mentioned that word "activist." Because in the conclusion of your lengthy opinion, you say "Those who disagree with our holding will likely mark it as the product of an activist judge. If so, they will have erred as this is manifestly not an activist Court. Rather this case came to us as the result of the activism of an ill-informed faction on a school board, aided by a national public interest law firm eager to find a constitutional test case on ID who, in combination drove the Board to adopt an imprudent and ultimately unconstitutional policy." It is extremely unusual for a court to say in advance that "There's going to be criticism of me, and I am an activist judge. So let me make it clear, right now: I'm not." Why did you feel the need to do that?

JEJ: Because I knew what was coming. I didn't know how pronounced it was going to be. I didn't know where it was going to come from. But I was not blind to the fact that a ruling as sweeping and as stark as this was going to evoke controversy. And I would get one shot at this. I can't write a follow-up opinion and answer my critics.

JC: Why do you need to answer your critics at all?

JEJ: Well, you don't have to answer your critics. But I think it's a license that a judge can take to anticipate the misuse or the misinterpretation of the judge's opinion. And I took that license in the conclusion, rightly or wrongly. I thought that was appropriate, and for me maybe it provided an element of psychic satisfaction to put it in there. It was not essential to the decision itself, obviously.

JC: But it also suggests that you were somewhat angry at the school board members and the lawyers for seeking out an "imprudent constitutional test." Were you angry at that point?

JEJ: Angry is too strong a word, Joel. Understand, when I wrote the decision I was entirely aware that looming ahead was a fee fight and that, in effect, the school board had taken the district over the cliff, exposing it to millions of dollars in fees and costs. The case was a rout—not at all a close call. The challenges for me involved how to write the decision, and how expansive or not to be in how I wrote it. But if there's heat in that conclusion, the heat is because this is a lovely community filled with good law-abiding people who, I suppose, were largely embarrassed by the scrutiny from the nation and the world as a result of this policy. And as I said in the conclusion, I think that the citizens were very poorly served by the school board. They had been told by their solicitor not to do this.

JC: Did you know that from the litigation?

JEJ: Oh, yes. In fact, the email from the solicitor to the superintendent was made part of the evidence. It wasn't privileged. They waived the privilege because they disseminated it—there wasn't even a claim of privilege. And the solicitor—a very experienced school board solicitor—said "Don't do this. You're going to get sued, and you're going to lose if you do it." They blew through every reasonable stop sign put up in front of them. And as I said in the opinion, they lied under oath. I thought it was craven behavior, and it didn't inure so much against them personally, other than perhaps their reputations. It was the taxpayers that would have to foot the bill.

JC: So what do you think the school board was trying to do—shove a religious doctrine down a secular school's throat?

JEJ: The record revealed that when the school board that developed this policy had a retreat at the inception of their term on the school board, they began to talk about how evolution was taught and why there was no prayer in school. In the face of generations of developed law, they had a considered purpose to make a statement. They got right into the science teachers' wheelhouse on this, and there was significant community opposition even as the policy was developed. It was editorialized against in the local newspapers, but they simply didn't care. They solicited information about Intelligent Design from outside sources. The depositions and testimony at trial made it quite clear that they would not and could not explain what Intelligent Design was. They didn't have a clue. They couldn't even parrot the so-called scientific explanation in support of Intelligent Design. They simply wanted to write evolution out of the curriculum, even though evolution is part of the state standards in Pennsylvania.

JC: What is the principal religion of the community?

JEJ: I don't know for a fact, but I'd have to say probably Protestant. That's my guess.

JC: Evangelical?

JEJ: I'm not sure, but I think the main actors were all Protestant.

JC: I've been direct in my questioning. As this is a rare opportunity for me, I should continue. Meaning, you've done something unusual in the aftermath of the case. You've spoken on it, you've been interviewed, including by myself. You've actually done a NOVA program in which you voice recorded various paragraphs from your decision. It almost seemed to me, as I was preparing for this interview that—although this may be overstated—that you were almost running for office, campaigning based on your decision in this case. And I find, interestingly, that you did earlier run for congress, and thought for a while of running for governor . . .

JEJ: For about a minute.

JC: I hear you. But that seemed to be what was, if not going on, a reasonable perception of what was going on.

JEJ: I'll answer this way. I think that we all have our strengths and our weaknesses, and I do have a political background. I did have a public speaking background. I'm not afraid to get out and to talk to people. I don't view the bench perhaps as confining as some do in terms of going out and talking about judicial independence issues. I've always been that way, ever since I arrived on the bench. It's just that you don't get as many speaking invitations when you don't have a remarkable case. Part of it is that people just assume that you don't want to go out. I've gone out every Law Day every year. I've given the requisite speeches. You may not believe this, but it was never within my contemplation that I would ever get a speaking invitation after deciding this case. That sounds naïve, but I just didn't think that I would.

So two things happened after I decided the case. The first was the spate of criticism that I received from various commentators, Phyllis Schlafly, Ann Coulter, Bill O'Reilly—some other sort of usual suspects. I thought that they blatantly misrepresented me, and did a great disservice to judges and how judges decide cases. And as I've said, frequently in public, I think it helps to dumb-down the public about these things. And then I received an invitation, as these things were happening, and I weighed whether to accept it or not. It was the Anti-Defamation League's executive conference in Florida. And I had a background with the ADL because I'd emceed some dinners way back when, when I was a lawyer. So, I accepted the invitation and I went down and I gave a speech. And it was the first time that I had any opportunity to really speak publicly about what I had been through and what I had done in the case.

Now, to be sure, that's a friendly audience in terms of the issue of separation of church and state. There's no question about that. It was not a hostile group. But I finished my remarks and I still wasn't sure how they'd be received. And I remember I looked up and I was receiving a standing ovation. And it's not that I'm so great, but I struck a nerve. I'm sure that I did, and you have to know your audience, I guess, about judicial independence. And I really felt that I found a voice.

Then I started to get other speaking invitations and I couldn't and wouldn't accept them all. I would have had no time to work. But I thought it was appropriate for me to pivot off what I had done and to try to educate and enlighten the public about how judges work. And it's been one of the most salutary, wonderful circumstances of my life that's really taken me to all parts of the country to meet not just people who agree with the decision but people who disagree with the decision as well. And to talk to them, not so much to attempt to explain the decision itself, although you put me through that today in some of your questions. But to talk about how judges go about deciding cases. Because, frankly, as judges, we don't get out as much as we should. Sometimes we're not asked. Sometimes we simply don't want to go out and talk about these things. And I think if we have a voice, we ought to feel obligated to do it.

JC: Have you heard other judges do what you've done in this case?

JEJ: You mentioned Vaughn Walker to me as one of the judges you've interviewed. He's now left the bench; but that's an example of somebody who wasn't bashful about going out and talking about his experiences.

JC: It's a lot different in Walker's case. He's no longer a judge.

JEJ: Judge Midge Rendell who serves on the Third Circuit never misses a speaking opportunity to talk about judges and judging. Sandra Day O'Connor, for example, who's still imbued with judicial power even though she's not on the Supreme Court any longer, has made a career out of speaking about these things.

JC: Well, I once heard at a Federal Bar dinner, Justice Harry Blackman—and I'm told he did this frequently—read aloud some of the hate mail he received after he decided *Roe v. Wade*. And he did that in the context of talking about the importance of independence. But you're actively talking about the case.

JEJ: Well yes and no. You've compelled me to do that today by your questions; but that's not the substance of the speeches that I give at all. You raise a good point and you ask a good question. I don't think, unless we're sort of inside baseball as we are today, that it's good policy for judges to go out and do some kind of apologia or an explanation for a case.

JC: Why is that not good?

JEJ: Because I think that it cheapens your work. If I can't explain my thinking in 139 pages, then I shouldn't be out trying to augment the explanation. You can get sucked into—as I am today—answering some questions about some of the minutiae in the case. But when I give a speech—understand, I very quickly pivot from a description of what the dispute was and the essential holding to the larger lessons. This is the theme of every speech that I've ever given—the need for a better civics education in the United States. And this dovetails with Justice O'Connor.

The role of the punditry, as I said before—and how the punditry tends to synergistically combine with that lack of a good civics education—it's kind of a witch's brew that, I submit, dumbs-down the public. Frankly, there's a need for better science education, although that's not my main area of commentary. I think it flows naturally from the case. So the title of the speech that I have given for years now is "Our Constitution's Intelligent Design." And it has to do with Article III, the proper role of judges, the separation of powers. It's intended to be a civics lesson. You may leave my speech and have a sense that I was involved in a controversial case, but still not know much more unless you did your own research about the inside baseball in the case. That's not the purpose of my speaking out.

JC: Based on your decision in *Dover*, should a litigant representing the religious side of a dispute before you in an unrelated case be concerned about you presiding in the case?

JEJ: No, they shouldn't be concerned at all. Because if you look at my career written large, I don't believe that I have a leaning or bias. And I think, to the extent I've been objectively evaluated, that's pretty clear. I call them according to the law and the testimony that I hear.

JC: You said in your opinion—"the Court is confident that no other tribunal in the United States is in a better position than we are to traipse into this controversial area" and decide the case. That's kind of a remarkable expression.

JEJ: It depends how you take it.

JC: How did you mean it?

JEJ: Let me tell you how I meant it, and I can tell you how it was misinterpreted. Take my friends at the Discovery Institute—which is a sort of worldwide proponent of Intelligent Design in Washington State. They took that as an arrogant statement, saying that I thought I was so great that I could undertake this analysis. I didn't mean that at all. That statement pertained to the fact that I held six weeks of trial and that I saw through the testimony something that no one else had been privileged to see. Which was putting Intelligent Design to its test to stand and deliver.

And remember, now, at the time, Intelligent Design proponents were approaching sympathetic minded school boards and state education board people across the Unites States. And they were somewhat piecemeal feeding them information on Intelligent Design, telling them that this was a very viable alternative to evolution. But there had been no searching analysis. I think we agree that there's few better crucibles in which to test something than the inside of a federal courtroom, particularly when you have experts on both sides and extensive scientific testimony. And after all, as you know, another aspect that the public generally doesn't know—judges decide what's good science every day through the *Daubert* touchstones that we utilize. So what I meant was—perhaps I said it inartfully and walked into a propeller by the way that I said it—was that I was as funded with information, or better funded with information, than anybody else was on that particular issue. So I was in a better place to take a swing at it than anybody else had been.

JC: Other than perhaps writing that phrase differently, is there something that you would have done differently in the case with the hindsight of seven or eight years?

JEJ: No. One of the reasons I wrote as expansively as I did was that I thought it was necessary to say what I had heard and seen in the courtroom for the benefit of any school board or board of education in the United States that wanted a primer on Intelligent Design. They could read the opinion. They might not agree with it, but they would see an expansive treatment of what I saw and heard. They, after all, might not have time to sit through a presentation. So I wrote at least parts of the opinion with that in mind.

JC: Who is the sitting judge, or judge in history, that you admire or would like to be the most?

JEJ: Probably Sandra Day O'Connor.

JC: What particular trait of hers do you admire so much?

JEJ: I'll never hold a candle to her legal abilities or her intellect; but I think that on a far larger scale than I'll ever achieve, she went through sort of the same progression that I did. Marked as a conservative from the inception of her tenure and then excoriated through the years because she supposedly drifted and was not true to her school. Her adherence to the rule of law. Her essential fairness. Her distaste for extraneous nonsense, which I've learned through getting to know her a bit through the years. Her sense of humor, which I count as an attribute that I hope every judge should have. I find all of those things so terribly compelling.

JC: Thank you, Judge.

Chapter 8

Judge Charles P. Kocoras

Now, I recognize that any expert called by either side has a degree of advocacy in him. But if you want to testify as an expert, you can't abandon your discipline—I actually think I used the word "shill" at some point. You can't come in and shill for one side, just because you have this wonderful reputation, credentialed background, etc.
—Judge Charles P. Kocoras, March 6, 2013

Since being appointed to the District Court bench for the Northern District of Illinois by President Jimmy Carter in 1980, Judge Kocoras has presided over numerous compelling matters.

In addition to In re Brand Name Prescription Drugs Antitrust Litigation, *the subject of this chapter, Judge Kocoras presided over a matter in which 46 male college athletes who were secretly videotaped in locker rooms and showers sued the sellers of the tapes, the college, and the Internet providers. The sellers sold the tapes through the Internet, advertising "hot younger dudes." Judge Kocoras dismissed the suit against the defendant college and the Internet provider but, as against the sellers, he awarded each athlete $1 million in compensatory damages and $10 million in punitive damages— more than $500 million, which was likely uncollectible.*

In a controversial matter, Judge Kocoras terminated a 20+-year-old mandate requiring the integration of Chicago public schools. The initial 1980 desegregation consent decree was designed to resolve the federal government's lawsuit against the Chicago Public Schools, which alleged discrimination against African American and Hispanic students. The decree required the Chicago School Board to operate under a detailed court order that required a prescribed racial mix in magnet and other selective schools. In determining that the mandate was obsolete, Judge Kocoras noted that it was "time for Big Brother to bow out."

In another matter, in a suit brought by a marketing company against an Internet-monitoring company, Judge Kocoras issued a default judgment that barred the defendant from blocking the plaintiff's e-mails as "spam." Notably, Judge Kocoras awarded $11 million in compensatory damages and directed that the defendant maintain a message on its website for a period of six months indicating that the plaintiff was erroneously listed on the defendant's website as a "spammer." (The Seventh Circuit reversed this ruling.)

The son of Greek immigrants, Judge Charles Petros Kocoras grew up on Chicago's South Side. His father, who had been in the wholesale produce business, died when Judge Kocoras was 18. The judge attended a junior college and graduated from DePaul University—working at a liquor store throughout. After college, Judge Kocoras worked for the Internal Revenue Service and remained employed by the IRS while attending DePaul University College of Law at night, from which he graduated valedictorian. During college and law school, he also served in the Illinois Army National Guard. After two years in private practice, Judge Kocoras worked as the First Assistant U.S. Attorney for the Northern District of Illinois and was thereafter chair of the Illinois Commerce Commission. He has continuously taught at John Marshall Law School since 1975. Appointed to the District Court in 1980, he presided as Chief Judge from 2002 through 2006 and currently holds senior status.

Judge Kocoras sits in Chicago, Illinois.

The Failed Expert

In 1994 the plaintiffs, on behalf of a nationwide class consisting of retail sellers of brand name prescription drugs, initiated a huge, $45 billion Sherman Act price-fixing case against the defendants—basically the suppliers of those pharmaceuticals, meaning the wholesalers and manufacturers of the drugs. The case was assigned to U.S. District Judge Charles Kocoras sitting in the Northern District of Illinois in Chicago.

The gist of the claim was that the wholesalers conspired to set a structure of differential pricing for these drugs. That is, the retailers, typically drug stores or pharmacies, would pay X for the drugs, whilst hospitals, HMOs, and other managed care facilities to which the drugs were sold—the so-called favored buyers—would pay X minus Y, or lower, more competitive prices. On its face, clearly, the pricing scheme was discriminatory against the plaintiffs, or so it seemed. The case was a big deal in the pharmaceutical world—after all, the giants of the pharmaceutical industry were at war.

The defendants, facially, had a simple answer: most managed care organizations and hospitals create "formularies" (i.e., restrictive lists of drugs). Meaning, their doctors are *required* to prescribe drugs to their patients and plan members from those lists. The defendants basically responded that the "favored buyers" used the formularies to control access to patient populations—thereby negotiating discounts and rebates from the manufacturers. Given the sheer size of the managed care organizations or the hospitals, they had the market power or capacity to gain discounts on brand name drugs.

So, for example, if a particular hospital network demanded that Searle Pharmaceutical sell a particular anti-inflammatory at, hypothetically, $4.00 per unit, rather than $5.00 per unit, at penalty of the network taking its business elsewhere (that is, by prescribing another brand or a generic drug with the same qualities), the hospital network had the clear leverage to negotiate a price reduction or rebate. Retail pharmacies, according to the defendants, simply didn't have the "juice" to accomplish the same result and, therefore, had to pay higher prices.

The plaintiffs disagreed. They argued that, indeed, they too had the power to move the market just as much. And this is how the case was joined.

In the face of this controversy, which lasted a number of years before trial was scheduled to begin, with several interim appeals to the U.S. Court of Appeals for the Seventh Circuit, a large number of the defendant drug manufacturers, including Abbott Laboratories, determined to settle in advance of trial without admitting any wrongdoing. The settlement for these manufacturers was in the neighborhood of $750 million.

Of course, the reason why particular defendants choose to settle isn't always clear. Still, one can assume that a cost-benefit analysis is typically implicated: Is it worth the risk of losing a potentially massive verdict? Is it worth the negative publicity that would certainly follow a negative verdict? Whatever the reason, however, a number of the manufacturer/defendants, most notably, G.D. Searle & Co.—clearly, a corporate fat cat—chose to go for broke. In so doing, they risked an almost unimaginably sizable verdict at trial, more so as the plaintiffs held in their arsenal an extraordinary forensic weapon prepared to testify on their behalf—a Nobel Prize–winning economist and tenured University of Chicago professor, in the person of Dr. Robert Lucas.

His lawyer and partner, Perry Goldberg, had trotted Dr. Lucas out before—and presumably his mere name on a witness list had scared defendants enough to yield large settlements to the suing plaintiffs. Consequently, Dr. Lucas never had to actually testify. But not this time—in *In re Brand Name Prescription Drugs Antitrust Litigation* before Judge Kocoras, Dr. Lucas would be forced to testify.

No settlement. Imagine. The defendants would have to challenge a Nobel Prize–winning genius in the complicated field of economics telling a jury that plaintiffs were the victims of an antitrust conspiracy at the hands of the pharmaceutical companies. In fact, his scholarship in economics was so great that the presiding trial judge—who clearly relished the prospect of seeing Dr. Lucas on the witness stand—would actually deny the defendants the often-granted opportunity to present his expertise to the judge in advance of trial, thus keeping plaintiffs from "poisoning" the jury with his erudition.

It was evident that plaintiffs were putting their eggs largely in Dr. Lucas's basket. For a period of ten weeks, the jury heard mostly (typically boring) deposition testimony read to them, along with four witnesses who testified live but were hurt considerably in their testimony during cross-examination. So if the case could be made, it had to be done by Dr. Lucas. But who would have been better?

What happened? Dr. Lucas saved the day for the plaintiffs, right? We shall never really know what the jury actually thought because, notwithstanding the great promise that Dr. Lucas held—at least for Judge Kocoras—His

Honor never let the jury deliberate on the plaintiffs' case. After observing the plaintiffs' case deteriorate and faced with Dr. Lucas's patently inadequate testimony, Judge Kocoras took the almost extraordinary step of directing a verdict against the plaintiffs, thereby taking the case squarely away from the jury and awarding the defendants a complete victory.

But Judge Kocoras not only dismissed the case. He offered a litany of Dr. Lucas's shortcomings; indeed, he went so far as to say that Lucas "abdicated entirely the concept of independence of expert witnesses, and simply became the sponsor" for plaintiffs' theory of the case. He found Lucas "ignorant" of what witnesses upon whose testimony he relied had said. He found Dr. Lucas's opinions not only *not* based on the evidence, but inconsistent with it, and without scientific basis or "the subject of economic methodological testing." And Judge Kocoras found that Dr. Lucas missed the core distinction between the market share that hospitals and managed care facilities could command compared to that of retailers.

But Judge Kocoras went further. He found that Dr. Lucas had a "disdain for reality," for example, in failing to show interest in how frequently retail pharmacies received discounts from manufacturers. And Dr. Lucas showed an "ostrich approach" in his hypothesis that competition in the pharmaceutical industry should drive the prices to all classes to the same level. Furthermore, Judge Kocoras wrote that, despite his superior academic knowledge, "Dr. Lucas never studied key concepts. Finally, rather than affording a basis for denial of defendants' motion for judgments of acquittal . . . Lucas's testimony clearly shows how vacuous the Class Plaintiffs' evidence of conspiracy really is."

It was also not lost on Judge Kocoras that Dr. Lucas had charged $600 per hour for his time while he spent only 40 hours preparing for his testimony. Did this lead Judge Kocoras to believe that, given the intricate and complicated issues, Dr. Lucas merely echoed his clients' position without substantial analysis? And how did Judge Kocoras react when he learned that the plaintiffs' lawyers entirely rewrote Dr. Lucas's "expert" report on which the plaintiffs' case relied?

And what did the jury think? And how would it have decided the case? We'll never know.

The Dialogue

JC: Judge Kocoras, how was the *Brand Name Prescription Drugs* case assigned to you?

CPK: Purely a random selection process in the Northern District of Illinois. The first case was assigned to me. As is routine, subsequently filed, related cases were hooked up to me.

JC: Will a case ever be assigned to a judge because of his or her particular area of expertise?

CPK: No.

JC: Before you were assigned the case, did you have any expertise in antitrust litigation?

CPK: None whatsoever. A few antitrust cases before—no particular expertise. No deep antitrust knowledge on my part.

JC: Do you see *Brand Name* as a complicated case among those assigned to you over the years?

CPK: It started out fairly complicated, by the sheer number of parties, the issues implicated, and the fact that the entire pharmaceutical industry was involved. There was a lot going on—many different issues and tributaries, albeit with antitrust in the main. In the end, though, the economic issues that governed the case's outcome were reduced to fairly simple concepts, which even I, as a non-expert in either economics or antitrust law, understood.

JC: When you started out, though, did you feel the need to do additional work on this case—more so, for example, than in a routine tort or contract action, or a motion to suppress?

CPK: Absolutely.

JC: As a result, did you conduct research beyond the parties' submissions?

CPK: No, but I did carefully read everything presented to me. If I didn't understand it, I'd read it a second time. In fact, the "complexity" that attached to the case was not only because of the case's subject matter and the parties involved. Early on, I heard that a Nobel Prize winner in economics would appear. No one wants to look stupid to any witness who appears before him. So, I wanted to be sure, whatever the economic issues, that I would be able to understand them and then extrapolate them onto the antitrust law that would govern the outcome. Clearly, the specter of the Nobel Prize winner off on the sidelines waiting to swoop in and educate us was surely a constant.

JC: Would it be inappropriate for a judge, in your view, to do research beyond what the parties presented? Perhaps, for example, Google searches to check into it whether your knowledge could match up to, say, a Nobel winner?

CPK: Yes. Take out Google and Wikipedia and whatever is available . . .

JC: Easier to take out Wikipedia—

CPK: Well, easier, but I don't think Judge [Richard] Posner takes it out. He thinks it's perfectly proper to consult Wikipedia and other sources.

Back to your question, I do think it's appropriate. You read a law review article on a topic. You'll read an educational treatise on economics. I don't think there is anything inappropriate about getting educated in an area where you need it. There is the fear that you'll get proselytized, or set in some direction by the choice of material you read. Of course, one never knows what hidden meaning lies in this material. But if it's a recognized expert treatise or source not on one extreme or another, I think, yes, it's entirely appropriate to gain knowledge about what you should know—in any way you can.

JC: If you do that—say, seek learning from perhaps a pro-plaintiff or pro-defendant source—do you think that you're obliged to tell the litigants: "Hey, I've done research beyond what you guys have presented, and I think you should know that?"

CPK: I'm not sure that's called for. My approach here was to learn as much from the papers and oral arguments. That would determine if I needed more. This is what a judge needs to know before I did any serious research on my own. I wouldn't jump into an area of economics or antitrust just because that's the subject matter. I'll let the lawyers educate me—lawyers are great at teaching you what you need to know.

JC: You mentioned a Nobel Prize winner in the person of Dr. Lucas. Before him, though, you'd had experiences with experts in various fields testifying before you, right?

CPK: Plenty.

JC: Did you have a view before dealing with Dr. Lucas that perhaps experts are overrated in what they bring to a litigation?

CPK: No pre-disposition about that. Some experts are good, some not so good. I will take them as I listen to them, both in direct and on cross. I'll decide who I can rely on—whose opinion warrants predicating some resolution on him, and who I should ignore.

JC: Have you ever appointed an expert to assist the Court?

CPK: No.

JC: Put aside your considerable experience on the bench, do you see judges generally better able than juries to find facts in complex cases?

CPK: I don't know about better, but I have a high opinion of juries, even in complex cases. There is a school of thought, some within the Seventh Circuit, that juries can't comprehend complicated cases and resolve them. I don't share that view. I think if you put a group of people with varied educational backgrounds and intellectual capacities in a room, and they each contribute to the resolution of the problem, I think that they generally do very, very well. So, I wouldn't exalt myself over a jury. Maybe over certain jurors, the judge has the better of it. But in my experience we don't know when a jury decides, whether the verdict is right—because "right" has an abstract connotation of perfection. But I have agreed almost always with the way my juries decided. In this case, after ten weeks of trial—and I directed the verdict to take it from the jury—my sense of the jury from some comments I heard, was that they agreed that the complainants' case wasn't there.

JC: Do you think that your experience—that your personal "verdicts" are typically consistent with your juries'—is largely explainable by the fact that you are sort of a "man of the people"? You don't present yourself as seated on a throne or in an ivory tower. Some judges do. They may have different views than a jury might.

CPK: No, I may be a man of the people and . . .

JC: I mean that in the finest sense of course.

CPK: Well, I know, but there is some arrogance at work. I'm dumber than some people, and smarter than others, okay? I'm no genius. I don't sit on the Court of Appeals and write today for the future. Had I been appointed to that Court, who knows. So I don't think that it's unique to my capacity or personality that there is this compatibility between my views and those of my juries. Candidly, there is a bit of arrogance in saying "I'm superior to a group of people who have been commissioned to resolve a case."

Many who level criticism at jury results and jury usage don't have much experience on how juries actually do their jobs and decide. A lot of professors—some, anyway—have that view. Definitely an ivory tower thing at work there.

JC: Is your view partially because you look at juries having practiced law for many years?

CPK: Well I was indeed in private practice. A prosecutor for a long time. A criminal defense lawyer.

JC: You tried cases?

CPK: Yes. I really don't think that's a prism that leaves some imprint that makes you see things in a certain way. It's just, my view, an experience factor. I don't think I'm better or worse by virtue of that experience. Rather it's because I have seen juries for 30 plus years, and before that when I tried cases. I know how they decide cases, in a generic sense. They listen when they're instructed, and generally obey the commands. Look, no human institution is perfect but I think that the jury system works very well.

JC: You say you ultimately found that the issues in this case weren't all that complex, once you had studied what was before you. Are some cases better handled by judges with expertise in the field? For example, tax cases, trademarks, patents?

CPK: There might be some highly technical or specialized cases where that would apply. I'm a former internal revenue agent. I used to teach tax law to new agents after I had done it for a while. The tax code can be very, very complex. Try to have a juror with no particular expertise in tax law decide a complicated tax case—you're asking for trouble. I share the view that that juror will not be as well-equipped as somebody else. Some cases, patent cases especially, because they're highly technical and have certain either singular or multiple disciplines that you have to study hard. And so there may be cases where the superior method of resolving the dispute is with someone steeped in the discipline of the subject matter. I don't think that's the normal kind of case that we deal with. But there are some cases that I will definitely concede—the more you know about this subject, the closer the result will be to what it should be.

JC: So let's get to the *Brand Name* case. Obviously, there had been considerable litigation up and down before the actual trial began. The trial evidence was ultimately a lot of deposition testimony, and 4 or 5 live witnesses including Dr. Lucas. Before the jury was seated, was it your sense that the case wasn't all that the plaintiffs had cracked it up to be?

CPK: No.

JC: Even though you had seen all of the pre-trial papers and . . .

CPK: Papers and points of view, and you get selected presentations of the record in terms of at least the facts. So you have a sense of the case and its issues. But I didn't have a sense of the strengths or weaknesses of the case. It's interesting that you ask me that question. I didn't have any predisposition of how this case would come out—where the strength or weaknesses were, and who would win. None of that. And the idea of directing a verdict in an antitrust case after 8 or 10 weeks of trial was furthest from my mind.

Here's what happened. The plaintiffs called four live witnesses and each got chewed up. One guy even admitted that he had lied. And in some instances, pharmacy-connected people had employed the same economic strategies that the defendants employed. So they were condemning the defendants for discriminatory pricing, and yet, when they could, they would do the same thing. Not all the witnesses—but the four.

Obviously, the plaintiffs' lawyers became aware that their witnesses were being hurt. So for the next number of weeks, until Dr. Lucas came along, we heard deposition testimony. Those depositions were mostly industry people. One after another, after another, and I'm thinking: "Why are we getting all these depositions instead of live testimony?" Everybody knows live testimony is a lot better than someone reading what someone else's answer was. Beyond that, the contents were of industry people. And unless they were going to confess to some nefarious activity, it will take a lot to put the pieces together. Civil or criminal—it's the same thing—same concepts. Someone agrees to fix prices in an illegal sort of way. Whether you call it civil or criminal, it kind of gets condemned in either branch of the law.

So I started to wonder: "Why are we getting all of this stuff?" And I'm trying to figure out how these pieces fit together to make an antitrust case, when a lot of the information is coming from the defendants or employees or representatives. So I started to think about that, because we are already in the middle of the trial: "Okay, if we don't have a smoking gun, we ought to have at least something else." The more I searched, the more I tried—and I started to think maybe something is missing that belongs here in the plaintiffs' case.

There's a vacuum of information. No employee of a drug company saying: "Oh yes, by the way, we had this meeting and here's what we talked about." That didn't happen. So you had to ask: "Who was at the meeting, what was the topic?" We had so many pieces, and a lot of them didn't go together. The more this went on, the more Lucas became more prominent as to what he might be able to do.

JC: A number of the companies had settled before the trial?

CPK: Yes. To the tune of 750 million dollars!

JC: Were you starting to wonder why those companies settled?

CPK: Just a little, because I know settling has a lot of different prompts to it. One is to not risk a verdict that is simply too overwhelming. Or one may be just compare dollars and cents and say look this is going to last a long time—this kind of litigation is not designed for a low budget analysis. It'll cost a lot of money. Lots of people settle for different reasons. Some lawyers see things in a certain way, some clients see things differently. So there are so many variables why in a large case like this people settle, that I wouldn't and couldn't give any credit to it, although it was intriguing that so many settled paying so much.

JC: Did you give any thought before Lucas testified to saying that there is something missing here: "Maybe you guys should consider talking to a magistrate and working out a settlement"?

CPK: No, sir. Not my role.

JC: Inappropriate for a judge to do that?

CPK: Once you start a trial you not only have to be impartial, but you have to give off the vibe of "appearing" impartial. If you make that kind of suggestion, you're giving your view of the case. That doesn't make you impartial. I've had lots of settlement conferences. I like them and I think I'm fairly good at it. Still, my view is that once the trial starts and the gauntlet comes down, if they want to settle that's their own business. Here, because it was so large and the lawyers were so good, I didn't even offer a settlement conference. These are big boys and girls. They know what they're doing. And if they want to talk settlement and want my assistance they'll ask for it. It wasn't a run of the mill civil case where you have a strong sense that settlements are really a good idea. In a lot of cases that becomes obvious. But this case was too big, populated by too many smart people and lawyers for me to say: "Let's sit down and talk settlement, because I don't want to try the case that will run two to three months." Most important, I wouldn't do it once the trial began.

JC: Getting to the core issue, you basically found Dr. Lucas not credible. Your opinion says: *"First it is proper to recognize Dr. Lucas's eminent and distinguished credentials. He is affiliated with the University of Chicago, indisputably one of the finest education institutions in the world. He is also a past recipient of the Nobel Prize in economics, an award equal in recognition of the scholarship and contributions to his chosen discipline. It is with high expectation that the Court anticipated his testimony and denied requests from the defendants to preclude his testimony or to conduct a separate Daubert hearing out of the presence of the jury."* So obviously, Judge, you relished the opportunity to see Professor Lucas on your witness stand.

CPK: No doubt about it.

JC: By all accounts, at least as of the first day he testified, he's a really big deal?

CPK: No question.

JC: Why did you deny a *Daubert* hearing?

CPK: Well, two things would cause a witness's disqualification as an expert. One, if he lacks credentials. Two, if whatever opinions he proffers aren't scientifically or equivalently arrived at. Dr. Lucas's credentials were sufficiently strong—you could simply take judicial notice that he is an expert without hearing a word from him. He teaches economics. And he received the Nobel Prize in economics. Am I going to question his credentials? The other part is deciding and evaluating the facts. I'm going to assume he did his homework and that he applied economic principles through a reasonable degree of economic certainty. So I don't want to waste my time because I know . . .

JC: You're going to let him testify . . .

CPK: I'm going to let him testify. And it made me, quite frankly, a little surprised that it didn't go well for him. But I didn't have a predisposition—my predisposition was the opposite. If I had any predisposition at all, it's that he'd done his homework. He's an able economist, and his opinions are going to be considered and admitted.

JC: So, is it unfair to say that you ultimately concluded that Dr. Lucas didn't know what he was talking about?

CPK: That's kind of strong, but it comes down to that. He didn't do his homework.

JC: What do you mean?

CPK: Well, he testified, it took him *only* 40 hours to reach his opinions. He also testified, essentially, that the lawyers redid his draft report. So, essentially, he became a parrot for the view of the lawyers and their clients. Now, I recognize that any expert called by either side has a degree of advocacy in him. But if you want to testify as an expert, you can't abandon your discipline—I actually think I used the word "shill" at some point. You can't come in and shill for one side, just because you have this wonderful reputation, credentialed background, etc.

So, the cross-examination showed two things fundamental. First, he was ignorant of much of the material evidence upon which he had to predicate his opinion. The facts of the case, that's the jumping off point. Two, he was just wrong in some of his opinions—demonstrably so. He didn't do his homework. He really didn't independently author his report. He didn't study the industry as you would expect. And that was clear from his testimony.

JC: So, on one hand you are saying he didn't spend enough time because he admitted he only spent 40 hours. On the other hand, you're saying that he was sort of in the hip pocket of plaintiffs' lawyers. If he's looking for money and the plaintiffs are willing to pay it, why would he only spend 40 hours? He could've spent two, three hundred hours and been compensated at the $600 bucks an hour he was receiving. Was there some arrogance in it all?

CPK: I wouldn't call it an arrogance. By the way, this was the first time Lucas ever had to testify. And I think he had been used before, maybe by these plaintiffs' lawyers. So if you want to just hypothesize what happened, which is quite dangerous—it may have been thought that he would never have to testify: that his presence and stature would suffice to produce a settlement that, I think, had been the case whenever he had been listed as a witness before. All surmise on my part. It may be that he didn't do his homework. Everyone else who listened to him thought he hadn't. He didn't do it because he didn't think he had to, thinking he would never testify, defend his positions to lawyers who, although not economists, are pretty bright, good on their feet, and armed with their own experts.

So, the only thing I can think of—and the analysis of a financial column in Chicago supports this—why Dr. Lucas faced these problems at trial is that he was being used by these lawyers as this big potential clout. And when they needed him to wield his club, he wasn't prepared to do that.

JC: You employed somewhat "extravagant" verbiage in your opinion, to describe Dr. Lucas. You say that he was sort of "ostrich-like," with a "disdain for reality." Pretty extreme terms . . .

CPK: Are those the terms I used?

JC: Yes.

CPK: "Reality"?

JC: Yes.

CPK: He did have a little disdain for the reality of the pharmaceutical industry.

JC: In using such language, did you think you needed to justify the strength of your opinion? Or is that typical of the kind of language in your opinions?

CPK: I called it the way I saw it. I didn't put anything in there just to buttress my conclusions—that's the way I saw it. I was extravagant in praising him without ever having seen him—calling him a product of a great school, which I believe is so. So it's not that. You want to know—I was disappointed in his testimony. Disappointed.

JC: Disappointed because you thought he would be able to make out the case that plaintiffs were bringing.

CPK: No, not for that reason.

JC: What then?

CPK: Because he couldn't defend his opinions. He didn't do his homework in terms of knowing the evidence in the case—knowing the industry.

I understand he had a Nobel Prize. I bow to that. But if you charge $600 per hour, those who pay that money deserve for you to—please excuse my expression—"work your ass off" to earn it. He didn't do that. I was seriously disappointed at that.

I didn't care if the plaintiffs won or lost—not my affair who wins or loses. Judges are passive at trial. Great advocacy and great witnesses make great trials. That's what I wanted to see. I didn't see that. I had the fullest expectation that I would get the cat's pajamas of economics. I was going to be a guest at the lecture of discourse, and learn something. If anybody does something great we all appreciate that. I didn't get that. Nobody else did either.

That was my disappointment. Whether the plaintiffs' lawyers or the plaintiffs themselves were foolish enough to put a lot of their eggs in his basket, that's their business. Doesn't affect my life. But I wanted him to be good because he had all of his credentials. I wanted to hear an eminent economist tell me things I didn't know or study.

JC: This question has been burning at me since I read your opinion, and I guess I'm in part the devil's advocate in asking it: Since, generally, in your experience, your "verdicts" match those reached by your juries, why didn't you just let the *Brand Name* case go to the jury? Since you believe juries are typically as smart as judges, why wouldn't you let the jury decide— let the plaintiffs have their "full" day in court? If their verdict then seems wrong, set it aside.

CPK: Easy to answer: I'm duty bound *not* to do that. If the law commands me to evaluate the evidence and make a determination—I've done what you suggest in other cases, but that isn't the best way to do it. If you're convinced after you give the breadth of the evidence its proper due, proper strength or lack thereof, and you are convinced that no reasonable jury can predicate a finding of guilt based on this evidence, it's your job to deal with it. And given what this case was about and how much time we had already invested, I felt duty bound to do what I did. I didn't do it lightly.

Do you think that for a second I didn't think that there was going to be an appeal, and how treacherous what I was about to do after 10 weeks of trial? I don't care if it's eight weeks of reading depositions, whatever it is—we've got a lot of time invested and the jury has a lot of stuff to chew on. So as I told you before, I didn't start out thinking "I'm going to go one way or another on this case. I'm going to let the evidence tell me where I've got to go." So when the evidence came in it was so lacking and an expert offered opinions that were so badly impeached, I couldn't let that case go to the jury. And if the Seventh Circuit says, "You should've done this or you could have looked at this evidence or sustained that," it's an easy reversal. But if I'm going to be fair to the defendants, and if they've done a good enough job to make it clear, they have to win the case now. I won't let the jury decide, and make my ultimate decision later. No, sir!

JC: You led me to believe earlier that in other cases you did let unsustainable cases go to the jury?

CPK: You might have a short case where you think maybe you should take it away, but you're not quite sure. You kind of lean that way. So I'll let it go to the jury. However, I don't remember ever letting a case go to the jury where I had doubts about whether I should—where I let the jury decide and then I took it away from the jury. I've had some cases where I let it go to the jury. I had some doubts about it. But when the jury decided it, they decided it in the right way—meaning, the way I think it should've come out. So they've taken care of my failure to rule.

JC: I think you're saying that if the *Brand Name* jury had not voted for these defendants, the result would have been "irrational" or "unreasonable"?

CPK: Yes. If I had let them decide—let's say the defendants didn't put on any case at all, because that's the realm we're dealing with . . .

JC: I mean if the case was just the depositions, the four witnesses and Dr. Lucas.

CPK: Yes, that would not have been a "reasonable" verdict, and I almost would have been compelled to take it away, had it happened that way. As I said, I thought my duty was to evaluate the elements and apply the standard that the law commands me to apply.

JC: One of the standards under [Federal] Rule [of Civil Procedure] 50 is that you, as a judge, can't make factual determinations in deciding that motion. Is it realistic that you can't make factual determinations? You basically said that the jury could not have believed Dr. Lucas's testimony.

CPK: I wouldn't let them rely on it.

JC: Oh, is that right?

CPK: Yes, because of the second prong of *Daubert*. His opinions were not formed either in a scientific way or a scientifically equivalent way. The jury couldn't have relied on Lucas. His opinions were thoroughly discredited. Even though I didn't hold a *Daubert* hearing before trial, I essentially did it at trial. And I took away the jury's ability to rely on him. Besides, even if somehow his opinions were allowed to stand—this is a kind of tricky, intellectual exercise—whether those opinions, without any foundational support in the evidence, could have been allowed to support a verdict for plaintiffs, I'd have to think about that. But I'm leaning that I wouldn't do that.

JC: You said earlier that, whatever the result, given the lawyers involved and the nature of the plaintiffs and defendants, you anticipated appeals.

CPK: Correct.

JC: And you already knew that a particular Circuit Judge would probably author the opinion, correct?

CPK: You could guess that it would be Judge Posner. He's an antitrust guy. He has seniority. He might also have been Chief Judge at the time, empowered to assign the opinion.

JC: It seems that he wrote all the Circuit opinions in the *Brand Name* case. So, anticipating that Judge Posner would probably author the decision, did that influence you? I mean, Judge Posner is an economics expert and, loosely speaking, believes that all litigations should be viewed through the prism of economics.

CPK: Wouldn't affect me one bit. At that point I felt the economics principles weren't so complex as to be beyond my comprehension or anybody else's. It was readily understandable why manufacturers discriminated against the retail druggist and favored the so-called "favored" purchasers.

JC: Because the favored purchasers—hospitals and HMOs—could affect the market due to the formularies?

CPK: Absolutely. And all the evidence supported that the retailers could not do that. And some evidence was that it was actually unethical for them to attempt it. When you walk into a drug store you hand the druggist the prescription and he's got to fill it. He can't tell you "By the way, your doctor is right, but I have another drug just as good, a brand name drug, not a generic. It has a little different property, but does the same thing and it's cheaper." Druggists can't do that.

The formularies for HMOs and hospitals—they can look at this pool of drugs, which essentially do the same thing and don't have any material differences in the effect on the patient, and say: "If you don't give us a discount, you are not on our formulary, and our doctors therefore won't prescribe them." In that way they influence the prescribing decision.

JC: So, who the judges are who might sit on the appeal would not be of interest to you, and wouldn't influence how you might decide a case?

CPK: It might be of interest to me, but whatever it is, it is. If I think I'm right, I don't care who's reviewing it. And, I've never talked to Court of Appeals judges on my cases. I don't do that. There were times that I would have liked to have. [laughter.]

Would I talk to an appeals judge after the case is completely over? No. We go on to the next case. Maybe you'll learn something, but it's over. It's a project. It's completed. I had my role, they have their roles. It's not personal. I'm not going to nitpick or quibble, or tell them they did great when they affirmed me. It's not the way the system works. I'm friends with these guys, good friends with Posner. Nothing personal about it, they review our work. We do what we think we have to do. We do it the best we can, they do it the best they can.

JC: Do you think that appellate judges, whether on a circuit court or the Supreme Court, are typically better judges if they had prior experience as trial judges?

CPK: Yes.

JC: Why?

CPK: They would have a better appreciation for what we do. Pressures we are under. That doesn't justify a bad decision, you understand?

JC: Right.

CPK: In fact, I was Chief Judge in this Court for four years. One of the judges from the Court of Appeals regularly wrote to me, saying "Can I come down and try some cases?" It was Dick Posner, and I accommodated him. Dick liked to try the hard intellectual cases. He's done that a number of times, and I admire him for that. Now, why he does it? I don't know if he does it to be a better appellate judge. But I think he has an interest, and likes to sample things that he's not done.

JC: Turning back to the case, some of the things that bothered you were that the lawyer rewrote Lucas's position paper, that Lucas had not studied some of the witness's testimony and that he had spent too little time in formulating his opinions. What if those things weren't in the case? That he had studied the witness's opinions. That he had written his own position paper without significant edits by the plaintiffs' lawyers, and that he had spent more time on it. It's sort of difficult to reconstruct, I understand, but would you have let the case go to the jury under those circumstances?

CPK: And the other facts stayed the same?

JC: Yes.

CPK: I don't know if I can answer that question. But if you want more speculation on a hypothetical that didn't happen—my purely off the cuff thought would be that the expert couldn't save the case. The facts would dictate the outcome. The facts being the lay testimony, if you will, and all the other documents and so on. They would dictate the outcome of the case, and I don't think the expert opinion would salvage that case. That's my present opinion, but I would have to give that a lot more thought and time.

Because, you know, experts come in and they give you their opinion and it's supposed to help the jury. One of the prongs of expert testimony is that it helps the jury understand non-run-of-the-mill stuff—so we're going to help you understand it. So maybe the jury's understanding improves. But if you start with ground zero—zero being the facts—you can multiply it by a factor of 10. 10 times 0 is still 0. Now that's too simplistic of an equation. But that's how, I think, I might come out if I gave it a lot of thought: that a good expert, even if you let his opinions in, can't change what's fundamentally necessary for the plaintiffs to win a case. That's my present answer. Tomorrow might be different.

JC: This last answer seems to be the news: the hoopla about the case is that you declared a Nobel Prize winner to not be credible. But what you are saying here, when you really analyze it with your robes off in chambers, is that the case itself was inadequate.

CPK: I think that's right. I don't mean to leave the impression that because Lucas didn't sustain his position, that's why the case disappeared. The case wasn't there before he hit the stand, and I was hopeful that somehow he'd make it better. He didn't. He isn't the reason the case went away, because I had both things to deal with. You couldn't predicate anything on what he had to say because he wasn't that good, and the facts weren't there, so that was an easy call.

In my general view, the evidence—the testimony and documents—are more important in the equation than the expert. And if you don't have that, the expert can't make it better. He can make it more understandable, more compelling. But if it's non-existent in the first place, the expert can't salvage it.

That's what I think is the right answer, but I don't want to take a test on it right now.

Chapter 9

Chief Judge Alex Kozinski

Breadth of experience in general is important for judging. But no matter how broad an experience any judge has, it will never encompass even a small percentage of the experience of all the litigants before us.
—Judge Alex Kozinski, April 9, 2013

Alex Kozinski is the Chief Judge of the U.S. Court of Appeals for the Ninth Circuit. A self-proclaimed libertarian, Judge Kozinski has a reputation for nonmainstream thinking, which is reflected in his witty, often controversial, and pointed opinions, many of them dissents.

Among Judge Kozinski's more far-reaching opinions is his dissent in U.S. v. Ramirez-Lopez, *a 2003 case involving an illegal immigrant accused of smuggling people across the border. Before his attorney could interview most of the witnesses who could exonerate Lopez, the government deported them yet detained those testifying to his guilt. Although the Ninth Circuit upheld Lopez's 78-month prison sentence, Judge Kozinski dissented and criticized the majority by offering a fictional dialogue between Lopez and his attorney in which Lopez's attorney sardonically explains to his client that he received a fair trial despite being deprived his due process rights. The opinion resonated so strongly that Lopez's sentence was suspended and all charges against him were dropped. Judge Kozinski's position on this issue eventually became the law in the Ninth Circuit in 2012 after prosecutors employed similar tactics in another matter.*

In another matter, Judge Kozinski dissented from an order denying a hearing en banc (as he did in the case that is the subject of this interview) in an action in which Vanna White sued Samsung when it produced a commercial with a robot dressed in a wig, gown, and jewelry posed next to a Wheel of Fortune-type board. White claimed Samsung had appropriated her identity. The Ninth Circuit determined that White had pleaded claims that could be tried. In Judge Kozinski's humorous and unrelenting dissent in which he argued that a hearing en banc should have been held, he criticized the court for stifling creativity and famously acknowledged that the Ninth Circuit is the Court of Appeals "for the Hollywood Circuit." In the "Barbie" case, Mattel sued MCA for producing and marketing the song "Barbie Girl" (which made it to the top 40), claiming MCA had turned Barbie into a sex object. In determining that "Barbie Girl" was protected speech, Judge Kozinski discussed the importance of satire, humor, and editorial comment. In that vein, he concluded the decision: "The parties are advised to chill."

Judge Kozinski's judicial philosophy, as well as his general worldview, is informed by his upbringing. Born Jewish in Bucharest, Romania, to Holocaust survivors, he was a self-described "committed communist" in his early years, hoping to bring those tenets to the West when his parents announced they were moving to Vienna. Upon arrival, however, he became an "instant capitalist," having discovered advantages that did not exist in Romania. His family moved to the United States when he was 12 and settled in California.

Judge Kozinski received an A.B. degree from the University of California, Los Angeles, and received his J.D. from UCLA School of Law in 1975. He clerked for future Supreme Court Justice Anthony Kennedy while Justice Kennedy sat on the Court of Appeals for Ninth Circuit, and then for U.S. Supreme Court Chief Justice Warren Burger from 1976 to 1977. While Judge Kozinski was in private practice, he served as deputy legal counsel for President-elect Ronald Reagan and then became Assistant Counsel in the Office of the Counsel to the President. In 1982, he was appointed Chief Judge of the then-newly formed U.S. Court of Federal Claims. When he turned 35 in 1985, President Reagan appointed Judge Kozinski to the Ninth Circuit Court of Appeals. At the time, he was the youngest federal appeals court judge.

Judge Kozinski was appointed Chief Judge of the Ninth Circuit on November 30, 2007, and currently serves in that position. His chambers are in Pasadena, California.

Judging from the "Bully Pulpit"

In January 2012, the U.S. Supreme Court, in *U.S. v. Jones*, unanimously decided this: if law enforcement agents choose to attach a Global Positioning System (GPS) tracking device to an individual's vehicle to remotely surveille the perpetrator's travels, they must obtain a search warrant to do so and comply strictly with the warrant. Having obtained a search warrant to attach a GPS device to the undercarriage of Jones's vehicle—authorizing its installation in Washington, D.C., within 10 days, but not having installed it until the 11th day and, in fact, in Maryland—the Court held that it violated Jones's Fourth Amendment rights. It was an unlawful search and seizure as if there had been no search warrant in the first place.

Accordingly, the Supreme Court suppressed the considerable evidence collected over the four-week period that the GPS device was active. Importantly, this was the Court's ruling, even though the police installed the device while Jones's Jeep was parked in a *public* parking lot—where no claim of trespass onto private property could be made. In short, even though such a GPS device is about the size of a bar of soap, and the police did not need to actually enter the individual's vehicle, the owner's expectation of privacy was violated.

The GPS device was at stake in *U.S. v. Pineda-Moreno,* decided by the Ninth Circuit two years before *Jones*; however, the dispute in *Pineda-Moreno* was different from that in *Jones*. Pineda-Moreno, you see, was a small-time marijuana grower and trafficker. After Drug Enforcement Administration (DEA) agents in Phoenix, Oregon, noticed him purchasing a large quantity of fertilizer, known to be used to grow marijuana, they observed him driving his Jeep to a "home" he was renting.

The precise nature of that "home" was critical: it was a trailer. Trailer homes typically don't have garages that are attached to or adjoin them. So when Pineda-Moreno arrived home one day, he parked his Jeep in his shared driveway near his trailer. When the DEA agents discreetly observed Pineda-Moreno's driveway, they saw no fence, no gate, no "No Trespassing" signs discouraging them from entering the property. So under cloak of night, between 4 and 5 a.m., they entered the driveway and attached the GPS devices to the undercarriage of the Pineda-Moreno Jeep.

These devices enabled the agents to track Pineda-Moreno's travels remotely—again, without the need to physically intrude inside Pineda-Moreno's Jeep. Finally, when information from the GPS device alerted the agents that Pineda-Moreno's vehicle was leaving a suspected marijuana grow site in Oregon, the agents followed it, pulled him over, smelled the odor of marijuana, and gained Pineda-Moreno's consent to search his trailer, where they found two large garbage bags full of marijuana. When Pineda-Moreno moved to suppress the evidence—arguing that the agents violated his Fourth Amendment rights by attaching the device to his Jeep parked within his curtilage—the District Court denied his motion. Consequently, Pineda-Moreno pleaded guilty conditionally, which reserved his right to appeal his Fourth Amendment claim.

The Supreme Court had not yet heard the *Jones* case or decided upon the need for a warrant to install a GPS. Thus, the issue in *Pineda-Moreno* in the Ninth Circuit was this: did the agents violate Pineda-Moreno's rights by going onto his driveway and attaching the device without having first obtained a warrant?

The Court, and later the majority in denying a hearing that would have allowed *all* of the active judges on the Court to hear the issue (a hearing *en banc*), decided that Pineda-Moreno simply had no "reasonable expectation of privacy" in his semiprivate driveway. There were no enclosures, no barriers, no lack of visibility from the street. Indeed, if an individual wanted to deliver a newspaper or visit someone, he or she would have to go through the driveway to get to the trailer. If a child had walked up the driveway or crawled under the Jeep to retrieve a lost ball or runaway cat, for the three-judge panel that heard the case, "Pineda-Moreno would have no grounds to complain."

But what was the opinion of Chief Judge Alex Kozinski—a philosophically libertarian immigrant from Romania? For Judge Kozinski, the Court's ruling and decision to deny an *en banc* review of the case were but a further effort to "dismantle the zone of privacy we enjoy in the homes' curtilage and in public. The needs of law enforcement, to which my colleagues seem inclined to refuse nothing, are quickly making personal privacy a distant memory. 1984 may have come a bit later than predicted, but it is here at last."

Notably, in describing Pineda-Moreno's driveway as "part of his home's curtilage," Judge Kozinski barely even mentioned that his home was actually a trailer. It seems that Judge Kozinski was determined to make a much more dramatic point. For him, the very rich could still protect (buy?) their privacy with electric gates, tall fences, security booths, remote cameras, motion sensors, and roving patrols. However, the "vast majority of the 60 million people in the Ninth Circuit" lived differently. They have open driveways, unenclosed porches, basement doors left unlocked, yard gates left unlatched, and garage doors that don't quite close.

But here is what really irked Judge Kozinski:

> There's been much talk about diversity on the bench, but there's one kind of diversity that doesn't exist: No truly poor people are appointed as federal judges, or as state judges for the matter. Judges, regardless of race, ethnicity or sex, are selected from the class of people who don't live in trailers or urban ghettos. The everyday problems of people who live in poverty are not close to our hearts and minds because that's not how we and our friends live. Yet poor people are entitled to privacy, even if they can't afford all the gadgets of the wealthy for ensuring it. Whatever else one may say about Pineda-Moreno, it's perfectly clear that he did not expect—and certainly did not consent—to have strangers prowl his property in the middle of the night and attach electronic tracking devices to the underside of his car. No one does. When you glide your BMW into your underground garage or behind an electric gate, you don't need to worry that somebody might attach a tracking device to it while you sleep. But the Constitution doesn't prefer the rich over the poor; the man who parks his car next to his trailer is entitled to the same privacy and peace of mind as the man whose urban fortress is guarded by the Bel Air Patrol. *The panel's breezy opinion is troubling on a number of grounds, not least among them its unselfconscious cultural elitism.* [Emphasis added.]

"Unselfconscious cultural elitism"? Was Judge Kozinski saying that his colleagues who voted against Pineda-Moreno were cultural (or economic) snobs who couldn't or wouldn't relate to the common man? Was he asking for a sea change in how federal (or state) judges are selected? Was he using provocative concepts simply as a way to throw out a relatively unimportant "two garbage bag" marijuana case? Or was he, rather, boldly bringing his innermost view of the unfair disparities between American society's "haves" and "have nots" onto the bench?

Still, until this point in his dissent, Judge Kozinski hadn't yet directly "personalized" it. So this was the pièce de résistance that ended his opinion:

> I don't think that most people in the United States would agree with the panel that someone who leaves his car parked in his driveway outside the door of his home invites people to crawl under it and attach a device that will track the vehicle's every movement and transmit that information to total strangers. There is something creepy and un-American about such clandestine and underhanded behavior. *To those of us who lived under a totalitarian regime, there is an eerie feeling of deja vu.* [Emphasis added.]

What was the purpose of all of this? Chief Judge Kozinski had clearly failed—if it was his intent—to persuade a sufficient number of his colleagues to grant an *en banc* in the case. In writing a passionate, personal dissent that, frankly, members of the bench and bar, and even law school students, infrequently read, was he simply intending to pour out his heartfelt thoughts about the judiciary in general and his colleagues in particular? Was he doing this merely because his life experiences (whether or not you consider them unique) guided him to say all of this? Or, in discussing his world views about the judiciary and society in general, was there something else altogether going on?

The Dialogue

JC: Before we discuss *Pineda-Moreno*, Benjamin Cardozo famously said that "The great tides and currents which engulf the rest of man do not turn aside in their course and pass the judges by." Also, he said, everyone comes to the bench with a "stream" or "tendency" that goes into their decision making. Do you agree?

AK: Other than being tautological, I don't know what it adds to . . .

JC: I'll ask this way. The conventional wisdom—the smart money, if you will—is that your judging comes from the place of your personal philosophy of libertarianism. Fair statement?

AK: It depends on what you mean by "comes from."

JC: The principal influence in your decision making.

AK: I'm influenced by many things. My philosophy is one of a vast number of things.

JC: I imagine. But what does that "libertarian" philosophy mean in the context of your judging?

AK: Suspicion of big government and authority. A tendency to favor individual action over collective action. A tendency to believe in individual initiative over collective initiative. Not being particularly awed or impressed by expression of authority.

JC: Did something in your life bring you to that place?

AK: Probably having lived under communism. Living under communism, and then leaving communism, is a big change. You feel the weight of government lifted off your shoulders in a way you didn't even know existed. A subtle decompression, but one that's quite noticeable.

JC: I read that you do not oppose the death penalty.

AK: No, I don't.

JC: Is that not somewhat inconsistent with a philosophy suspicious of big government?

AK: Not at all. The death penalty is just one form of punishment, and being suspicious of authority certainly doesn't mean you believe government should never act. Or that certain conduct should not be punishable. If you accept that regime, which I do, the death penalty is no different from anything else the government does.

JC: Isn't a "suspicion" of big government somewhat inconsistent with being a Chief Judge over, say, fifty million people in this Circuit?

AK: Not at all.

JC: But you do believe that law enforcement has basic flaws in how it imposes punishment, correct?

AK: No.

JC: Interesting. So when you say suspicion of big government, what do you mean?

AK: All exercises of power are subject to corruption and bias. No difference between government and anything else. Any aggregation of power is like that. The thing about government is that it has a monopoly on the lawful use of force. And so one must be particularly suspicious of it because there is no competition. There's no second government or different government that you can go to. No checks like these exist in the market economy, where corporations have other corporations to compete with, employers have other employers to compete with. Or, employees have other employees that might take their job if they don't do well. Those things don't apply to government. So we must have other kinds of constraints. One constraint is that those who help apply the government's force, which is what we as judges do when we approve when and how the government can take somebody's liberty, we ought to be reluctant and leery of its use.

JC: Are the courts better equipped to that than the legislature?

AK: For individual cases, certainly. That's why we don't have bills of attainder. Ultimately it's the legislature that provides the authority for the government's use of force. We apply it in individual cases. We are best suited to apply it in individual cases because we can find the facts in cases to ensure that it's actually suited to the individual case. But the exercise of power is by the executive and the legislative branches acting together.

JC: Let's talk about *Pineda-Moreno*. You were terribly concerned that law enforcement abused that particular defendant.

AK: Correct. I was concerned about their use of a particular method of tracking the defendant.

JC: An abuse in how they enforced the law relating to him?

AK: You say abuse of the defendant. I think the abuse was in the powers the investigators were given.

JC: The case was a marijuana case. Two garbage bags full, a fairly substantial amount of marijuana. Still, marijuana. Would you have viewed law enforcement's actions differently were it two garbage bags full of heroin?

AK: I see no difference in what crime the investigator was looking at. I didn't remember, until now, what they were tracking him for. Not even sure I ever knew. I am sure it was out there for me to know; but if you gave me a multiple choice exam I don't think I would have gotten it right.

JC: These law enforcement officers went into the curtilage of his property, such as it was. He drove his car into a driveway right next to his trailer. You say, tell me if I'm wrong, that if it were a rich guy with a house who drove his BMW into his driveway—you take pains to mention BMW—that the Court would treat that defendant differently. That judges might be more concerned about him than about Pineda-Moreno.

AK: I don't think I said that at all. What I said is that most of us park our cars behind locked gates, so our curtilage is not open to the kind of abuses that the police engaged in with Pineda-Moreno. When you are behind a locked gate, the police won't sneak in and put a GPS unit on your car. It's just not possible. In some sense we are shielded from the same kind of problem that Pineda-Moreno faced. I didn't say we'd be more concerned. I said that some problems poor people have rich people don't, and most federal judges are fairly well off. So the idea of living in a trailer and parking your car in your open driveway where police actually can go in and attach a GPS unit are just not problems most of us face in life. I park my car way off the street.

JC: Your opinion said that most judges suffer from "an unselfconscious cultural elitism."

AK: Did I say that?

JC: You did. What does that mean?

AK: It means that we are all captives of our environment, our upbringing and lifestyle. We tend to see the world from that perspective. So when we think about somebody whose life is very different, we can't really see it the way they do. And to someone like us, for example, parking a car in an open driveway, even though the government admits that it was a curtilage, just doesn't strike us as being very private. When you park your car at home, you will go into a garage.

JC: You did write that opinion in which you said that. Four judges agreed, and signed on. What does that mean—the five of you don't suffer from that "unselfconscious cultural elitism"?

AK: I think that what it means is that in this particular case—this one instance, this one situation—we were able to look past that and overcome it. I think most of us can and have overcome it in particular situations. That doesn't mean that, on a daily basis, we are not captives of it. You always have to struggle to escape your own point of view and try to view things from the perspective of people not like you. It's a constant struggle. You have to escape your background if you want to judge people different from yourself.

JC: In *U.S. v. Kras*, the Supreme Court heard the case of a man who didn't have the filing fee needed to file a bankruptcy petition. Justice Marshall, in dissent, said that "It's disgraceful for the interpretation of the Constitution to be premised upon unfounded assumptions of how the poor live." Similar to what you were saying in *Pineda-Moreno*?

AK: I think so. I'd have to know more about the context, but it sounds like it. Justice Marshall, who himself came from a disadvantaged background and suffered discrimination, knew a thing or two about different points of view that maybe some other federal judges know only theoretically, not practically. There's a big difference between practical knowledge and theoretical knowledge.

JC: Was your dissenting opinion moved by some personal experience? Or were you able to overcome the "unselfconscious cultural elitism" that others suffer from, but can't overcome?

AK: Hard to say. I may have just stumbled into this in *Pineda-Moreno*. Any of us can do it in any particular case, if you think hard enough about it or make the effort to step out. I think the majority of the judges in that case probably didn't, and maybe I thought about the case and saw this aspect of it.

JC: Is it advantageous for judges generally to do something in their lives while or before becoming judges, to gain a perspective that they might not otherwise have?

AK: Breadth of experience in general is important for judging. But no matter how broad an experience any judge has, it will never encompass even a small percentage of the experience of all the litigants before us. It's just not possible. No matter how broad your experience has been, you will deal with people who are not like you. So I think it's important to remind ourselves every so often that many people are not like us, and sometimes when we talk about what's going on with them we are really projecting what's going on with us. And we need to stop and ask ourselves: "Is that a fair statement of their situation, or is that really a projection of who we are?" Lots of times it's a projection of who we are.

JC: I remember reading of some dispute arguing that you should recuse yourself from death penalty cases because you had visited in prison someone facing the death penalty.

AK: It was actually the Attorney General of California who complained.

JC: Should judges do that kind of thing to get a better sense of what really happens?

AK: I do what I think is right for me. For example, I sit as a district judge regularly, taking one or two cases a year. I did it when I started out because I hadn't been a trial lawyer and needed experience. I thought it was useful for me as an appellate judge. I continue to do so, because I keep learning things as a trial judge that I don't learn as an appellate judge.

Some judges do, some don't. Some excellent judges have never sat as trial judges. And there are some excellent judges who don't need to because they have lots of life experience. So I don't make prescriptions for other judges. I can't get in their heads; I don't know all of their life experiences. I personally find it useful. Doing things and staying in touch with people and participating in community functions and generally being open to contact by various people in the community is something I find useful to my judging. I can't judge anybody else's situation.

JC: When Justice Sotomayor was nominated by President Obama there was a brouhaha over the President having said something like—"It's a very important quality for a judge to have empathy." Was it empathy you were showing to Pineda-Moreno in the vigor with which you articulated your views?

AK: My dissent had nothing to do with Pineda-Moreno himself.

JC: You were basically talking about poor people.

AK: I was talking about poor people, but also all people. Some aspects of the case had nothing to do with being poor. There were two issues: the curtilage issue and the GPS tracking issue. The curtilage issue certainly applied more to poor people than to people who can surround themselves with walls, security kiosks, gated communities and the like. Obviously, they don't have the same problems. But the other issue had to do with tracking.

Of course all of us who carry cell phones and fast tracks and things like that can be tracked. Anybody who drives a car to which the police can attach a GPS unit could be tracked, at least until the Supreme Court decided *Jones*.

Remember, this was a dissent from a denial of an *en banc*. So, those things are seldom about the individual. Maybe in a death penalty case it would be about the individual. This was not about Pineda-Moreno. It was about us in society and how the police can track us. The first part of the opinion dealing with curtilage was more directed to poor people. But once they go after poor people and get them, the rest of us are not far behind. So really, this was about all of us.

JC: In a Supreme Court dissent in *California v. Hodari D.*, Justice Stevens was bothered by the majority opinion's "gratuitous" cite from the Book of Proverbs that "the wicked flee when no man pursueth." He was troubled because many people in minority communities actually fear the sudden approach of strangers. Justice Stevens didn't come from a world where that would have been his personal experience.

Or perhaps, you remember a judge in the Southern District of New York, Harold Baer, who said something similar, but far more boldly, in a suppression case. President Clinton and Senator Moynihan suggested he should be impeached for basically exhibiting (my word) that kind of "empathy" for a particular defendant. Should judges be criticized for deciding cases relying on things they don't necessarily know from the bench, but from life?

AK: Judicial opinions and expressions are often misconstrued or taken out of context. Very often they are denounced in the press by people who haven't bothered to actually read them. A classic example was after the panel of our Court decided that the Pledge of Allegiance was unconstitutional because it said "Under God." Within less than a day it was taken up in the Senate, and ninety-eight senators voted to condemn the opinion. I'm on the Court and hadn't yet gotten the slip opinion.

Now this was before the days when you could download it from the internet instantly. I am reasonably sure that ninety-eight of those senators, or some significant number, had not actually had time to read and understand the opinion, in order to be able to condemn it.

At the same time, we're a public institution. We speak what we speak with the authority of government. I'm not going to say that it's inappropriate for somebody to comment on what we say in our public utterances. So if the President wants to come after us, or the Senate wants to vote ninety-eight to nothing to condemn one of our opinions, they're entitled to. I certainly won't say it's inappropriate. Part of being a public institution is being criticized, maybe being criticized unjustly.

JC: You say that sometimes judicial opinions are misconstrued. Accepting that, how about your statement in *Pineda-Moreno*: "I don't think that most people in the United States would agree with the panel that someone who leaves his car parked in his driveway outside the door of his home invites people to crawl under it and attach a device that will track the vehicle's every movement and transmit the information to total strangers. There is something creepy and un-American about such clandestine and underhanded behavior. To those of us who have lived under a totalitarian regime there is an eerie feeling of *déjà vu*."

There was something in your life experience that was unique to the members of your Court. You lived and suffered in a totalitarian, communist regime.

AK: That's right.

JC: What impact did it have on your thinking as a judge? Do you think it's possible that that will happen again here, given the kind of behavior engaged in by the DEA in this case?

AK: It's somewhere along the spectrum. I don't think we'll get to communism or to the kind of totalitarianism regime we had in Romania. But there are degrees of power and intrusion. And now with an electronic age, it's so much easier for the government to keep track of everybody. Twenty years or thirty, fifty years ago, even if the government had wanted to, just keeping track of a single individual would require a team of undercover agents following and tracking. There was no way to do it effectively, and certainly not for large masses of people. Now, we are subject to all sorts of electronic monitoring, constantly. Our phone company knows exactly where we travel because of the cell phone. And there are all sorts of records of things we do on-line that disclose a great deal about who we are and what we do, our patterns and habits. It's now very cheap for the government, and fairly easy to get information and track all of us.

To me, this poses a new kind of danger that we need to think about if we want to protect the same level of liberty that we had in a pre-electronic age, when we were protected by the fact that it was just too tough to track us. The basic thing is that the world doesn't stand still, nor does life. Things are forever changing and part of what it means to protect our liberties is to anticipate and to be aware of these changes and how they affect our lives. That's what's going on there. This is a new danger. GPS tracking couldn't exist ten, fifteen years ago.

JC: You write an opinion like this. You're extremely articulate, assertive, maybe aggressive, in how you state these concepts. You say pretty strident things. You make the "totalitarian" comment. You make the "unselfconscious cultural elitism" comment; that the Fourth Amendment was being "decimated." You refer to "the needs of law enforcement to which my colleagues seem inclined to refuse nothing," and you say that the Majority was "quickly making personal privacy a distant memory."

Using these means, are you trying to get other judges to vote with you? Are you rather making a statement for society?

AK: I think I cited some of my early dissents in that . . .

JC: Okay. So what are you trying to do with strident remarks like that?

AK: Several things. One thing is that I was trying to take this case *en banc.* I fought a battle internally, and lost. So the next step was *cert.*[1] The most immediate thing, I was trying to raise the visibility of the issue to make or help make it *cert*-worthy. Some issues can't be made *cert*-worthy, but sometimes you can help. The lawyers were pretty good, although I thought there were arguments they could have made that they didn't articulate as clearly as I could. But I also wanted to show that the Ninth Circuit's view, as articulated by the majority opinion, was not the unanimous view of the court. And that losing the *en banc* battle didn't foreclose the issue in the future. So I tried to articulate it strongly, and bring judges with me to show a division in the ranks—which signals something to the Supreme Court.

---

1. Author's note: The grant of a writ of certiorari ("cert"), requiring the vote of four Justices of the U.S. Supreme Court, enables that Court to hear a case.

But I also wanted to alert people outside of our Court that this is an issue worth pursuing. So if I write something like this, I expect that lawyers will read it, and they may have cases where they say: "This is an important issue." Maybe in a different circuit or in state court, they might say, "Well we're still at a point where we can make a different decision. So we'll read this dissent and try to avoid some of the pitfalls or problems that plagued this opinion, and try to set this up for a better challenge in the next case."

I thought that if I did not manage to get a *cert* grant in our case, at least I would try to avert a similar result in another circuit, and thereby precipitate a circuit split which could cause *cert* to be granted in that case. I didn't know that when I was writing this that the *Jones* case was already in the works and soon to be issued by the time I wrote my dissent.

I don't communicate with judges in other circuits, so I didn't know there was a circuit split about to happen. I hoped other courts and legal scholars, lawyers and advocates would pick up on it and push back. I wanted to give them the tools.

JC: I think readers will be astonished to see this. Most lawyers, I think, believe that a judge has a case he's deciding or dissenting in—unless he has a particular interest in the issue—and he looks at the facts and the law and that's it. As opposed to having a "world view" of where they want it to go beyond the immediate case.

AK: [Judge] Learned Hand certainly had a world view. [Judge] Henry Friendly had a world view.

JC: Aren't they exceptions, although you're in good company? Do you think that most judges, say, your colleagues, have a view beyond the case, similar to what you've just articulated to me?

AK: My colleague [Circuit Judge] Stephen Reinhardt has a view. [Circuit Judge] Harry Pregerson has a world view. [Circuit Judge] Carlos Bea has a world view. I can't say that about all of my colleagues. I think many have world views. Some apply them to judging, but perhaps others don't. They have views on certain issues. And I certainly don't have views on every issue. The Fourth Amendment happens to be an area where I have very strong views. There are other areas where I have strong views—for example, contracts, or the "takings" clause. I don't have a mega-view on all issues, but certain areas interest me and worry me.

I can't speak for other judges very knowledgably, but I'm guessing that every judge, to some degree, has areas that he is particularly concerned about. They may be broader, or narrower.

Some of my colleagues do take the view that you've expressed. That you decide this case for today and that that's our job—our job is to decide this case for today and the mega-theory is then stitched together by a series of individual decisions made by judges in individual cases. I think judges who hold strictly to that view are in a distinct minority. Most of the appeals judges I know, to some extent, have areas where they feel strongly—they have an overarching view or theory, and then cases come along which fit into that pattern.

JC: Let's take *Pineda-Moreno*. You conference the case with your colleagues after argument. In looking at the facts—you personally experienced, you say, a *déjà vu* experience, having come from the communist world, and having been the son of Holocaust survivors. Do you take that up with your colleagues? Do you say "Hey, guys, you don't understand. Let me tell you about an overarching experience in my life that influences my thinking. You guys just simply aren't sensitive to it—you all need think about it?"

AK: Words like that would just alienate them. I don't do that very often. Part of the problem is that I've been here for a very long time. Most of my colleagues know my story and my *mishugas*. And I don't have to tell them I come from communism and that I'm bringing a message. Most of my colleagues have lived with me a very long time and are very tolerant. I must say, I've never gotten any flak from them about anything I've said. They understand where I come from, so I don't think I would need to do that. It's a little patronizing, I think, to say "Look, I know . . . "

JC: Is it patronizing to say that most federal judges come from an "unselfconscious cultural elitism"?

AK: There are things you can say in an opinion that would be patronizing if you said them in conference, face to face, yes.

JC: Is it patronizing to say that in an opinion?

AK: I don't think so. Face to face interactions are inherently different.

JC: What do you think your colleagues say when they see that kind of thing?

AK: "There he goes again!" [laughter.]

Opinions are bully pulpits to some extent. Particularly, dissents. Was it Justice Douglas or Justice Frankfurter who said that they're "a call upon the future." You're speaking to the future. Future generations, future readers, future decision makers. You've lost this battle; you've lost the current set of decision makers and now you're speaking to the future. And you're trying to do your best to make sure that their work product gets as little respect and following as possible. It's advocacy! This is why we went to law school.

JC: Do you prefer to be in the dissent?

AK: I love dissenting. I like winning but . . .

JC: But winning doesn't provide the opportunity to use the bully pulpit the same way.

AK: Oh, I do that sometimes too. But majority opinions are inherently limited because they have to be quite responsible. For one thing you have to put in enough facts to make sense of the ruling. You also have to be mindful of precedent. Dissent, you can disagree with precedent. You also have to be very careful in a majority opinion because what you say will be cited as precedent and get applied in future cases. So that inherently limits how far you can go in a particular case, because you don't want the case to make a bigger impact than it deserves. Whereas a dissent, or even a concurrence, but particularly in a dissent, you can be as grandiloquent and as expansive as you want. It has no precedential force. People follow it only to the extent they're persuaded by it.

JC: Concerning the "elitism" business, if President Obama and Senator Feinstein were to read your dissent in *Pineda-Moreno*, what should be their takeaway? If they find a guy as smart as Kozinski who clerked for Warren Burger, as you did, but lives in a trailer park, "we should consider appointing him to the Court because we need more judges who don't suffer from that unselfconscious cultural elitism"?

AK: I have no problem with the basic proposition. Except, I have a hard time imagining a guy who is that accomplished and smart who went to law school and lives in a trailer park. You'd have to ask: "Why is he living in a trailer park? How did he wind up there with a law degree?"

JC: Perhaps, you're culturally elitist yourself concluding that. Maybe he's happy to live in a trailer park.

AK: That wouldn't be the same. Living in a trailer park as a life choice is not the same as living in a trailer park because you have to. So that guy would have said, "Well, I've got lots of money, I could live in Bel Air, but I choose to live in a trailer park." It's not the same thing, because he can get out of the trailer park at any time at all. So I'd have to ask a few more questions about why the guy lives in a trailer park.

But accepting your premise and assuming that his choice is not made irrationally—say, the guy is *meshuga* or crazy—or has committed a felony along the way, I think, yes, getting judges with diverse life experiences is important.

Far more important than, let's say, gender diversity on the bench. My experience has been that my male colleagues and female colleagues are no different as a group. They are all different from each other, but I can't at all say I detect a "female view" or a "male view." Not at all. I have many colleagues of both sexes. So I think that is a less important distinction than other kind of things that we don't consider for diversity. Such as income level, such as . . .

JC: How about race?

AK: I think, for sure, race matters more than gender. I think having been on the Court with [Judge] Jerry Farris—who grew up in Alabama, and wound up going to law school in Washington State because the State of Alabama paid him so they wouldn't have to integrate their law school—was an eye-opening experience. So I think race matters a lot more than sex.

But even that is becoming less significant. Diversity of background, diversity in law school; my not having gone to one of the top five law schools in the country; having gone to law school or college in different parts of the country; having grown up in different parts of the country, all make a difference. I think growing up in Southern California or Arizona is very different from growing up in Maine and New York City. Those kinds of differences matter. And I think in general, diversity is a factor that those who appoint judges should consider giving serious attention to.

JC: Because you believe there are no poor judges on the federal courts, do you have a greater obligation to protect that wing of society—because you yourself seem not to suffer from that elitism that concerns you?

AK: I do think one has a particular obligation. We deal with people and situations that we haven't experienced.

JC: After the decision denying *en banc* in *Pineda-Moreno*, the Supreme Court decided, in *Jones*, that a warrant was necessary to place a GPS on a car, either within or outside the curtilage. *Pineda-Moreno* went back up to the Circuit where your colleagues on the original panel decided that there was still sufficient evidence without using the GPS and its fruits. Why didn't you try for an *en banc* the second time around?

AK: I don't exactly remember. I do remember thinking it was not an *en bancable* issue. I may have been wrong. I've since learned more about it and wish I had called for *en banc*.

JC: Once the case was decided by the Supreme Court which basically said that you were right, whether within or outside the curtilage, why would you even have any interest after that?

AK: Not because of that issue. There was another issue, and I was just not attuned to it. I have since heard criticism of it, and wish I had been aware of it. I'm not sure it's right. I just would have looked at the case from a different perspective. But it's now gone and nothing we can do about it, so I'll just wait until the next case comes along.

JC: It was my view that you had already issued your jeremiad about this. Maybe having lost the *en banc*, you simply ran out of steam in a sense—that you took your best shot and it was time to move on.

AK: No. Those two issues were gone, so there was nothing else to say on the curtilage issue and the GPS issue. But there was this other thing lurking. I just was not aware of how important it is. I should have taken a closer look at it. I'm not saying I was wrong; I'm just saying I have since read more about it.

Incidentally, just this term I was vindicated on the curtilage issue too—a case involving the dog that was brought onto somebody's porch to sniff for drugs. I think it was Justice Scalia who wrote the opinion. He said that even though the curtilage is open to the public, you expect the mailman to come knock on the door but you don't expect people to bring a drug-sniffing dog.

To me that's the situation in *Pineda-Moreno*, where they said a little boy could bounce a ball under the car and go there to retrieve it, so it's not private even within the curtilage. What I said was, of course, it's possible that a little boy might do that, but you don't expect the police to go in and attach a GPS device. So I see a perfect analogy there and I think I was vindicated on that issue as well.

JC: Since you brought up Justice Scalia, I have to ask: it seems that he isn't typically interested in garnering votes to his position. He writes an opinion—very ably, of course—to articulate his point. Your philosophy seems different. You try to get votes.

AK: I can't tell you his philosophy. I don't know what happens before the opinion comes out. A misleading thing about looking at just the public record is that you don't see all the things that happened where somebody succeeds in persuading people internally. I've got a fairly large stack of dissents and memos, objections and jeremiads, that have never seen the light of day because my colleagues have changed their minds. Or they've said, "Rather than have Kozinski say this or that about me, I'd just as soon change my mind." [laughter.] And that has happened. It happens to all of us, not just me. I've changed my mind in light of other judges' dissents. That's an important part of the process.

So to try to judge Justice Scalia's view based on what we see in the published record, is somewhat like looking at the tip of an iceberg. I have no information on what happens internally; but my guess is he is quite effective internally. But that's merely a guess.

I know that here on the Ninth Circuit we have quite a bit of discussion and often change our minds. It's very common for judges to—a lot of cases aren't close, and there's nothing to change your mind about. But where there are differing views, it is very common for our judges to yield or be persuaded to change positions, or to shift in light of a strong contrary view by a colleague.

I'm also in a different position from Justice Scalia. When he dissents, there's no place else to go. That's the ultimate, and the best he can do is make a plea to a future court to overrule the current majority. By contrast, I've got lots of options. I can hope to persuade the Supreme Court, or other Circuits to go a different way. I can hope to persuade state courts, and very often state courts will look at our dissents, and will choose not to follow the Ninth Circuit majority, but rather the dissent.

This has happened to me over the years, for example, in the *Vanna White* case—a high publicity case involving intellectual property. I think many more courts, including state courts, followed my dissent than have followed the Ninth Circuit majority opinion. So I still have people I can persuade where it will make a difference.

Whereas, I guess, on the Supreme Court, when you dissent . . .

JC: That's the ball game?

AK: Yup. That's the ball game!

Chapter 10

Judge Jed S. Rakoff

But what overcame all this was the truly mind-boggling nature of DNA exonerations. When I was a prosecutor I took it almost as a given that the government virtually never prosecuted the wrong guy. Even as a defense lawyer, I might think that the government was overbearing, but not that my client was innocent. The DNA exonerations, though, established clearly that such confidence in the system that prosecutors like me had was misplaced.
—Judge Jed S. Rakoff, January 29, 2012

Appointed District Court Judge of the Southern District of New York by President William J. Clinton in 1996. Much has been written about Judge Jed S. Rakoff, he is known to be scholarly, thoughtful, blunt, witty, and unconventional.

Judge Rakoff does not shy away from controversy. His many notable rulings have made him a hero and a foe; his opinions might seem apostasy to his former colleagues. He has been called a radical and, at times, an "activist judge." In addition to the Quinones *opinion, in which he held the death penalty unconstitutional (discussed in this interview), he refused to rubber-stamp settlements involving the Securities and Exchange Commission (SEC)—in one he rejected a settlement that would have had Bank of America pay $33 million but ultimately approved the settlement when it was increased to $150 million. In another, he refused to approve a $285 million settlement between Citigroup and the SEC, noting that, to Citicorp, $285 million was nothing more than "pocket change." In other matters, he*

211

directed the Department of Defense to turn over unredacted transcripts con-
cerning Guantanamo detainees; severely criticized the sentencing guidelines,
citing circumstances where they "have so run amok that they are patently
absurd"; and refused to sentence former attorney Marc Dreier to 145 years
for securities fraud, stating that it would demean the 150-year sentence
imposed on Bernie Madoff.

A Philadelphia native, he received a B.A. from Swarthmore College, was
awarded a Masters in Philosophy from Oxford University, and graduated
from Harvard Law School cum laude in 1969. He clerked for Judge Abra-
ham Freedman of the Third Circuit and then became a federal prosecutor
in New York for seven years, ultimately heading the Southern District's
Business and Securities Fraud Prosecutions Unit, the principal such unit in
the United States. Thereafter, he worked as a litigation partner in two pre-
mier Wall Street law firms, handling primarily criminal matters and civil
RICO cases before being appointed to the bench, where he now holds senior
status. He has served on the Governing Board of the MacArthur Founda-
tion's Law and Neuroscience Project and chairs the National Academy of
Science's committee on eyewitness identification. He has coauthored five
books, published more than 100 articles on the law, and has taught numer-
ous courses at Columbia Law School for many years. Because he once
sentenced a Russian pilot to 20 years for drug trafficking, in 2013 Russia
banned him from entering the country.

Judge Rakoff sits in New York City.

Death Is Different

On June 26, 1999, Alan Quinones, a career narcotics trafficker in Bronx, New York, was arrested shortly after a meeting with an undercover narcotics detective to whom another drug dealer, Eddie Santiago, had introduced him. Having been "set up," Quinones decided with his confederates to ambush Santiago and murder him in cold blood.

The murder was brutal. Santiago was handcuffed and hog-tied while a violent death was dealt him, blood running from his mouth. If the savage nature of the murder itself wasn't enough to demonstrate Quinones's barbaric persona, a coconspirator, acting at Quinones's direction, brought a can of gasoline so that Santiago's remains could be burned. When the horrific acts were done, Quinones pushed a shopping cart from the building and loaded its bundled contents into a van. Quinones would boldly and happily brag to others—witnesses who would later testify against him—that they had "burned the guy." Santiago's charred dead body was later found in a vacant lot in the Bronx—remnants of a comforter remained around the body with duct tape covering his nose and mouth.

The extensive drug trafficking and the homicide, the crime for which Quinones and his less-involved lieutenant, Diego Rodriguez, would ultimately face the death penalty, were not the crimes of the century. No one, not even Santiago, deserves to be murdered in cold blood. But life is apparently cheap in the Bronx—rarely is a death penalty carried out. In fact, Santiago's murder would not have been punishable by death in New York *state* court, where the death penalty (presently in abeyance) is limited to only certain kinds of murders. This case, however, was before a federal court, where no such limitations interfered.

Santiago was a "rat" in the patois of the street—a paid drug informant of the police. Such informants are the lifeblood of narcotics enforcement; they "hand up" other drug dealers in exchange for prosecution "amnesty" or leniency. Thus, even though few, if any, will have shed tears for Santiago, federal prosecutors take murders of registered informants almost as seriously as cop killings.

Still, the murder was virtually commonplace—it was nothing new for the constabulary of hardened New Yorkers. Perhaps the U.S. Attorney, a Clinton appointee, was viscerally opposed to the death penalty, except in the most repugnant of cases. Maybe she would have been against death for the convicted offender, even if Mother Teresa was murdered while doling out alms to the poor. (Death penalty abolitionists or opponents typically oppose its use across the board.) Either way, she and her staff recommended against the death penalty for Quinones and Rodriguez.

But she was overruled. Given President George W. Bush's doctrinaire approach to the death penalty, having campaigned hard for its use, Attorney General John Ashcroft directed that the U.S. Attorney's Office seek death. Once the office received its marching orders from above, it carried out its duty unambiguously: it advised the court and the defense that it would ask for the death penalty if the defendants were convicted, making the defendants "death eligible." Thus, the prosecution would diligently and resolutely pursue the case and the death penalty—no matter their personal feelings or that the presiding judge would later provocatively label the death penalty "state sponsored murder."

The case against Quinones and Rodriguez was easily not the strongest case in the courthouse that year. Still, though largely circumstantial, it was clearly sufficient. Even the absence of intact, compelling evidence of Santiago's cadaver (corpus delicti)—accomplished through the gasoline torching of his body—would likely not bother a jury. True, there was no DNA, no recorded confession, no unimpeachable witness of consummate rectitude. That such hallmarks of "slam dunk" prosecutions were lacking would likely mean nothing to a jury—there was more than enough to convict. Jurors typically bring common sense to the table. They usually don't need videotapes of a crime in progress to truly "know" what happened, even though a skilled defense lawyer might suggest or argue otherwise to them.

Under the Federal Death Penalty Act enacted in 1994, a federal district judge's role in imposing death is largely ministerial, no matter what personal feelings he may have. If a jury convicts based on the trial evidence presented, in a second-stage deliberation, the jury is procedurally asked to choose between death and a life sentence. There are typically no other choices.

Curiously, under the law, a single juror can veto a death sentence voted by the remaining 11 jurors (although when selected, a juror must not be morally opposed to the death penalty). However, a federal judge, appointed by the President of the United States with life tenure, who heard all the evidence just as did the jury, cannot overrule the jury's verdict based on his own view of the case. So, if the jury has voted unanimously for death—that is, if the jury turns its collective thumbs down as might Caesar against a defeated gladiator in the Coliseum—the judge is procedurally reduced to formally "announcing" death for the now-convicted accused. While perhaps wiping away the inward (or even exposed) tears for the awful duty imposed on him by law, he must stoically look the defendant in the eye: "I sentence you to death."

Not in *Quinones*. Long before the jury was empaneled, indeed, as soon as the trial judge learned that the government would ask for the death penalty—some 24 months before any trial would take place—Judge Rakoff asked the parties to address whether the federal death penalty statute was unconstitutional, though it had never been held to be by any federal court in the nation. In so doing, he did not seem concerned about the nature of the charge before him. Nor did he raise as constitutionally questionable the likely cross-racial makeup of the jury pool, or whether the mechanism to impose death—an intravenous needle—was barbaric ("cruel and unusual," in the lexicon of the Constitution). Nor, importantly, did the judge show a specific concern, based on anything he knew at the time, that one day it would be "too late" for evidence to come to light *in this case*, that would cast doubt on the verdicts ("death is different").

No, stripping aside the legal technicalities and niceties of his novel and articulate decision, on July 1, 2002, Judge Rakoff decided that the statute was unconstitutional precisely because too often in recent years, largely based on scientific breakthroughs such as DNA, guilty verdicts in death cases had been set aside (sometimes just prior to execution) due to "actual innocence." He basically said—though two justices of the Supreme Court had maintained in another case that a claim of innocence alone might be legally inadequate to warrant a reprieve from a death penalty verdict—trial convictions *generally* were no longer sufficiently reliable. Judge Rakoff, therefore, without hearing one word proving guilt or innocence or demonstrating reasonable doubt in the *Quinones/Rodriguez* trial, declared the death penalty unconstitutional simply because the prosecution said it would seek it if the defendants were convicted. He did not have at that time, and maybe he never did, any reason to believe that the evidence would not be sufficient.

The U.S. Attorney promptly appealed the judge's decision, and a three-judge panel of the U.S. Circuit Court of Appeals unanimously reversed it and reinstated the case as death eligible, disagreeing fundamentally with Judge Rakoff's *sua sponte* analysis of the law, which argued that the Federal Death Penalty Act "cut off the opportunity for exoneration" and created an "undue risk of executing innocent people." Quinones and Rodriguez were once again death eligible.

But this wasn't the first time a federal defendant in New York was death eligible under the 1994 law. On another floor in the same austere U.S. courthouse in Foley Square, another judge, also appointed for life, was presiding, at the time of Santiago's murder in 1998, over the indictment of death-eligible defendants—there, entitled *U.S. v. Osama bin Laden*. That judge, a thoughtful man indeed, irrespective of his inward thoughts on the death penalty or whether the government was wise in that case to seek it, did *not* declare the death penalty unconstitutional.

Bin Laden was the lead defendant, but, of course, he had not been apprehended (he later received a death penalty of another sort on May 1, 2011, in Pakistan, which, incidentally, no one seemed to challenge). And this indictment and the trial upon it predated 9/11 and the arrests of Quinones and Rodriguez. Bin Laden along with the others had been charged with the August 1998 bombings of the U.S. embassies in Kenya and Tanzania—murderous acts of terror against the United States on foreign soil. Whereas the government sought death for the accused terrorists who had been captured and would later be convicted, in the second stage of the trial the prosecutors could not persuade the jury to sentence them to death. Would the jury—reportedly concerned that a death verdict would have made the defendants "martyrs"—have decided differently if the verdict had been reached *after* the 9/11 attacks? It is impossible to know.

More pertinent, would Judge Rakoff have declared the death penalty unconstitutional if bin Laden, or even bin Laden's lesser-known terrorist codefendants, had stood trial before him—particularly if bin Laden had been arrested for the 9/11 World Trade Center attack, recognizing that the U.S. courthouse where Judge Rakoff sits was, but no longer is, in the shadow of the Twin Towers? After all, Judge Rakoff's decision to set aside the death penalty for Quinones and Rodriguez, before his decision to do so was reversed on appeal, had nothing whatsoever to do with the nature of the crime charged or the ignominy of the defendants.

Was there anything in the judge's life or training that informed his decision to take the highly unusual step he did? And whereas he was reversed by an appellate court, which put the death penalty back in play for Quinones and Rodriguez, would that be the end of it for Judge Rakoff? Or would he somehow use the extraordinary power of the trial judge to make rulings that might, as Justice Harry Blackmun would describe it in another context, "tinker with the machinery of death" as it related to Quinones and Rodriguez?

Stated differently, does an appellate reversal mean that a judge must—or this judge must—move on? Or, if death as a penalty is wrong in a judge's mind, must one/should one/will one go to the wall to deny death its victory? In other words, suppose that, after the death penalty eligibility had been restored for Quinones and Rodriguez, they had actually pleaded guilty or the parties agreed to a nonjury trial and Judge Rakoff, not a jury, alone had to decide whether a death sentence should be imposed. How would the judge's personal view of the death penalty have impacted his decision?

The Dialogue

JC: In the *Quinones* case, when you got on to the bench, you knew nothing about the case, except perhaps from reading the indictment. Yet, out loud you questioned the constitutionality of the death penalty before the defense even had an opportunity to speak.

JSR: True. And I was very concerned about doing that. This was the only case in 16 years on the bench where I raised an issue not raised by the parties, except for those situations where a judge is by law supposed to exercise a third-party view of the case. But, normally, it's central to the adversary system that a judge shouldn't inject his own views. He should simply try to decide which party's arguments are better under the law and facts. There are a lot of good reasons for that—providential reasons, fairness, and the like. Still, as the Supreme Court has frequently said "Death is different." And, reflecting on this, I believed I had a view that was relevant and important and should be discussed, considered by the parties. Not meaning to be melodramatic, this case was about a person's life.

JC: You weren't concerned, were you, that the *Quinones* defense, particularly in a death penalty case, wouldn't raise every possible argument, and that's why you needed to offer your own views before it did?

JSR: It's somewhat strong to say it was "my own" view. At this point, mine was an idea that I wasn't sure I would finally accept or reject, and I ultimately went to great lengths to ensure that everyone was heard fully on it. But, death penalty jurisprudence had been in something of a rut. The Supreme Court held the manner in which "death" was administered was unconstitutional back in the '70's, but in ways that were quickly remedied by statute. That jurisprudence was largely about the Eighth Amendment's "cruel and unusual punishment" clause and the Fourteenth Amendment's "equal protection" clause.

JC: But, since you chose to raise it, obviously you were concerned about potentially innocent defendants having been convicted who couldn't prove their innocence because they were already executed. The exonerating evidence came too late. Did something in your past as a prosecutor, defense lawyer, or even as a judge, raise large concerns for you that some convicted defendant was truly innocent, or at least there were real questions about it?

JSR: Well, several aspects of experience bore on my approach—although they cut in opposite directions. To begin with, I had never been an ideological opponent of the death penalty. Nor, strangely, in favor of it either. No strong anti-death penalty views going on the bench, or even after I got there. I had read many studies about deterrence. And while it was commonplace for death penalty opponents to argue that there was a scarcity of evidence that it actually provides added deterrence, contrary studies, especially those by James Q. Wilson, a very respected, conservative social scientist, cut the other way.

The argument for the death penalty, if you put aside ideological, emotional or even religious views, is that, if imposed, society will save lives. Meaning, would-be killers will just think twice, knowing death may ensue for them if they are caught. And a degree of folk wisdom supports that. You see dramas and movies all the time where, when someone is about to pull the trigger, he thinks twice in a way that he otherwise wouldn't—although whether the death penalty or a Hollywood director causes the second thought is altogether another question.

Another aspect of my experience that kind of cut in favor of the death penalty but that is hard to talk about it, is that in 1985 my older brother was brutally murdered in the Philippines, bludgeoned to death by an intruder, who then set his apartment on fire to cover his tracks. The murderer confessed but the system of justice in his case didn't fare well. The killer got off far too lightly—three years—with at least a hint of corruption in the way the case was handled by the Philippine authorities. And, when he was murdered and the case came to trial, if the Philippines had the death penalty I would have been all in favor of it.

In hindsight, thinking about that during *Quinones*, I needed to recognize that my feelings about my brother's case were borne of similar emotion to those who support the death penalty. In particular, juries confronted with vicious crimes feel those emotions that obviously consumed me because it was my own brother. There's sort of an instinctive desire to see an awful crime go punished—harshly.

But what overcame all this was the truly mind-boggling nature of DNA exonerations. When I was a prosecutor I took it almost as a given that the government virtually never prosecuted the wrong guy. Even as a defense lawyer, I might think that the Government was overbearing, but not that my client was innocent. The DNA exonerations, though, established clearly that such confidence in the system that prosecutors like me had was misplaced.

This wasn't just my mistake: most judges thought likewise. Let me read what the famous Judge Learned Hand, in rejecting an appeal, once said: "Our procedure has always been haunted by the ghost of the innocent man convicted. It is an unreal dream. What we need to fear is the archaic formalism and the watery sentiment that obstructs, delays and defeats the prosecution of crime." For Hand, an innocent who is convicted almost never happens.

And that's what *I* thought, too. Probably for the same reasons, because I had seen our system work so well. I had seen federal prosecutors so scrupulous, maybe to some, overly scrupulous. I saw the high burden of proof, and so many things that would prevent an innocent man's conviction. I also saw acquittals where the defendant was clearly guilty: further evidence for me that the system protected the innocent, as it even protected the guilty. I saw, too, close cases where convictions were often reversed on appeal. All these things persuaded me that the system worked extremely well.

Suddenly, through DNA, we learned that there were not just one or two, but dozens, of cases where the jury had found guilt beyond a reasonable doubt, and where the appeals court said the proof was not only beyond a reasonable doubt. Beyond all doubt! Then, even after numerous *habeases* had been exhausted, suddenly the guy is shown by science to be actually innocent. And this almost always in death-penalty cases. The very viciousness of the crime blinded the prosecutor, the judge and the jury to the facts. They had the wrong guy. To me, this was mind-blowing.

JC: Interesting, but when you tossed out the death penalty across the board, you didn't know *anything* about the evidence against Quinones. No reason whatsoever to question his guilt. Aren't I right?

JSR: True, but that's not the way the law works. The question is not what should be the rule in a given case. General legal principles must govern across the board. There will be cases where the proof will be unbelievably strong. Others, more questionable. And many, whether they fall into Category 1 or Category 2, will depend on your own perceptions as to the evidence at the time. So you can't decide about the death penalty's applicability based on the facts of a given case if your point is that in an unknown, but substantial, number of cases it will appear that there is proof beyond a reasonable doubt, but nevertheless the appearance is erroneous.

JC: *Quinones* was the first case to hold the death penalty unconstitutional after it was reenacted in 1994. Did you have any case law on which to base your thinking that the number of cases establishing "actual innocence" long after a conviction would justify the almost strident constitutional attack you made?

JSR: Strident? That term is somewhat extravagant. But I don't think I would have raised the issue without reading *U.S. v. Herrera* when this idea first occurred to me.

I looked into the law to see what the courts—the Supreme Court, in particular—had done before DNA exonerations, where actual innocence claims were raised. The dispositive case, not so long before, was *Herrera*. In *Herrera*, the question was framed directly: you could seek post-trial relief long after you had exhausted all your appeals and your *habeas* claims that had been rejected—but only where you now had new evidence to show your actual innocence. Not some wishy-washy procedural or tactical attack, but real proof that you were innocent. That was *Herrera*. The way I read it is what got me going on the "due process" approach. Five justices, led by Justice O'Connor in a pivotal concurring opinion, held that it's "never too late" to raise actual innocence. They found it unconstitutional—it violated due process—to execute the innocent.

I still believe that that is the proper meaning of *Herrera*, as I said in my opinion. The Second Circuit didn't agree. That was basically why it reversed me. But when I first read *Herrera*, long before I had said anything in court, it gave me a legal framework to address this DNA situation that so troubled me.

JC: Did you read Justice O'Connor's opinion in *Herrera* when it was first published, or only when *Quinones* landed on your docket?

JSR: Once *Quinones* was assigned to me, and even not quite then. I mean the chronology was, first, the motions came in from the defense, consisting of familiar stuff. They didn't really address the DNA business at all. In fact, nothing aside from the Eighth Amendment. I'm thinking, "Gee, because of DNA exonerations, here's a huge development in how we should look at it. And, in my view, not just the death penalty, but how we should look at how we determine guilt or innocence. Because once you get into the reasons why the jurors make those mistakes, you see other implications." And I'm not seeing any of this in the papers submitted to me. It seems to me maybe, if it's unconstitutional, if innocent people are being executed, we've got a real problem here. So that's when I started looking at the books and that's when I closely looked at *Herrera*.

JC: You declared the death penalty unconstitutional, the government appealed, the Court of Appeals decided you were wrong, and then the case returned to your docket as "death eligible." The jury convicted and was then asked in the second penalty phase to decide for or against death.

But couldn't you have assumed from the outset that the odds of a New York City—more liberal than most—jury voting for death was no greater than 50–50? Couldn't you have simply waited until the jury convicted (if it did), and if it then voted for death, *and only then*, decide to hold it unconstitutional? Why decide a difficult and extremely troubling issue that may not have been necessary?

JSR: I could have. My opinion gave several reasons why I thought I shouldn't wait. Judge Leonard Sand of this Court had reached that issue in an earlier case. He had decided that certain procedural aspects of a case would be affected by whether a defendant was death eligible at trial—such as in selecting a jury. As a defense lawyer, if you know in advance there's no death penalty, you will select the jury differently. Also, a death eligible defendant will have more juror challenges. Thus, a number of procedural differences in a death case would make it appropriate to address this matter first, although one is not compelled to.

JC: So, being the devil's advocate—my friends and detractors (often the same people) would say "the devil is well represented"—one could say that your decision to hold the death penalty unconstitutional pre-trial might be seen as "*Activist*" in helping the defense to better prepare for trial.

JSR: I'm not sure. Well, first of all, you've used the "A" word—Activist. Oh no! Not another Activist Judge!

JC: Well, to some you're leader in the field, aren't you?

JSR: It's such a meaningless term. I see argument, articles, from the left saying that the *Roberts Court* is the most activist court ever. And, of course, when I was young, the *Warren Court* was attacked as activist. I'm not quite sure the term has any meaning left. But if your question is "Was my raising this issue sooner rather than later intended to favor one side in indirect ways," the answer is absolutely "No." Obviously, the decision favors the defense on its face—although, frankly, I think it benefited both sides to resolve it sooner. Suppose the jury had voted death and I had only raised it then. There would have been no time, or it would have been much more difficult to find the time. I had extended arguments and briefings of this issue. It was easier early, when I decided it—because the way death penalty cases work, there's always much time pre-indictment. The defense goes to the Justice Department in Washington to argue for mitigation; and, if they fail, they come back to court and make all sorts of motions. It's a much slower process than normally. Now, it is also true that after a death penalty is imposed and after the direct appeal, things will slow down for many years through *habeas* proceedings. But that's not what I'm referring to here.

JC: You mention Judge Sand—a very distinguished judge with probably twice as many years on the bench as you. This is an inside baseball question: Would you talk to other judges, particularly ones you greatly respect, to seek out their views on an issue they have already faced, perhaps in a very informal chat? Or indeed, might you talk to a judge from the other end of the spectrum who you respect?

JSR: Normally I don't. Other judges don't know the facts of an individual case. I've learned from much experience at judges' lunches, some judges will say, "Oh, I've got this difficult issue. What do you guys think?" Nothing wrong with that. But I'm always uncomfortable giving my views because, without being there and knowing the real facts, you're often missing vital facts, and you may give views not really as narrowly addressed to the case as they might need to be. That's just my personal feeling.

JC: But in dealing with a *legal* issue . . .

JSR: Sure, yeah. In this case. And it's the only case. I went to one judge when I drafted my first opinion and said "What do you think?" That person was in fact Leonard Sand. And the reason was the same reason why I gave the prosecutors several bites of the apple here. I knew that this was, at least in its initiation, my idea, and there's a natural tendency of any human being to think, "You know the idea I just raised is a great one!" And I was concerned that since this was the only case in which I had in any major way raised my own idea—other than later cases like *Bank of America*, which are procedurally different—that I might be more in love with my theory than was warranted. And, so, Judge Sand is one of the judges of this Court whom I most respect, and he was also one with death penalty case experience. So, I thought he knew the jurisprudence, and that he was someone who would give me a candid view. We also knew each other well enough that he wouldn't hesitate to tell me if he thought I got it wrong. As it happened, he agreed with me, and that gave me more confidence in my view.

JC: It was common knowledge at the time that the Bush Justice Department was fervently in favor of the death penalty.

JSR: Yes.

JC: In fact, the United States Attorney decided against death for Quinones, but was overruled by her superiors at Main Justice who instructed her to seek execution if a conviction eventuated.

JSR: Right.

JC: In some cases, other district judges actually wrote to Main Justice in their death penalty cases, or asked the United States Attorney to convey to Main Justice their view that the death penalty should not be pursued in a given case. Something you might have considered in this or another case?

JSR: I can't speak to every case. First, as a general matter, I don't think judges should inject themselves into the Executive Branch's decisions. Separation of powers and all that. I don't hold that to be the Holy Grail; but, as a general matter, not something I'm comfortable with. But much more important, I didn't know the facts well enough to offer such a view. This was a vicious murder by two men. The lead defendant, Quinones, basically claimed in his defense: "I wasn't there during much of what went on." So, I had no basis pre-trial to evaluate that. One important thing I've learned on the bench is that you don't really know the facts until trial.

JC: You could have written such a letter between the conviction date, and when the death penalty phase began.

JSR: Yes, but that's a very short window. They follow each other almost immediately.

JC: Things can move fast at Main Justice.

JSR: Not really. But, in any event, it never occurred to me. I didn't see that as my role. This is a question I haven't thought about, like most of your questions. Moreover, I really doubt such a letter would have accomplished anything. The main effect of such a letter in that circumstance, after Washington had repeatedly turned down requests to reject the death penalty not only from the defense but also from the U.S. Attorney, would be to make me feel good, salve my conscience. But no practical effect.

JC: Suppose Quinones and his lawyers decided that the case was so overwhelming that he should plead guilty, thereby to make a better argument for leniency at sentence because of the remorse generally inherent in a guilty plea. Thus, to better try to defeat the death penalty. If he had pleaded guilty, the "death" decision would then have been yours alone.

JSR: Is that right? Where were you when we needed you?

JC: Thank you. But assume that hypothetical and assume, too, that you had already been reversed, reinstating the death penalty potential. What would the reversal of your decision have done, given your personal view that imposing death was bad policy on constitutional grounds, or even just bad policy? In other words, if the death decision was yours alone, would you have "pulled the trigger" if the facts warranted it?

JSR: You're really asking a variation on a problem that judges face constantly. At times we are called upon—even required by law—to impose sentences that we feel are unjust for many reasons. For example, mandatory minimum sentences. And some judges have literally resigned from the bench rather than do that. I guess I don't feel quite that way, although there's nothing worse, and no judge doesn't feel terrible if he or she must impose a mandatory sentence which they feel is unjust under the facts of a particular case.

But that would not have quite been the situation here. I would have had the option to go either way given the considerations that may be taken into account in a death penalty case, at the penalty stage. There are virtually no limitations on what one can look to in making the decision. Thinking aloud, I probably could have looked at the DNA history. It's one of the things I could have considered. Even though under your hypothetical he pleaded guilty, I imagine I could have harbored a concern over whether he had pleaded guilty just to avoid the death penalty. It certainly can happen. Although that would not have been my main focus, I am quite confident of that. I would have looked at all sorts of things about his upbringing, about the culture in which he was raised and things like that—things that actually led the actual jury to vote against the death penalty.

As you know, if even a single juror votes against the death penalty, that single vote vetoes death as a sentence; but in *Quinones*, the jury was actually unanimous against death. So, certain facts led twelve reasonable people to vote against death. It's likely that those same facts would have persuaded me to decide against death. Also, interestingly, in a death penalty case a judge must very carefully scrutinize jury selection so that no one says, "I'll never impose the death penalty" or "I am ideologically opposed to the death penalty." This was a jury of twelve people who said they would vote for death in the appropriate case, but unanimously concluded that this was not that case. So, it's quite plausible to assume that I would have reached the same conclusion for the very same reason.

JC: The *Quinones* victim wasn't a pillar of society. He had been a drug dealer himself. But, let's assume, the death penalty case wheeled out to you had a different murder victim. Assume, the indicted defendant was Osama bin Laden, hypothetically captured in Pakistan and extradited to New York for trial. Let's assume your death penalty defendant wasn't Quinones, but bin Laden himself for having blown up the World Trade Center. More than 3,000 victims. That's your case. What would you do? Same thing?

JSR: Makes no difference from the standpoint of my ruling.

JC: Aren't you a little cavalier with your answer, Judge . . .

JSR: It wouldn't be the first time.

JC: You're saying that you could hold the death penalty unconstitutional with the survivors of 3,000 people murdered on 9/11 in your courtroom by video, phone or some hookup, basically saying, "Judge, are you crazy? How can any thoughtful or decent human being, how can a judge who deserves to be on the bench, do what you're planning to do?"

JSR: Even when I made the decision in *Quinones*, I knew, as I told my wife at the time, this ended any chance for me to reach the Second Circuit Court of Appeals. I'd be a political pariah to certain members of Congress. And there was testimony, moving testimony from the victim's mother during the penalty phase that really tore at my heart. I mean it reminded me very vividly of how I felt when my own brother was murdered—how devastating this case was to her. And while, as you say, Quinones's victim was not a pillar of society, he was a man who was trying to do the right thing by reversing his past and cooperating with the government as an undercover operative when he was murdered. That's actually why he was murdered.

But, sure, if it had been Osama bin Laden, would I have had the courage to follow my principles? I hope so, but I would have been vilified everywhere. But that's what one must understand about the law. I mean the basic principles of the law have to be the same for all cases. Rich or poor, good or bad, every person deserves to be treated equally by the law. If you don't believe in that you don't believe in the rule of law.

JC: That would have literally been *the* single most unpopular judicial decision in American history, if you held the death penalty for Osama bin Laden unconstitutional—especially in New York City.

JSR: So, I should consider myself fortunate that was not my case. But, to repeat, who knows how far my courage would have taken me, and whether it would have faltered. And there are so many easy way outs. I could have said, "Well, it's just my idea; I'm not going raise it. We have the adversary system." Or I could have said, "Well, let's wait to see if the jury imposes death, although in that case the likelihood would have been high indeed." But I don't see how you can be a judge if you're not devoted to the notion that the law must be the same for everyone.

When I was a criminal defense lawyer, I was very unpopular with some good friends for a period of time because I represented a particularly bad guy. Nothing of the order of bin Laden; but, you know, one case where I represented a man who murdered his wife who was a very dear friend of my very close friend's wife. For a year she wouldn't even speak to me, even though we had been best friends ("How could you represent that guy?"). And so you just would multiply that up the scale for a judge. But the point is—our system would just be hypocrisy if we had one law for defendants generally, and another law for really bad defendants. So I don't see how a judge—if you deal, as I was, with an issue that cuts across all death penalty cases—can do it any differently regardless of who the defendant was. Having said that, I'd like to believe I would have been true to my principles. But you never know.

JC: At least two, maybe three judges in this Courthouse have needed bodyguards for the rest of their lives for having presided over terrorist cases. You, however, would have needed it in the hypothetical bin Laden case, for having *rejected* death for him.

JSR: I actually received a few death threat letters after I decided *Quinones*. The Marshals thought they weren't serious. One obviously drunk guy called me one night. Generally I answer my own phone in chambers in the evening. He said, "I read your decision in the X case [not *Quinones*], and I'm gonna kill you." It became ever clearer that this guy was just a complete drunk, and that the case that troubled him wasn't mine—rather, another judge's. I was so tempted, although I didn't, to say, "May I transfer your call?"

JC: Since I used the "Activist" word before, I did notice in your *Quinones* opinion, you said that if the death penalty were imposed against him, it would be a form of "state-sponsored murder." That's a fairly provocative word. You certainly didn't believe that the government was seeking the death penalty as an act of "murder," however unhappy you were with the potential punishment he might suffer. Why would you use the expression: "state-sponsored murder"?

JSR: I don't think I said that about Quinones himself. I referred to broader problems presented by current awareness about the death penalty. By the time of the *Quinones* case, we knew that significant numbers of actually innocent people were sentenced to death, our legal system was flawed in a much larger dimension than most of us had contemplated. I was deeply troubled that the government, knowing that, knowing that they're going to therefore execute a certain number of innocent people if they persist in pursuing death as punishment, are engaging, harsh as it sounds, in "state-sponsored murder."

JC: I'm beginning to sound like an apologist for the death penalty (although I'm not). But do you actually believe there has been a serious issue in the United States over the last 30 years, where prosecutors bring cases with a death potential where they have significant reservations about guilt?

JSR: No, but that's the whole point of the DNA stuff.

The system is less accurate than prosecutors and lawyers generally have believed, and they need to adjust their beliefs and presumptions accordingly. So, what are the problems? And we ought to discuss them, because it colors the answer to the point you're making. The single, biggest cause of wrong death decisions is erroneous eye witness identification: A witness gets up in the court, often someone who didn't know the defendant, just saw him for maybe seconds at the time of the event, and says, "That's the guy," and points him out in the courtroom. Many studies suggest that such evidence is fraught with so-called "false positives"—with errors, substantial possibilities for errors. In fact, the New Jersey Supreme Court recently instituted certain limitations on eye-witness identifications precisely because of that. But it's powerful evidence.

Now, do prosecutors sometimes portray that evidence as even more powerful than it really is? I have to say, occasionally they do. I think more often, though, it's the witness himself or herself, at the time of the event or the initial lineup or the initial photo array. They may think in their minds, "I'm pretty sure it's him." By the time they reach the stand, they have convinced themselves, "Yes, it's definitely that person." So they express no doubt whatsoever. So there you have a person with no motive to lie, saying flat out, "He's the one who pulled the trigger." That's powerful, persuasive evidence.

The jury, which in my view already has a tendency to want to find someone guilty because of the horrific nature of the crime at issue, feels very accepting of that evidence. So I don't suggest the prosecutor is pulling the wool over the jury's eyes. I'm suggesting that there are ways that none of us suspected 20, 30, 50 years ago, that evidence is much more frail than we all believed.

JC: Last question. You raised your brother's murder in the Philippines. It's hard for me to ask you about it. But he suffered a brutal murder, tortured and bludgeoned with a metallic object. When you sentenced one of Quinones' confederates, and the victim's mother addressed you in court at that defendant's sentence, you told the story about your brother. Why? What was your purpose in raising that very personal . . .

JSR: I had no purpose. It was surely an emotional reaction. I had never mentioned my brother's murder to anyone outside the family before then. I've become more able to talk about it in later years. The victim's mother was in such obvious distress in ways that just rushed out. It's the closest I've ever come to crying on the bench. It sounds so trite or cliché, but I actually could feel her pain. And so I wanted her to know that she wasn't alone; that this can happen to any of us. That's why it came pouring out of me as a way of trying, in some very small way, to help her feel more accepting of that terrible event.

JC: I see you actually choking up now as you relate the incident. Let me ask: if your brother's horrible murder had happened now, after *Quinones*, and the prosecutors allowed you, as his surviving brother or perhaps his next of kin, to decide for or against the death penalty, would you be able to show the consistency—perhaps, I should say, the integrity—to veto death for your own brother's murderer?

JSR: Oooh. Tough question. I don't know. [Long pause.] Everyone is a blend of passion and reason. When someone you love is taken from you, your passion, your remorse, can overcome everything. But one of a judge's roles to emphasize reason and defuse passion. When I go on the bench I know it is my duty to act like a judge. Off the bench, I'm just another guy.

Chapter 11

Judge Emmet G. Sullivan

No one has to prove his innocence. The standard is whether or not the government has proven guilt beyond a reasonable doubt. That's the standard that I'm obligated to follow.
—Judge Emmet G. Sullivan, November 5, 2013

Judge Emmet G. Sullivan is the only person to have been appointed to three District of Columbia judicial positions by three presidents. He served as a Superior Court judge at the behest of President Ronald Reagan and was elevated to the position of Associate Justice of the D.C. Court of Appeals by President George H. W. Bush, where he served until he was appointed to the federal District Court for the District of Columbia in 1994 by President William J. Clinton.

Judge Sullivan is known to be smart, courteous, tenacious, and formidable, and he does not hesitate to hold lawyers accountable. The Ted Stevens case (discussed here) is not the only time Judge Sullivan has challenged, and criticized, the parties and their counsel. In one matter, he reluctantly approved a settlement, but not before he directed the Department of Justice to demonstrate why causing Barclay's bank to pay only $298 million was a "penalty," when the bank obfuscated transactions for more than a decade, allowing customers in Iran, Cuba, and other sanctioned nations to move some $500 million into the United States.

In another case, Judge Sullivan imposed a sentence four years longer than that requested by the prosecution, calling a former Army Corps of Engineers' employee's actions in a $30 million bribery and kickback scheme *"shocking, vicious and cruel." He dismissed a case against Iran that was brought by the Americans who were held hostage there from 1979 through 1981, upholding—at the request of the intervening State Department—the accord entered into that freed the hostages and protected Iran from prosecution (thus rejecting Congress's post-1981 attempt at passing laws that would have permitted the suit to proceed). Judge Sullivan also tackled the issue of global warming in a comprehensive 116-page decision and—ruling against the competing interests of environmentalists and businesses—upheld the classification issued by the U.S. Fish and Wildlife Service that the polar bear was "threatened," but not "endangered," deferring to the agency's jurisdiction to make such a determination.*

Judge Sullivan is the consummate "Washingtonian," having been born, raised, and educated in the District of Columbia. He received his B.A. from Howard University and his J.D. from Howard University School of Law. As recipient of a Reginald Heber Smith Community Law Fellowship (Smith was the author of the 1919 treatise "Justice and the Poor," which argued for free legal assistance for those in need), he worked in Neighborhood Legal Services in Washington, D.C. He then served as a law clerk to Superior Court Judge James A. Washington Jr. in 1972. Judge Sullivan entered private practice until being appointed by President Reagan to the Superior Court of the District of Columbia in 1984, when he began his judicial career. He taught as an adjunct at Howard University School of Law, served as a visiting faculty member of Harvard Law School's Trial Advocacy Workshop, and is currently an adjunct professor at American University Washington College of Law. Judge Sullivan has served on countless committees and commissions and is the recipient of numerous awards, most notably the Thurgood Marshall Award of Excellence (awarded by the Howard University School of Law Alumni Association); he was inducted into the Washington Bar Association's "Hall of Fame" in 2012.

Judge Sullivan currently sits in Washington, D.C.

Guilt, Innocence, and Prosecutorial Misconduct

When a defendant has been indicted by a federal grand jury, counsel typically believes his client has one foot in prison with the other lagging shortly behind. When the defendant is a public official, even having served ably—regardless of whether you agree with his political ideology—for more than four decades, counsel will likely see his client's chances as even worse. Still, through all of this, what does the *judge* think of the defendant's guilt or innocence? Or is guilt or innocence beside the point—is the real issue what the parties can demonstrate within the parameters of what the law allows, and indeed requires?

Ted Stevens was the longest serving Republican U.S. Senator in history—he served from December 1968 until January 3, 2009, and had actually been engaged in local politics before Alaska was a state. He lost his seat, which had accorded him the chairmanship of the powerful Appropriations Committee, following his conviction by a jury on October 27, 2008, a mere eight days before his final Election Day. Parenthetically, it may be that the loss of that election, and thus his position, gave the Democrats a super majority in the Senate, allowing it to later pass the Affordable Care Act. Yes, the conviction of Senator Stevens had great impact, indeed.

The "corruption" indictment of Stevens had been filed in Washington, D.C., likely brought there to avoid the venue of Alaska, where Stevens was a very popular figure. Although running 28 pages and containing seven counts, its substance was uncomplicated: Stevens had failed to list on Senate disclosure forms approximately $250,000 in goods and services he had received—mostly in remodeling his elaborate chalet home in Girdwood, Alaska—from an oil services company, VECO Corporation. Bill Allen, Stevens's friend and CEO of VECO, clearly aware of Stevens's enormously powerful position in the Senate and capacity to influence legislation and appropriations, spearheaded the remodeling effort and would accordingly be the government's principal trial witness.

Because of the upcoming election and the potential influence of a pending criminal case, Stevens's robust—take no prisoners—defense team, led by legendary Washington lawyer Brendan Sullivan (no relation to the judge), demanded a speedy trial designed so that Senator Stevens could be acquitted before Election Day. Judge Emmet Sullivan promptly granted it. The prosecution team, composed principally of seasoned prosecutors from both the U.S. Attorney's Office in Alaska and the Public Integrity Section of Main Justice in Washington, D.C., would prosecute. The guts of the case, indeed, to be carried largely on the shoulders of Allen's testimony, was that Stevens simply never paid that $250,000—ergo, the disclosure violation of not reporting the "gifts." At trial, though, the case morphed into something else: Stevens had asked to be billed. Was this because he wanted to actually pay the sum? Or did he ask to be billed, just "covering his ass" in so doing?

Because the case was fast-tracked, deadlines for motion practice and discovery were fast and furious, and soon Judge Sullivan himself became obviously incensed with the prosecution for what he perceived as a lack of professionalism—if not worse. He, at times, excluded evidence because of late disclosures. At one point, Judge Sullivan actually considered declaring a mistrial, but he ultimately decided against it.

Allen's testimony—and the prosecution's treatment of contrary statements—seemed to push Judge Sullivan to the brink. Prosecutors told defense counsel before the trial that Allen told them that he believed Stevens would not pay the invoice. But in prior interviews, memorialized in FBI memos, Allen said he believed that Stevens would pay. The court had ordered the delivery of all *Brady* materials (i.e., the disclosure of exculpatory or impeaching information).[1] Notwithstanding the court's order, these reports—one of which had actually been redacted from previously delivered materials—were not delivered until approximately 11 p.m. the very night before Allen was to be cross-examined. Thus, although not the most uncommon occurrence in criminal practice, the prosecutors first produced to the defense those exculpatory memoranda—evidence directly in conflict with what Allen told the jury when questioned on direct examination—shortly before cross-examination was to begin. A clearly agitated Judge Sullivan saw this late disclosure as "probably intentional"—even though, while deprived of an opportunity to "open" on the conflicting statements, Stevens's attorney would still have the opportunity to cross-examine Allen with this extremely helpful, documented conflict in his story.

---

1. Brady v. Maryland, 373 U.S. 83 (1963).

But not only that, here was a letter from Stevens to Allen in which Stevens asked for a bill, thanking him for the work on the chalet: "You owe me a bill—remember Torricelli, my friend. Friendship is one thing—compliance with the ethics rules entirely different." Clearly an extraordinarily helpful letter for the defense, "Torricelli" being a reference to a U.S. senator from New Jersey who was accused of receiving gifts from a campaign donor. Allen's direct testimony, however, was that Stevens's letter was simply an effort to "cover his ass"—the "proof" being that Stevens's friend told Allen to ignore it, as it was merely a slick effort by Stevens to protect himself.

But when did the prosecutors first learn that they could rely on Allen's comeback to the exculpatory letter from Stevens? Specifically, when did they first know that Allen's state of mind was that Stevens didn't really mean what he said in the letter—that he didn't really want a bill but was just intending to create a record that he had asked for one? More distressing, did Allen make up that story late in the game and only then tell it to the prosecutors? Was Allen influenced by his (improper) relationship with a female FBI agent? No matter; despite Judge Sullivan's continuing infuriation with the prosecution team, the case went to the jury, and Stevens was convicted on October 27, 2008, a few days before the election.

Defense counsel Brendan Sullivan almost immediately demanded that the Department of Justice conduct a full investigation concerning the failure to produce *Brady* materials. Soon thereafter an FBI agent, Chad Joy, wrote Judge Sullivan saying that the prosecutors had deliberately withheld evidence from the defense and actually hid a government witness from the defense—sending him back to Alaska without telling the defense or the court. The handling of this Joy letter by the prosecution—was it a "whistleblower" letter that would have afforded Joy certain protections?—actually led Judge Sullivan to hold two government attorneys in contempt. Further, the judge took the extraordinary step of directing Attorney General Michael Mukasey, himself on the verge of leaving office as a new president had been elected, to submit a declaration explaining the "pattern of belated revelations" by the government and its unsatisfactory explanations for same.

In the end, although the then-new Obama administration Attorney General Eric Holder directed an investigation by the Department's Office of Professional Responsibility, that was not enough for Judge Sullivan. He appointed a special prosecutor—one with no ties to the Department of Justice—to conduct his own investigation.

And what was going through Judge Sullivan's mind when the prosecution team continued to ignore his order to turn over documents? When three Department of Justice lawyers conceded—as there was no credible alternative—that there was no reason they had not complied with the court's discovery order, Judge Sullivan declared their conduct "outrageous" and held them in contempt as they sat at counsel table.

Whether one ultimately concludes that the conduct of Stevens's prosecutors regarding their discovery obligations, including under the U.S. Supreme Court's decision in *Brady v. Maryland*, was intentional, reckless, negligent, or even innocent, the conduct is not necessarily isolated. Prosecutors, defense lawyers, and judges alike recognize that there is at least a certain amount of gamesmanship on the part of prosecutors in complying with these obligations. But judges typically don't exact extreme measures or penalties for such violations; instead, they take corrective measures intended to put defense counsel and their clients on a level playing field—recesses, exclusions of evidence, curative jury instructions.

Although, occasionally, prosecutors are indeed remonstrated in court opinions for *Brady* violations, almost never are they held in contempt, disciplined, referred for discipline, or placed under the microscope of a special prosecutor appointed by the aggrieved judge. And rarely (has it ever been the case?) is the Attorney General of the United States directed by a judge to submit a declaration in a case about something he can't possibly know about firsthand, even if Judge Sullivan later relented when General Mukasey was going out of office a few days later at the end of the Bush administration.

For Stevens, these legal matters ended on April 1, 2009, when, prior to sentencing, Attorney General Eric Holder moved to dismiss the Stevens indictment with prejudice, which was granted a few days later by Judge Sullivan.

But what of the report by the special prosecutor—514 pages of findings issued three years after the case was dismissed? Did the *Stevens* debacle, or the findings made in the report, help judges and counsel to take preemptory steps and address *Brady* disclosure early and frequently, demanding explanation of all actions taken to make sure materials were timely delivered?

And what was unique about this case that led Judge Sullivan to take the extreme actions he took, which experienced defense counsel all over the country would say prosecutors have done to them at least once in their career, with no such ramifications? Was it something about the visibility of this case that would place experienced prosecutors in the judge's cross-hairs? Was it that this case had presented Judge Sullivan with a platform to address a problem that he saw as institutional to the Justice Department? Was there something inherent in Judge Sullivan that made him take the actions he did—actions that few others in his shoes would have?

Or was it because Judge Sullivan harbored doubts about Senator Stevens's actual guilt? Or is that the wrong question; is it better to ask whether Judge Sullivan had doubts about whether the government had met *its* burden to demonstrate guilt beyond a reasonable doubt?

The Dialogue

JC: Before we turn to the *Ted Stevens* case, Judge: Harvard Law Professor Alan Dershowitz, in his book *The Best Defense*, some years ago and somewhat controversially, said that "Almost all criminal defendants are, in fact, guilty." When he met with criticism over it he basically, paraphrasing, responded with this: "Isn't it better that the people that we prosecute are guilty, rather than the specter of law enforcement prosecuting significant numbers of individuals who are actually innocent?" Do you share that sentiment?

EGS: I just don't view it that way. Anyone who comes before me in my capacity as a federal judge is presumed innocent and entitled to a fair trial. I don't have any pre-formed opinions about guilt or innocence. Everyone's going to be treated the same way—fairly. Everyone's going to get a fair trial. It is not the role of a judge to determine who the government should prosecute.

JC: When you were a [District of Columbia] Superior Court judge handling an extensive docket and the defendant had able counsel and the system was working, a decision about guilt was basically for the adversary process to work out. It wasn't necessarily in a judge's capacity, except in unusual circumstances, to consider the defendant's guilt—other than, of course, if you were sitting in a non-jury trial. Correct?

EGS: My job was to make sure that an individual had competent and effective counsel, that there was a level playing field, and that the trial would be fair. Of course, at the Motion for Judgment of Acquittal stage, I had to determine if a jury could find a defendant guilty based upon the evidence presented.

JC: Do you think that when you were elevated to the [Federal] District Court—with a smaller docket and perhaps more experienced counsel—did you see your role change, according you a greater ability to consider guilt or innocence?

EGS: First of all, the presumption of innocence remains with a defendant unless and until the government proves beyond a reasonable doubt each and every element of an offense that a defendant is charged with. No one ever has to prove innocence. I stress that particularly when I take a plea. There, I tell people, "Look, you want to go to trial, you'll get a fair trial. You don't have to prove any innocence. The burden always rests with the government." My job is still the same—district court judge, superior court judge. Those scales of justice behind the bench [the judge physically pointing] are behind my bench for a reason. And they're always balanced. That's what I stand for—a fair system of justice. Regardless of the court I have served on, my role has remained the same.

JC: Turning to the *Stevens* case, that was probably the most high-profile criminal case that you've ever handled.

EGS: I have had a number of high profile cases. But, yes, that's one of the most significant criminal cases I've presided over.

JC: Do you think you handled that case differently than, perhaps, a run-of-the-mill case, given its high profile nature? The defendant, after all, was a long-tenured United State Senator up for re-election at the time.

EGS: No. I handled it the same way I would handle a case against anyone else.

JC: This defendant was armed with as fine a criminal lawyer as exists in the country. The defense—given the impending election campaign of Senator Stevens—wanted an immediate trial.

EGS: That was unusual. No one had ever appeared before me and insisted on a speedy trial. It's always the opposite. Everyone wants more time, and you can appreciate that. This was truly an atypical case in which Senator Stevens demanded a speedy trial because of that impending election.

JC: And I take it you're saying—since you treat all defendants alike— you would have granted an out of turn, a speedy trial, to pretty much anyone with extenuating circumstances?

EGS: Absolutely. When the issue comes up, and it comes up on a daily basis in this Court, I explain that no one is under pressure to waive speedy trial rights. If you want a trial within the speedy trial timeframe, you'll get it. That's my promise to everyone. No one ever takes you up on that. Ted Stevens was the atypical defendant who wanted to. There were compelling reasons. And the government was asked to weigh in and had no problem with that.

JC: How soon after the case was wheeled out to you did you actually get to know what the government was accusing Stevens of?

EGS: Quite soon. I recall very vividly the day I received notice that the indictment had been returned and the case had been randomly assigned to me. I actually was in the jury room behind this courtroom. I had presided over a series of hearings involving Guantanamo defendants and someone entered the room and said "You've received the Senator Stevens indictment."

Quite candidly, I had not been following press accounts of investigations of Senator Stevens. It was with a fair amount of interest that Addy Schmitt, my brilliant career law clerk at the time, without whom I could never have gotten through the *Stevens* case, and I started reaching out to social networking media to find out just what the media were saying about the Senator. So it was a very short period of time in which we attempted to arm ourselves with information about the allegations. I had the first status hearing within a few days, because speedy trial rights become implicated very quickly.

JC: You were resistant a few moments ago to the notion that judges might consider innocence as opposed to "non-guilt." In the private moments in your chambers when the litigants aren't present and the pomp and circumstance of the courtroom doesn't surround you, do you typically consider privately the innocence of a defendant?

EGS: I take very seriously the principle of law that the presumption of innocence remains with any defendant unless and until the government proves guilt beyond a reasonable doubt.

JC: Let me probe that a bit. Are you so structured in how you look at cases, that you only look at them through the Constitution's presumption of innocence as opposed to—"Well, the guy's before me. It's important if he's really innocent?"

EGS: No. No defendant has the burden to prove innocence.

JC: True, but, at bottom, you're a human being. When you read about cases that are *not* before you that are reported in the newspaper, don't you consider whether those defendants are innocent or not?

EGS: Again, the presumption of innocence remains with the defendant unless and until the government proves guilt beyond a reasonable doubt.

JC: Now that I'm asking you to think about it—Senator Stevens of course died tragically in an airplane crash several years ago after the trial and after his indictment was dismissed. Do you think, now pushed by me to offer your personal opinion on it, that the Senator was innocent?

EGS: My opinion is that had the government abided by its obligation to produce exculpatory information, I think there is a fair chance that Senator Stevens could have been found not guilty. I don't have an opinion about whether he was innocent of those charges.

JC: When you have a defendant in a particular case—let's put Senator Stevens aside for the moment—a hypothetical defendant in a jury trial who takes the stand. There will be circumstances where you're going to enhance his sentence if he's found guilty, because you have concluded that he perjured himself. Correct?

EGS: Correct.

JC: Suppose your conclusion is that he lied when he said "I simply didn't do what I'm charged with." You are then basically making a judgment about his innocence, aren't you?

EGS: I'm making a judgment as to whether or not someone told a lie under oath. That's obstruction of justice, and that's a basis for enhancing a sentence.

JC: But if he lied under oath about the "ultimate" issue in the case—e.g., "I didn't rob the bank"—that would go to guilt or innocence. Wouldn't it?

EGS: No one has to prove his innocence. The standard is whether or not the government has proven guilt beyond a reasonable doubt. That's the standard that I'm obligated to follow. If I determined that the defendant had lied under oath, that could impact whether the sentence would be enhanced.

JC: You're challenging, Judge!

EGS: Let me give you an example. I just tried a case last week. A colleague called me very early one morning and told me she was unable to proceed with the trial. She had selected her jury. It was a sting case. She said it was a one to two day trial. I had other things but carved out time to try the case. The defendant testified. And he was present during all sorts of discussions about an impending robbery of a liquor store. He said nothing; but he was present with other co-conspirators. Cops who set up the sting inquired, asking who's this guy? And the cops were told by the other co-conspirators that he's just a crash dummy, a junky—just a fall guy. And the guy sat there. He's charged with the conspiracy. He said one word—there was some question about a Plexiglas screen in a liquor store. What do you call that screen? And this defendant said: "It's called Plexiglas." That was the only thing he said.

I knew when that case went to the jury that it was going to be difficult for the government to obtain a guilty verdict because it was difficult to prove that he knowingly participated in this conspiracy. Yes, he was present when discussions were going on. But it was very difficult. And my law clerks asked me, "Do you think that the jury will find that he's not guilty?" I said they could; or on the other hand it could be a hung jury. I just focused on my job, the government's job, the defense attorney's job. Able defense counsel never advocated that his client was innocent, but rather that the government failed to prove guilt beyond a reasonable doubt, and he articulated a whole host of reasons. And the more I heard from the defense attorney during closing argument, the more I was convinced that it was probably a better than 50% chance that the defendant would be found not guilty. And he was found not guilty.

Was he innocent? You know I really don't have an opinion about that. But I do have a firm belief and opinion that the government failed to prove guilt beyond a reasonable doubt.

JC: Okay. Needless to say, you were tremendously troubled by the government's conduct in *Stevens* concerning compliance with its discovery and *Brady* obligations. Let me take one last stab at it. Do you think, and assuming that Brendan Sullivan had had all the exculpatory material on time with which to question the key witness, Bill Allen, in your heart of hearts do you think the Senator was guilty?

EGS: You're asking the same question in a different way. You're asking me if I think he was innocent of the charges.

JC: No. I'm asking if you think he was *guilty*.

EGS: My answer is this. If Brendan Sullivan had had all the material he was entitled to under the Constitution to defend his client, I think that Senator Stevens could have been found not guilty of the charges by a jury.

JC: Now, suppose *you* were the jury?

EGS: I'm not going to sit here and say, "Has this guy proven his innocence?" That's not my job; it's not the jurors' job. He would have had the same chance. Had Sullivan had all the material he was entitled to under the Constitution to properly defend his client, which he didn't—he did an excellent job, but he didn't have the material—there's a good chance that if the case had been tried non-jury, the Court could have determined that the government failed to prove guilt beyond a reasonable doubt. That's my story and I'm sticking to it! [Mild laughter.]

JC: Do you ever, when you sentence someone after a jury trial, say: "You're guilty of this offense and I'm sentencing you because I think you're guilty?"

EGS: [Long Pause.] No, the jury has spoken. I was listening to your question carefully. I was trying to think back. Has there ever been a jury verdict that I disagreed with? I can't recall one. At sentencing, I would never say "In my heart I know you're guilty." Because the jury has spoken. I never use those words. I would go through the evidence. This is what a jury considered, and it determined your guilt beyond a reasonable doubt. I've probably said in the past, "I have no basis to dispute that." That sounds like something I would say. But innocence, it's not something we deal with.

JC: It seems to me like your unwillingness or reticence to broach the issue of guilt or innocence is somewhat uncommon among the federal judiciary. I haven't done a study but it does seem unusual. Do you think that structured-ness on your part comes from something in your background— your prior practice as a lawyer, an experience in your life or, if I might even raise it, your experiences as a black man? Do any of these factors influence your concern about discussing "innocence" and making sure that, for you, the issue is instead whether the government proved its case beyond a reasonable doubt?

EGS: No, I think it's just as a result of my understanding of what my job is and what it requires me to stay focused on.

JC: In *Stevens*, obviously, you were concerned about the government's misconduct in withholding materials, or delaying production for significant periods of time. Why do you think that the prosecutors did that? Was it just a series of screw-ups, or were they doing it deliberately for a tactical reason—to have a better chance of convicting the Senator?

EGS: The reason why I appointed a special prosecutor was precisely to determine what happened. There was a basis in the statute authorizing the appointment of a special prosecutor, and for him to investigate and to determine whether contempt proceedings were appropriate. And I was concerned enough about the frequent revelations that exculpatory evidence had not been revealed that I took the extra step to appoint Hank [Henry F.] Schuelke [III]. I was ill-prepared to myself formulate an opinion because, first of all, I'm not an investigator. I didn't know what was going on in the minds of the prosecutors. I didn't know what was in their files. I didn't know what their instructions were. So I thought the better approach was to appoint someone above reproach who could conduct a fair and appropriate investigation and make findings—about what happened, what should have happened and what didn't happen. But I resisted the temptation to speculate about the reasons for the frequent revelations that exculpatory information had not been turned over.

JC: When you read all or part of Mr. Schuelke's 514-page report, did you come to your own conclusion as to why they did it?

EGS: The report speaks for itself. And I didn't appoint the special prosecutor so I could publicly disagree with him. I think reasonable people could formulate an opinion as to whether, for instance, there was an obstruction of justice. I think that a reasonable person could conclude that, indeed, certain members of the prosecution team were guilty of obstruction, and I believe there was even a footnote in the Schuelke report that reflects his own reluctance to speculate about whether or not there was an obstruction, because that was beyond his mandate. But I've not sat back and in my own mind agreed or disagreed, or attempted to take issue with his findings. I accept his findings. I think they're reasoned findings following a multi-year investigation. He and his colleague, Bill Shields, did a more than credible job in investigating, and I think their findings are well supported by the record.

JC: Was your step in appointing a special prosecutor to conduct an investigation a statement about the *Stevens* case? Or a statement by you, beyond *Stevens*, to address your concern that too many prosecutors engage in *Brady* games, for lack of a better word?

EGS: I think that what I said on that date that I appointed Mr. Schuelke speaks for itself. I had set forth all the reasons that day in April why I thought there was a need for a special prosecutor.[2] I really don't have anything to add to that. Those are my reasons. That was consistent with my job to administer justice—to find out what the heck happened in this case. Why was there this train-wreck? Why did the Attorney General on April 1, 2009, dismiss this case with prejudice? Why did it require three Federal prosecutors to be held in contempt of court for refusing to turn over documents and then to tell me that they could think of no reason why they hadn't turned over the documents? They earned that contempt citation. I had never in my career held anyone in contempt of court. Why did all these things happen? I thought it was consistent with the fair administration of justice to take it to the next level. I thought that the Department of Justice was ill-prepared to proceed with the type of investigation I thought was appropriate. So that's why I appointed a special prosecutor.

---

2. Author's Note: After specifying the government's numerous failures of production, and hearing counsel and Mr. Stevens, Judge Sullivan addressed the government's pending internal investigation: "the Court has repeatedly been told that the office of professional responsibility at the Department of Justice is conducting an investigation into the investigation and prosecution in this case . . . That was six months ago. The Court next heard about the OPR investigation when the Government assured the Court it need not take any action based on the [Chad] Joy complaint because OPR was conducting a thorough investigation. That was four months ago. And yet, and to date, the silence has been deafening." After commencing criminal contempt proceedings against the original prosecution team based on their failures to comply with his numerous orders and counsels' "potential obstruction of justice," Judge Sullivan, in the "interest of justice" and in accordance with his obligation to determine what happened in the case, appointed Mr. Schuelke "a non-Government disinterested attorney to prosecute that matter." U.S. v. Stevens, 08-231, Transcript April 7, 2009 at pp. 45–48.

JC: At some point while he was still in office, you ordered a declaration from the then-Attorney General Michael Mukasey. You ultimately relented on that when he was leaving office. Why did you want a declaration from the Attorney General himself? He clearly had nothing to do with these discovery abuses.

EGS: Because I was being spun by everyone else on the prosecution team, and I thought that the only way to get a straight answer was to require the Attorney General himself to give me that answer. I was not getting straight, truthful answers by members of the prosecution team.

JC: Did you have the same concern after the administration changed—when the "new kid on the block," Attorney General Holder, came into office?

EGS: First of all, I never had any conversations with Attorney General Holder—or Attorney General Mukasey, for that matter—about the *Stevens* case. I know Mr. Holder from the days when I served in the Superior Court and he was a Superior Court judge. So I do know him, but we have never discussed the *Stevens* case.

I've responded to things he's said in public. He's responded to things I've said in public. I had no preconceived notions about what he knew or what he was going to do. It was a complete surprise to me when I heard on the morning news that morning, April 1st, that he was dismissing the indictment. I had no prior knowledge of that.

JC: But in terms of whether he would have his staff conduct a thorough investigation of what occurred during the prior administration in the *Stevens* case, you wouldn't have been concerned about that would you?

EGS: I was concerned about that. It wasn't anything personal towards Eric Holder. It was that under the rule under which I appointed the special prosecutor, I made a decision that the Department of Justice was conflicted in being able to conduct a fair and impartial investigation. Otherwise I would have referred it to the Department of Justice for whatever consideration the Department wanted to give the case. So I made a decision that there was a need for an independent special prosecutor-type regardless of who the Attorney General was because, frankly, I had had it. I had been spun by the prosecution team. I was not getting truthful answers as late as February 13, 2009—the defense team still wasn't getting exculpatory information that I had ordered to be turned over. So it appeared to me that the only thing that I could possibly do to try to determine what happened—meaning, what went wrong—was to appoint someone who was independent of the Federal Government, regardless of who the Attorney General was.

I have the highest regard for Eric Holder, and he knows it. I think he's done a great job, and it was nothing personal to him. It was just that regardless of who the Attorney General was, I was determined to appoint an independent investigator. Because I thought that one was justified by everything that had taken place in the case up to that point.

JC: Is there something, in retrospect—if this kind of thing were to happen before you again—that you could have done or would do today to ensure that the continuing abuse pattern that existed in *Stevens* wouldn't happen in a new case?

EGS: A lot has changed. First of all, there's new training at the Department of Justice—a great step forward. I don't think it goes far enough. And I've altered the way I do business in my court as well. I have a standing order now that's issued immediately when an indictment is returned. It sets forth the bases for production on a rolling basis of *Brady* material, discovery material and impeachment material. And I make inquiries in court about the government's obligation. I don't have problems. In fact, I've been pleasantly surprised by the reaction of prosecutors in my courtroom to me and my procedures. It's not unusual for the government to affirmatively state "Judge, we're aware of our *Brady* obligations. This is what we've turned over, and this is what we're doing in an effort to locate additional information." And by and large, defense attorneys accept that. So things have changed. The attitudes have changed, and I've altered the ways in which I conduct hearings in my cases. And it starts with that standing order that I issue immediately upon the indictment in every case, before the attorneys even appear. So everyone knows what the ground rules are.

JC: Do you think things in general have changed in part because of what you did in the *Stevens* case?

EGS: I think, absolutely. It's not just me. It's other judges as well. Judge [Paul] Friedman in the *Safavian* case. It's Judge Mark Wolfe in his cases. Judge Don Molloy in his cases. And judges talk. We talk about these issues. So it's not just Emmet Sullivan. It's what other judges have done and are doing across the country. And I think there's a greater sensitivity on the part of everyone—on the part of the government especially. And on the part of defense attorneys also. Because defense attorneys now, at the earliest opportunity, are filing requests for scheduling orders in cases. Not only in my courtroom but in other courtrooms across the country. They're asking that judges issue orders requiring the government to do certain things. So that if there's a breach of that obligation to produce information, there's a penalty. And that penalty could be contempt of a clear and enforceable order. So things have changed. I think there's a lot more we can do. I still think there's a crying need to change Rule 16 of the Federal Rules, so that there's one uniform standard for producing favorable information in a usable format, on an on-going basis, and starting as soon as an indictment is returned.

JC: Do you think that more defendants are getting acquitted due to these innovations?

EGS: I don't have a basis to formulate an opinion whether more people are being acquitted or not. I just don't know. That is an interesting question you ask, but I think there are more implications than simply whether more people are being acquitted or not. I think that as a result of the innovations, the entire trial process is being implicated. I think more judges are issuing discovery orders. I think more defense attorneys are being aggressive about demanding discovery material, and the plea process stage has been dramatically implicated because attorneys are receiving more Brady material at an earlier time to enable them to be in a better position to evaluate plea offers.

JC: Turning for a moment to our discussion earlier: I assume, you believe that sometimes in your courtroom guilty individuals—or, using your more exacting phraseology—individuals that you might have concluded have been proven guilty beyond a reasonable doubt, were actually acquitted. Is that a fair statement? Or, you won't even give me that?

EGS: I have had cases in which I believed that the government would probably obtain a guilty verdict, and the jury in the end found "not guilty."

JC: That's as much as you'll give me. I hear you. So in such cases, and assuming the "alleged" conduct by the defendant was horrible, do you get annoyed? Do you say to yourself, "Here's a guy . . . I think the government has proven its case beyond a reasonable doubt, and he's walking away. And, frankly, I'm afraid he may do what he was charged with again?"

There's a long pause here on your part, Judge. Obviously, you're carefully considering your answer.

EGS: As hard as it may sound, I firmly believe that, regardless of the outcome, when a jury has spoken—guilty or not guilty—the system has worked. The system has failed to work when jurors cannot agree.

JC: Why is that? Reasonable minds can differ. Can't they?

EGS: When I say it's failed to work, it's failed to produce a unanimous verdict. That has happened, and it's happened recently—this past summer. And I have to retry the case. I accept that. Not always will twelve people be able to agree, and there may be some good reasons. A case was well tried. That's what I meant. I'm not casting aspersions or suggesting nefarious reasons for the inability of jurors to find the defendant guilty or not guilty, but I recognize that does happen and that's something you just have to accept and retry the case.

JC: Did it surprise you when the *Stevens* jury convicted him on seven counts?

EGS: No, I wasn't surprised. I didn't know, at that point, the level of the government's failure to produce exculpatory information. I struggled to make sure that the defendant received a fair trial, and it was a struggle—because at every turn we learned something more about what the government had failed to do. I was confident that I had done everything to balance the scales of justice before that case went to the jury, including instructions to the jury resulting from the government's misconduct, and I thought it was a triable case at that point. I thought the jury was properly instructed. And so I can't say that I was surprised when the jury returned a guilty verdict.

JC: How important was it that Senator Stevens was in the hands of such an able lawyer as Brendan Sullivan who was able to uncover the government's misconduct?

EGS: It's a combination of things. It wasn't until after the Schuelke report that we all learned the depths of what had happened in this case. So the Senator was very fortunate in having one of the best attorneys in the country representing him. And indeed he had a team. So that was not an insignificant factor.

JC: What about that? What does that mean for other defendants unable to have a combative gladiator like Brendan Sullivan?

EGS: In April 2009, when I appointed Mr. Schuelke, I would have appointed him or another special prosecutor-type for a John Q. Public case. It had nothing to do with the fact that Stevens was a United States Senator. It had nothing to do with who his attorneys were. It had to do with justice and what justice means. There were some serious problems in that case, and I wanted to determine what had happened. So it made no difference that it was Senator Stevens. It could have been John Q. Public. I would have done exactly the same.

JC: Let me take another stab at it, Judge. While Senator Stevens was on the stand—and I understand that it's not your job, at least at that point to make credibility judgments—did you have a sense as to his credibility while he was testifying?

EGS: I observed his demeanor on the witness stand. I thought he was struggling as best as he could to tell the truth. I didn't sense that he was deliberately not telling the truth. And again the presumption of innocence remained with him throughout the trial.

JC: And while the principal witness against the Senator, Bill Allen, was testifying, what was your sense about his testimony—recognizing, of course, that you had not seen some of the cross examination material that the government had withheld?

EGS: There were significant pauses between questions asked of him and answers given by him. Also, there was an indication at one point that a member of his defense team was coaching him while he was on the stand.

JC: If you had not been confronted, after the trial, with the misconduct that was uncovered, the Senator was 84 years old and had lost his Senate seat. Given his conduct, would you have sentenced him to any incarceration, assuming his health was okay?

EGS: I never thought about what the sentence would have been. We never got to that point. He would have been treated like anyone else. We would have gotten a probation report. There would have been a recommendation. I would have heard from his attorney, heard from the government and imposed a sentence I thought was fair and reasonable. I've just never thought about that. And really I'm not in a position to speculate about what the sentence might have been.

JC: I hear you saying—and, of course, accept it—that you would treat him as you would treat anybody else. Still, in a high-profile case with all the country watching, do you think judges are able to impose sentence on a defendant of that caliber as if he were just John Q. Public?

EGS: Sure. I think we are able to. I take very seriously the oath that I took to administer justice without respect to who the individual is. I think we're able to do that for the most part. It's not unusual at all to have to impose sentence on someone who is a high profile personality.

JC: Of course you want to impose it fairly. But knowing that he's been a sitting Senator for 40 years . . .

EGS: At least.

JC: Wouldn't you want to send a message to other citizens: "You run afoul of the law, look what happened to Senator Stevens"? So it is going to be different, isn't it?

EGS: It's going to be like any other case in that you'll consider the individual as a whole. You'll consider all the good he's done in his life, and what happened here. And you'll consider what other people think about him. He was well respected. There were high profile people who testified about his character during the trial. Sentencing in every case is difficult. They don't become easier over time. It would have been a difficult, challenging sentencing. But all a judge can do is determine what he's been found guilty of, his personal history, his criminal history and otherwise. He did a lot of good for the people of Alaska, and arguably for people of the country. Then you try to determine a sentence that's fair and reasonable. So, it would have been challenging. That's why my hair is grey now.

JC: Have you ever considered, when sitting back in your easy chair, that the result of this prosecution may have affected American society far more broadly than the *Stevens* case itself? As I understand it, Senator Stevens probably would have voted against ObamaCare [the Affordable Care Act] if he had stayed in the Senate, which would probably have led to the defeat of ObamaCare. So the impact of this prosecution—poorly conducted in terms of government misconduct—and Senator Stevens' marred conviction had an impact much broader maybe than just the case itself.

EGS: The fact that he was a United States Senator didn't give him any greater rights than anyone else. My job was to give him a fair trial. He had demanded a speedy trial. And had John Q. Public done that, he would have gotten a speedy trial too. So my job was to make sure that he got a fair trial and that that trial commenced and concluded well in advance of that election because that's what he wanted. He wanted an opportunity to stand for re-election and an opportunity to hopefully say he was found not guilty. That was my job. I didn't think about how he would have voted on things. And for people who don't believe that, that's their problem.

JC: No, I certainly don't think any decision by you was intended to influence how Senator Stevens' votes would line up. What I'm asking is this: when you sit back in your easy chair, maybe watching a Redskins football game, do you ever think about the impact of your decisions on society? You're appointed by the President of the United States with life tenure. So you potentially have great impact on the United States beyond the four corners of this courtroom.

EGS: I think a federal judge should always think about his decisions and the potential impact of those decisions on society. Nevertheless, a federal judge should not be result oriented.

JC: But have you ever thought: "I've done something worthwhile beyond what's impacted in my immediate, sanitized, courtroom."

EGS: Of course, we as federal judges recognize the implication and impact of our rulings. Sure. I think we all do.

JC: Does that give you happiness?

EGS: I don't think I measure it in terms of happiness. I think I measure it in terms of recognizing the impact of my decisions on the parties before me, and, at times, on the public at large.

JC: But if the impact is one that makes you happy as a citizen, does that . . .

EGS: But it doesn't factor into the decision making process, whether I'm going to be happy or not. So that's not something I focus on afterwards. There are decisions I've issued because they're consistent with the fair administration of justice. Period. And I've felt in my heart that justice prevailed. Whether I'm jumping up and down with joy about the decision is something different. But that's not a factor that I consider—whether I'm going to be happy after I've rendered a decision. That's not something that factors into it. Otherwise I'd be an activist and making decisions for the wrong reasons.

JC: That's fair enough. The reader won't know that we're actually sitting in your courtroom (alone) without your robes or your jacket on, and we're having a pleasant chat here. But it seems to me that you resist looking back on your rulings from the vantage point of just another person—that you seem to separate your personal self from your role as a judge. I'm not suggesting that you make decisions in a case to make you happy. Instead, I'm asking this: after the case is over and you look back at a case five or ten or even fifteen years later, don't you say to yourself "Gee, I used my judgeship to make things better for society or at least some subset of it. I did within the confines of the law and my judgeship, as I should have. But dammit—that was something good that I did." Do you ever consider that?

EGS: No. Maybe there'll come a time in my life when I'll write a book about that. But right now, no. I do my job. It's not about happiness or sorrow.

JC: So if I were to ask you are you happy with what you did in the *Stevens* case, you would say . . .

EGS: I think that what I did in the *Stevens* case, justice demanded. It wasn't a question of me being happy. It wasn't a question of me getting back at the government. It was a question of me doing what I thought was appropriate from a legal point of view to determine what went awfully wrong in the prosecution of Ted Stevens. It wasn't being spiteful. I recognized that I had the authority to do what I did, and I exercised that authority.

And I felt good in the sense that that was consistent with the fair administration of justice. Because I thought the public and the court should know what went horribly wrong in that case.

Chapter 12

Judge Vaughn R. Walker

I can understand that people could think those things, and perhaps there is a bit of self-delusion in thinking that, "No I don't have those kinds of emotions or feelings." And I'm not saying for a moment that one's background, life's experience, do not in some fashion or other color your outlook as a judge and perhaps color what you do as a judge. None of us ever escapes our past, our backgrounds and our life's experiences. But the very job of being a judge is to attempt to divorce yourself from extraneous influences.
—Judge Vaughn R. Walker, July 17, 2013

It was the liberal Democrats who successfully stalled Judge Vaughn R. Walker from being appointed to the U.S. District Court for the Northern District of California. Nominated by President Ronald Reagan in 1987, Democrats objected because of his perceived lack of sensitivity to homosexuals and others. They based their denunciation on Mr. Walker's forceful representation of the U.S. Olympic Committee in a lawsuit that, successfully, sought to prohibit a San Francisco athletic association from using the term "Gay Olympics" and on his failure to resign his long-time membership in the then all-male Olympic Club. Judge Walker was renominated by President George H. W. Bush in 1989 and confirmed without incident.

During his tenure on the bench, Judge Walker presided over myriad high-profile cases. In addition to the Proposition 8 case discussed here (for which Judge Walker will be forever remembered), he presided over the Apple/Microsoft copyright case concerning ownership and protection of visual displays typically associated with Apple. He refused to dismiss the antitrust suit stemming from the purchase by Hearst of the San Francisco Chronicle *and, using such terms as "inference [of] cronyism," flatly criticized the role played by the Department of Justice. Shortly before he retired from the bench, he ruled that certain counterterrorism policies implemented by President George W. Bush involving domestic surveillance were illegal. In making that determination, he rejected the government's attempt to have the case dismissed based on the "state-secrets privilege."*

Shortly before the Proposition 8 case, Judge Walker dismissed a case brought by a pilot—a gay man who was HIV-positive—even though the government had clearly violated his right to privacy with respect to his HIV status. That decision was reversed by the Ninth Circuit, which was itself reversed by the U.S. Supreme Court so that Judge Walker's ruling was reinstated, a ruling unmentioned by critics of his ruling in the Proposition 8 case.

As a judge, he has been described as independent-minded and, at times, unorthodox and unpredictable. Notably, Judge Walker sentenced a defendant to serve two months in custody followed by 100 hours of community service—the defendant was to stand in front of a post office with a board stating: "I stole mail. This is my punishment." This sentence was affirmed by the Ninth Circuit, noting the broad discretion afforded to a district judge.

Judge Vaughn R. Walker was born in Watseka, Illinois. He graduated from the University of Michigan and Stanford Law School. After Stanford, he clerked for Central District of California Judge Robert Kelleher from 1971 to 1972. He then went into private practice at an old-line San Francisco law firm, where he worked until his nomination to the federal bench was confirmed in 1989. Judge Walker became Chief Judge in 2004, a position maintained until shortly before he retired from the bench in early 2011. After leaving the bench, he publicly acknowledged his gay orientation, which had been widely politicized as an "open secret" during the trial. He has since returned to private practice, acts largely as a mediator and arbitrator, and is a frequent lecturer at Stanford University Law School and University of California, Berkeley School of Law.

Judge Walker currently practices law in San Francisco, California.

Same-Sex Marriage

On June 26, 2013, the U.S. Supreme Court in a 5–4 decision decided the so-called same-sex marriage case, *Hollingsworth v. Perry*, neé *Perry v. Schwarzenegger*. To the lay world, the decision invalidated on constitutional grounds state law bans against same-sex marriage.

In truth, the Supreme Court did not quite do that. Rather, the Supreme Court decided a matter of extremely important procedural law, but procedural law nonetheless. It held that those individuals who appealed a decision by a U.S. district judge sitting in San Francisco who had held that the California ban on such marriages—commonly known as "Proposition 8," for the amendment to the California Constitution enacted by a referendum—simply had no legal "standing" to appeal. Had, instead, the government of the State of California itself chosen to appeal, the Supreme Court might well have decided the case on the merits. In other words, it might have directly decided whether or not a ban on same-sex marriage violates the Equal Protection and Due Process clauses of the U.S. Constitution—whether refusing to allow same-sex couples the right to marry denied them "the equal protection of the laws."

Because of this procedural nuance, we may never know what the Supreme Court might have decided had it reached the merits of the controversy. Legal decisions have a way of taking on a life of their own, and it may be that the Supreme Court will never actually get to decide the merits, given that more and more states are validating such marriages, leaving the change in the national mores to become a fait accompli. Accordingly, the *Hollingsworth* decision will be seen as having de facto invalidated same-sex marriage bans. If that occurs, the Supreme Court will have effectively deferred to a trial-level decision by a lone district judge sitting on the federal bench in San Francisco—a venue particularly hospitable to the rights and interests of the gay and lesbian community.

The somewhat long, winding, and perhaps torturous road of gay rights, particularly in California, led ultimately to the doorstep of the courtroom of Judge Vaughn R. Walker. In 2000, Proposition 22, the California Defense of Marriage Act, codified the definition of marriage as "a relationship between a man and a woman." In 2004, however, in ostensible defiance of the proposition, the mayor of San Francisco directed county officials to issue marriage certificates to same-sex marriage couples. Soon, however, California's highest court—the Supreme Court—without addressing the constitutionality of Proposition 22, directed San Francisco to stop issuing the licenses. In 2008, however, deciding various appeals, the California Supreme Court invalidated Proposition 22, giving way to same-sex marriage.

Not to be outdone, Proposition 22 proponents went back to the referendum process. On Election Day, November 4, 2008, they accomplished the passage of Proposition 8, designed to invalidate same-sex marriage and the same-sex marriage licenses that had been issued. For perspective, some 18,000 same-sex marriages had taken place in the four and one-half months between the court's decision invalidating Proposition 22 and the passage of Proposition 8. Upon the passage of Proposition 8, those who believed that same-sex marriage should be permitted were back to square one.

That was the case until the opponents of Proposition 8 brought their case to the federal courtroom of Judge Walker. He—to the surprise of nearly everyone—chose to hold a full-scale evidentiary hearing to address the merits of the Proposition 8 opponents' claim, that is, to decide whether, indeed, the ban on same-sex marriage was merit-based or constituted discrimination, a violation of equal rights. In so doing, Judge Walker took testimony from proponents and opponents of same-sex marriage on core issues—the psychological and sociological benefits and detriments to all concerned of what has emerged as socially acceptable behavior. However, there was a complication. The lead defendant was Jerry Brown, the governor of California. He and other government defendants declined to defend the proposition, arguably giving plaintiffs their case. Except that Judge Walker granted the proposition's proponents leave to intervene and do precisely what the state government refused to do—defend the viability of the proposition on the merits.

We now know that Judge Walker, after two weeks of testimony, concluded this: "Proposition 8 fails to advance any rational basis in singling out gay men and lesbians for denial of a marriage license. Indeed, the evidence shows Proposition 8 does nothing more than enshrine in the California Constitution the notion that opposite-sex couples are superior to same-sex couples." He thus declared that Proposition 8 was unconstitutional.

Still, one must wonder what went through Judge Walker's mind when the case was randomly assigned to him. Would his thinking have been different if, as the Reagan nominee (and Bush appointee) that he was, he had taken the bench in, for example, Mobile, Alabama, not San Francisco? Or, what if he had been assigned the case in 1986 at the height of the HIV epidemic?

Furthermore, could Judge Walker not have anticipated that the case might ultimately have found its way to the U.S. Supreme Court, which would effectively leave standing his decision as perhaps the law of the land? Did he not consider that his own status as a gay man might complicate the perceived integrity of the decision? This is particularly important since Judge Walker had chosen to not disclose his status—even though it was informally known in the San Francisco legal community—until he had decided the case and retired from the bench. Was he concerned about a potential recusal motion if he were to make disclosure on the record, and therefore deliberately chose not to, precisely so that he would be the judge to decide the case?

On the other hand, why didn't the Proposition 8 proponents move for Judge Walker's disqualification? Perhaps they thought that they lacked sufficient basis to allege that he was gay and that, even if so, he would be biased against their position. Did they fear that Judge Walker would be offended by the mere filing of a motion that would air his personal life status—that if they filed and he denied a recusal motion, their chances of victory would have diminished? Were they concerned that Judge Walker might sanction them for having filed a scandalous motion?

Or was something altogether different at stake? Namely, did they believe that the way in which Judge Walker had chosen to live his life—quietly maintaining his sexual orientation—suggested to them that he would lean in favor of Proposition 8's proponents? Did his prejudgeship representation of the U.S. Olympic Committee in a lawsuit against the Gay Olympics—which actually held up his nomination as a judge—make them more optimistic? Did his decision—rendered less than one year earlier—to dismiss a case brought by a gay man even though the government clearly violated his statutory right to privacy concerning his HIV-positive status give the proponents confidence that Judge Walker would rule in their favor? When they rolled the dice and chose to not object to his sitting, did the Proposition 8 proponents conclude that they might indeed have a "secret weapon" poised to rule for them?

Perhaps more important, how would Judge Walker have reacted to such a motion? Would he have denied it outright, as had at least one Jewish judge sitting on the prosecution of a Palestinian terrorist (as in the case of Judge Michael Mukasey in New York) or as in the instance of a black jurist sitting on a civil rights case (such as Justice Thurgood Marshall of the Supreme Court)? Would he have done what California's Chief Judge James Ware did when faced with the proponents' motion arguing, after Judge Walker's decision was rendered, that Judge Walker's judgment should be vacated because he should have been disqualified—that is, write a 14-page, exacting decision denying the motion and, in doing so, admonishing, "The presumption that Judge Walker, by virtue of being in a same-sex relationship, had a desire to be married that rendered him incapable of making an impartial decision, is as warrantless as the presumption that a female judge is incapable of being impartial in a case in which women seek legal relief."

Or might such a motion have caused Judge Walker to look more deeply inside himself to assess his capacity for objectivity? Might a motion have caused him to better assess the potential appearance of impropriety in sitting on the case, particularly if the truth were to later emerge—as it did when he retired from the bench?

The Dialogue

JC: This book, Judge Walker, is of course about how judges think—and what is not reflected in the court record about the decision making. Because of the *Perry* case's very nature, I'll invariably ask some personal questions, trying to probe without being invasive. If I inadvertently stray across the line, please sustain an imaginary objection, and I'll move on.

VRW: So I get to make the objection and the ruling as well?

JC: Exactly. So: many judges occasionally preside over marriage ceremonies—typically for friends, colleagues, clerks or former clerks. Before *Perry* was assigned to you, did you preside over marriage ceremonies?

VRW: Yes, but not many. I can't tell you the exact number, but less than a half dozen. The first, and probably the second were marriages of former law clerks. Interestingly enough, the marriage that I presided over immediately preceding the *Perry* trial was a marriage of one of my former law partners who, at the time his marriage, was 95 years old and his bride was 83. So when, in the course of *Perry*, counsel for the proponents of Proposition 8 argued that the main purpose of marriage was procreation, I pointed out that I had performed this marriage but had not inquired whether they intended to engage in procreative activity. I asked counsel if I had missed something. I received no real answer.

JC: For a period of time before Proposition 8 and *Perry*, Mayor Newsom had directed San Francisco to issue same-sex marriage licenses when requested.

VRW: Correct.

JC: During that period of time, did anybody ask you to preside over a same-sex marriage?

VRW: I believe not. I was, however, asked to perform a marriage between two men after the California Supreme Court had found Proposition 22 to violate the California constitution. During that four and one half month period, there were approximately 18,000 same-sex marriages performed in California. In a subsequent California Supreme Court decision, where the Court upheld the right of the people to amend the constitution, it also provided that those 18,000 marriages would remain valid and in full force. I had been asked to perform a same-sex marriage during that period of time, between individuals one of whom I knew and had known for a long time. I did not know his partner. I did not accept the invitation and didn't perform that marriage.

JC: Why?

VRW: Little did I, of course, know that I would eventually draw the Proposition 8 case; but I was aware that the matter was going to be before the voters in November, and I just thought that perhaps something might come up in court and it was better not to perform that particular marriage.

In addition, frankly, I had never searched out the opportunity to perform marriages. I did very few. Didn't particularly like doing them. The only ones that I performed, as I say, were for former law clerks and persons I felt very close to over a long period of time. The individual who asked me to perform this same-sex marriage was a long-time friend but not someone I felt particularly close to.

JC: You seem like a rather gregarious man—did you not like doing so because, typically, someone who presides over a marriage remarks about what a wonderful institution it is and you had not been married? You're looking at me as if I'm asking you something that you probably haven't thought about before.

VRW: Correct, I hadn't thought about it in those terms. I don't get weepy at marriage ceremonies. And I just never felt comfortable with the trappings of such ceremonies. Not just marriage ceremonies, but such moments of sentimentality. I don't particularly like delivering eulogies or toasts at retirement parties. That just isn't something that I particularly revel in doing. Not my cup of tea.

JC: Fair enough, but to the extent that a judge who performs a marriage ceremony, at least in a legal sense, sanctifies the marriage, you would have had no problem in legal terms. In other words, you wouldn't have declined because you thought it was wrong for same-sex people to marry, am I right?

VRW: Yes, I didn't think there was anything wrong with people of the same gender marrying. So, my reservation about performing a same sex marriage was not based on that.

JC: That said—Cardozo spoke of it eloquently—however objective one might try to be as a judge, he comes to the bench with certain biases or prejudices, and I don't mean that in an *ad hominem* way. Did you have a particular view of same-sex marriage as an institution (or potential institution) before the case was wheeled out to you?

VRW: Not to any great degree. The concern that I had was really quite different. You may recall that in 1986 there was a retention election in California in which three of the four judges on the California Supreme Court who were on the ballot that year were not retained by the voters. The issue then largely centered on votes that these justices had cast in death penalty cases.

When the California Supreme Court decided the marriage cases in which it held that Proposition 22 was unconstitutional, I had a telephone conversation with an old friend of mine who is a California Court of Appeals justice, who had been involved in politics and was completely familiar with the 1986 retention experience. I expressed some concern that Chief Justice George and perhaps others on the California Supreme Court might be subject to a campaign in connection with retention if they voted to invalidate Proposition 22. I knew that George was on the ballot for retention in November of 2008. I can't remember precisely when I had that conversation, but the thought that was going through my mind had less to do with the issue of same-sex marriage than whether the California Supreme Court's decision on that subject might ignite a political backlash that would result in one or more of the justices not being retained. Justice George is a personal friend and an outstanding jurist. He did vote to invalidate Proposition 22 and decided ultimately to retire at the end of his term, but my concern was if he wanted to stay I did not want to see him defeated for retention. So to the extent I was thinking about these issues my concerns were quite collateral to the issue of same-sex marriage.

JC: The *Perry* case was ultimately wheeled out to you by random process, correct?

VRW: Correct.

JC: Was there any talk in the blogs or elsewhere that came to your attention saying that a gay judge would be sitting on this important case?

VRW: Yes. I can't pinpoint exactly when. But I did receive a telephone call from a reporter named Andy Ross who writes a column in the San Francisco Chronicle. Interestingly enough, to my recollection he was the first and only reporter who ever asked about my sexual orientation in the almost 20 years that I'd been on the bench. I can't remember exactly the question he posed, but he asked about my sexual orientation in the context of the case. My reaction was this was not really relevant any more than the gender of a judge would be relevant in a gender discrimination case, the race of a judge in a race discrimination case, or what have you. I believe I said I didn't have a comment on that. After hanging up the telephone I thought— "Well now, that doesn't sound too good. That will sound like I'm trying to hide something, and that's certainly not my intention." So I went down to the chambers of my colleague and good friend [Judge] Chuck Breyer. I told him of the conversation, and I said what worries me is not that Ross is going to run with a story that a gay judge has the case . . . .

JC: I take it that Judge Breyer knew you were gay.

VRW: Oh yes. I think all my colleagues did. If they didn't, they weren't paying attention. I said my concern was that the "no comment" would be seen as trying to hide something. And I don't think that was the appropriate response now that I've reflected on it. He said, "Don't worry. I'll do something." He didn't say what. But he did call Ross and provided a comment that said, in essence, that while Judge Walker has never hidden his sexual orientation, he doesn't advertise it. He doesn't kind of wrap himself in the rainbow flag. So when the column appeared it really carried Judge Breyer's comment more than mine.

JC: That was the last time it came up while you presided over the case?

VRW: Yes. It came up later, of course. Counsel for the proponents of Proposition 8 were asked, and were quoted in the paper saying that they were not going to raise a disqualification issue at trial or anything like that. And they did not.

JC: They were asked by Ross or some reporter?

VRW: By some reporter. I don't know whether it was Ross or another reporter but they were quoted as saying they weren't going to touch the issue. And they did not until after the judgment, and I had retired from the bench.

JC: Did you, either yourself or perhaps guided by Judge Breyer who was obviously a trusted friend, consider that perhaps the better path would be to straight out put it on the record and avoid any later second guessing?

VRW: I can't say that I didn't think about that. But I didn't think it really appropriate because, I will say quite candidly, I do think it's irrelevant to a judge's capability of being a judge. There are certain characteristics—gender, race, ethnicity, etc.—that a judge need not put that on the record. There are other things about one's background that may not be so apparent—and unless the judge has the feeling that that is going to color his work on the case in some fashion, I don't think it a disclosable matter.

And as you know, when ultimately the issue was raised subsequently, the judge who ruled on the matter, Judge Ware, came to that conclusion. That if a judge genuinely believes that the matter is not something that is likely to influence his or her decision it is really not a disclosable matter. Furthermore, as I said earlier, I think my colleagues all knew my sexual orientation. It was pretty well known at the bar.

I had been subject to a good deal of criticism when I was nominated to the bench because in private practice I had handled a trademark litigation on behalf of the United States Olympic Committee to prevent a group from putting athletic events under the trademark "Gay Olympics." We succeeded in that litigation. And at the time of the nomination I was criticized for the way I handled the case. And it was further said that I took the case in the 1980's and prosecuted it that way because I was a closeted gay man trying to cover up.

JC: Assuming that the many lawyers representing the Prop 8 proponents had done their homework and knew that 20 years earlier your Reagan/then Bush I nomination had been held up because of that—and I understand Senator Cranston and Ms. Pelosi were part of the attack against you—they may have concluded, "Well we have a judge willing to bend over backwards so as to keep his gay status under wraps. He may be a ringer. We may do better with Walker than with the next guy if Walker recuses himself."

VRW: Well, Joel, you've been a lawyer for a long time. You know full well that amateur psychoanalysis of judges is a very dangerous and risky business.

JC: For sure.

VRW: And perhaps that's how those lawyers perceived the situation. But I don't believe that it is up to the judge to speculate what may be going through the minds of lawyers in appraising the judge to attempt to rectify any misimpression that the lawyers may have. It's getting pretty speculative.

JC: I suppose a skeptic might say that a judge in such an important case, particularly in this community in California or some eastern states . . .

VRW: It's just as important in Idaho and Alabama and so forth . . .

JC: I'm going to ask about that in a moment. But that said, and being the devil's advocate, one might conclude that a well-respected judge who had been on the bench for 20 years, might really want to keep the case. If you had put your sexual orientation on the record it might have raised the possibility that maybe you wouldn't end up sitting on the case. That's what a skeptic might say.

VRW: There's another side to that skepticism on this particular issue. It was the contention of the proponents of Proposition 8 that the existence of the right of people of the same gender to marry jeopardized the institution of marriage—heterosexual marriage.

JC: Right.

VRW: Which would create exactly the same hazards for a heterosexual judge as would exist for a gay judge. The hazards of the same bias. If you spin out that theory of bias. So, in essence, there really isn't a judge who could surely be impartial, except possibly for a bisexual judge. And I think it's different from a situation in which a judge might be a member of a social group, club or some activity that would not be particularly well known and that might have some connection to the case. Those kind of disclosures are obviously often judgment calls depending upon the circumstances. But I just didn't think that this was matter that needed to be disclosed, so I didn't. And part of it of course was that, in actuality, everybody knew.

JC: Again I'm trying not to be too invasive, so cut me off if I am. I take it that at the time when you handled the Gay Olympics litigation, you defined yourself as gay.

VRW: Not really, no. That was in the mid-80s and I was not as open as I later became. I became much more open after I went on the bench.

JC: I seem to have read that your litigation on behalf of the Olympic Committee was fairly aggressive.

VRW: I was accused of being an aggressive litigator, correct.

JC: In what sense?

VRW: The primary accusation centered around the enforcement of a cost award in the litigation. I was accused of being vindictive. Of course, the client felt that it was entitled to collect those costs, and I, as the lawyer, was pursuing those costs . . .

JC: From time to time one will see that clients may want to retain a particular lawyer—say in the Paula Dean case these days, she may be an excellent lawyer but Dean's chosen lawyer happens to be black. Or a Swiss bank in a Holocaust litigation may deliberately retain a Jewish lawyer.

Did that that have anything to do with why you were retained by the U.S. Olympic Committee?

VRW: I'm quite sure that it did not. They didn't approach me in the first instance; they approached a significant partner in the law firm, and I had worked with this partner in a number of matters. I was hired as the junior partner on the case. I'd never been first on the masthead in any litigation at that point until then. After the firm took on the case, the senior lawyer bowed out of it and I moved up to first. Hence, I got all the "credit," as it were.

JC: As an aggressive litigator before you became a judge, if you were representing the Proposition 8 proponents and the case wheeled out to somebody like you, would you have been comfortable trying the case before such a judge?

VRW: If I had been representing the proponents of Proposition 8, I would have tried a quite different case from the one they tried, without regard to who the judge was. I don't believe that a motion to disqualify a judge drawn randomly, as I had been, because the judge was gay and the case involved gay rights would have been a very auspicious way to begin the litigation. Even if that motion had succeeded or if the gay judge had recused himself, it would have sent the case off on the wrong foot. And, say, a straight judge who had drawn the case subsequently I think would . . .

JC: Be pissed off?

VRW: Well, again we're engaging in some amateur psychoanalysis of judges which we agree is a dangerous business. But it would not have been a particularly good way to begin the litigation. And put yourself in an analogous situation in which a female judge draws a gender case of some kind and either recuses herself or is knocked off the case by one of the parties to the litigation and say, a male judge draws the case. It puts that judge in an awkward position as well. I would think litigators would recognize that.

Several years ago, I drew a challenge to an anti-affirmative action initiative measure that California voters had adopted. One of my African-American colleagues had the case re-assigned to himself on the ground that the case was related to a case he had previously been assigned. The notion of related was a real stretch. He found the initiative unconstitutional. His decision was reversed by the Ninth Circuit in a very sharply-worded opinion, made more stinging by the judge having seemed to reach out to get the case. Now this happens to be a fine judge and one stinging reversal from the Court of Appeals does not undo a long and distinguished judicial career. But recusing yourself from a high profile case or reaching out to get one or conjuring up a lot of reasons why people may presume judicial bias can be a very tricky business.

JC: My asking if you might try the case differently than might others leads me to this: Would you have felt comfortable representing the Proposition 8 proponents, had you been called upon to do so?

VRW: As a lawyer? Joel, I don't believe that as a lawyer you have to believe in the righteousness or goodness of your clients. Your job is to represent your clients as they are, whether you agree with their positions, whether you think they're innocent as the driven snow or not. Your job is to deal with the facts and the circumstances as they appear. I'd obviously have to know a good deal more about the funding of the Proposition 8 litigation than I know and exactly who had initiated the contact before I'd feel comfortable accepting that assignment.

JC: But assuming it wasn't some sort of political jihad and the proponents honestly believed—as I'm sure some of the proponents do—that marriage should be opposite sex exclusively, and they ask you to be their litigator, you would have felt comfortable?

VRW: I think I could have taken that case.

JC: Interesting. You said earlier that presiding over the case would have been of extraordinary importance, not only in San Francisco, New York or other major cities. But also you mentioned Idaho. Do you think you would have found it as easy to preside over the case and rule as you did, if the case were venued, for example, in Montgomery, Alabama?

VRW: Frankly, it's hard for me to imagine me sitting in Montgomery, Alabama. But I would like to think that I could handle a case that might be unpopular in the local community. After all, I did handle that "Gay Olympics" case—and a lawyer has a good deal less insulation from public criticism than a judge does—and I took a good deal of flak for it and never had any reservations about doing it.

So it might have been more awkward or difficult in Alabama or Idaho or Mississippi than San Francisco. But I think it would have been incumbent on the judge who drew the case to handle it as best he or she could. After all, I thought my job as the judge was to give the parties the opportunity to present the case that they wanted to present, put on the facts, argue the case and create a record. So many of these cases involving constitutional issues go up the appellate chain on the basis of these broad propositions that judges seem to distill out of their own experience, law review articles, ancient texts, or whatever.

But many of these involve facts that are in dispute. Many of these cases turn on issues that are disputed issues of fact. And this clearly was that kind of case, where the parties were throwing facts against one another. Propositions with respect to the institution of marriage, its role in society, its effect on people and so forth. And I thought my job, under those circumstances was to give them the opportunity to present the evidence that would support their conflicting factual assertions.

JC: Did you give them that opportunity because you thought you really needed to hear those facts or because you knew that this case would certainly go to the Ninth Circuit and in all likelihood, given its impact, would go to the U.S. Supreme Court? In truth, you probably could have decided this case without a factual hearing at all?

VRW: I don't know that I could have. Number one, I did think the case was going certainly to the Court of Appeals and in all probability to the Supreme Court. And I thought that if it's gonna go, let's have a record for the parties' factual assertions. So it seemed to me that a trial was the way to handle the case. I'm not sure the parties were expecting a trial. But obviously we discussed this at the case management conference and set the trial agenda. Could I have decided the case without a factual record? Well, what evidence or what basis would I as a judge have had to make a finding about the role of marriage in society, about the changing institution of marriage over time, about the importance of marriage, the history of marriage and so forth? How would I have made those kinds of determinations? I could have sent a law clerk to work in the library and come up with some scholarly articles on these subjects. But that's not really the judicial function. The judicial function is to give the parties the opportunity to make those showings and that's what I thought my job was.

JC: Let me be blunt. You knew where you were going to come out as soon as the case was rolled out to you, didn't you?

VRW: No, I didn't.

JC: Well, you certainly had no objection based on the example you gave of the gay man who wanted you to perform his marriage. You had no objection to gay marriage before the case was rolled out to you. I assume over the course of years you had discussed it with friends or colleagues or your partner or other people.

VRW: As a matter of fact, I had not.

JC: Is that right?

VRW: Correct.

JC: Not with your partner? Not with friends or colleagues?

VRW: Actually I had not. Certainly not with my partner. I recall a conversation with a friend about the cases in the California courts, but I don't believe I had expressed much of an opinion if any on the merits or lack of merits of the issue. It really had not been . . .

JC: That's surprising. I have two friends, one is now a retired state judge and his wife is a federal judge. Shortly before the O.J. Simpson trial they told me over lunch that before Simpson was charged with murder they had never heard of O.J. Simpson, and I laughed throughout the lunch over that. It sounds something like what you're saying here, that you too were living in a cocoon of sorts.

VRW: Don't forget there was another angle to it. I did use as the reason for not performing the marriage that this might conceivably be something that would come before me. I wasn't thinking of Proposition 8, of course. I was thinking of maybe a social security case or something along those lines that might come before me. The stated reason for turning down that request was that there might be something that would come before me; but frankly I was, on a personal level, not very enthusiastic about marrying this couple, knowing, as I did, only one of the two and not being particularly close to him.

JC: When the case was rolled out and you saw before you the sort of odd couple in David Boies and Ted Olson representing the plaintiffs in the case, did that mean anything to you in terms of the politics—or the sociology—of the case that was being brought before you?

VRW: Not particularly. I had met all three of the major lawyers at one time or other, when I came into the case. Olson, Boies and Chuck Cooper, but in completely different contexts. And long before the case so that I can't say that I knew all of them, but I was on a casual acquaintance basis with all of them.

JC: Did the fact that Olson and Boies were coming in, surprisingly given they're usually political opposites, suggest anything to you about an inevitability of the litigation's outcome?

VRW: Not other than that it was being treated as a high-profile case. We had these celebrated lawyers coming into this case which obviously was going to get a lot of public attention. It was not the first high-profile case or high-profile legal talent that I had before me by any stretch of the imagination.

JC: I'm talking about the fact that they were opponents in *Gore v. Bush*.

VRW: It was obvious that they had teamed up with the view of creating the impression that this was a bipartisan effort that reached across partisan lines. To the extent I thought about it, it seemed to me to be smart strategy on their part.

JC: In your encyclopedic 64-page opinion, you went into great detail about the witnesses for Proposition 8. Unless I'm reading between the lines, you seemed a little angry at some of the things they were saying. Am I right?

VRW: I think you're misreading it. Angry?

JC: Angry in the sense that they were treating gay marriage as second class marriages, and gays as second class people. I am talking about Mr. Blankenhorn.

VRW: Blankenhorn among other things testified that he had [previously] written that when gay marriage becomes legal in the United States, America will be more American. And obviously Boies did a very good job of exploiting that comment. Blankenhorn was not credible in terms of his qualifications on this subject. And his testimony, frankly, was incoherent. He has subsequently, as you may know, recanted his position [taken at trial] and now has publicly endorsed same-sex marriage in an op-ed piece in the New York Times.

If anything, what got my dander up about the litigation conducted by the proponents of Proposition 8 was not so much the evidence that they presented, but the evidence they didn't present. None of the proponents of Proposition 8 testified in support of the Proposition except one, and he was called as an adverse witness by the plaintiffs. This was the Reverend Tam. But the other proponents did not testify. The proponents did not call anyone to testify on the merits other than Blankenhorn. They had withdrawn two or three witnesses. Two that I remember from McGill withdrew on the pretext that they were concerned about their personal security because of the possibility that the trial might be broadcast. Revealingly enough, parts of their testimony was introduced by the plaintiffs as excerpts from these witnesses' videotaped depositions. There were no other witnesses that were called by the proponents, other than Blankenhorn and a witness who testified on the level of scrutiny to be given to Proposition 8. So these witnesses gave testimony helpful to the plaintiffs.

One would have thought that individuals who had engaged in a public, highly publicized campaign that had raised a great deal of money to put before the voters a proposition, would, when that proposition was challenged, be willing to stand up and explain their position. They were not willing to do so. Nor were they willing to present even a halfway credible case in support of the factual propositions which they contended were the foundation for the proposition that they had supported. So if anything got my dander up it was not the case they presented, it was the case they didn't present.

JC: So since you say with the right qualifications you would have been willing to litigate the case on behalf of the proponents of Proposition 8, what would you have done differently to persuade the likes of a Judge Walker?

VRW: Well, I would have attempted to put on a case which would have supported a secular justification for confining marriage to an institution between people of the opposite gender. And that would have been of the same kind of evidence, though obviously with a different result, of the sort that the plaintiffs presented. Academic testimony, perhaps some sociological testimony. I think that the proponents could have put on a significantly more impressive case than the case they did put on. Whether it would have prevailed or not is quite another matter. But they seemed not even to try. I was surprised at that, frankly.

JC: I take it that your decision to retire from the bench had nothing to do with the *Perry* case.

VRW: Nothing.

JC: You were just deciding to move on.

VRW: That's correct.

JC: There then came a point where you had a conversation with a newspaper reporter, I think it was Reuters.

VRW: I wouldn't exactly call it a conversation, but . . . I was beginning my new practice. I had talked to a trusted media adviser about how we'd kick this practice off. She said, "What you need to do is to prepare an announcement, a press release, and then make yourself available to members of the press to discuss the new practice that you've embarked upon." So I issued a press release and I thought the thing to do was to sit down with the reporters who had covered the courts and who continued to cover the courts for the papers, all of whom I knew. After all, sitting for 20 years on the federal bench you become acquainted with the press corps who follow the federal court. And we had a meeting, probably a half a dozen or so reporters, one of whom was Dan Levine of Reuters. I was there to discuss this new practice, and he asked about my sexual orientation and ran a story and that sort of ate up the whole purpose of the press conference.

JC: Were you bothered that had happened?

VRW: Well, I was irritated that had become the focus, when what I wanted to do was get my name out there as somebody who was available for mediations and arbitrations.

JC: But you said in the interview, as I recall it, that you'd been in a gay relationship for eight or ten years, as opposed to saying you were gay. Were you saying that so that people would understand that being in a gay relationship for a long time meant you had no marital intentions, as a hedge against a motion to invalidate the verdict? After all, Judge Ware relied on that fact when he denied the motion to invalidate your decision.

VRW: I think Dan's comment was something like there had been a news report I believe in the Los Angeles Times, and it was either during the Proposition 8 trial or maybe even beforehand, that Judge Walker attends bar events with his long-time companion, a physician. And Dan's question, if I remember it correctly, was: "Tell us about this partner of yours." Or something like that. That's how the subject began.

JC: But you didn't use the phrase "long-term relationship" in order to avoid the potential of the Proposition 8 crowd claiming that you were potentially a direct beneficiary of your ruling, as the Proposition 8 proponents later suggested.

VRW: No, I'm not sure exactly what you're driving at, but I was not thinking about my ruling.

JC: Would you talk—or did you talk—to colleagues whom you trusted, to get their views on the gut issue that was facing you in the case?

VRW: No.

JC: Is that something that you religiously avoided doing in cases, talking to colleagues about . . .

VRW: Not necessarily. It's unusual to talk to your colleagues about the merits of a case. You might talk to your colleagues about certain evidentiary matters; subpoena issues; or witness issues of some kind. Those are the sorts of things that you might talk to your colleagues about.

JC: I don't know if you're a churchgoer or the like. Do you seek inspiration in a church or from a spiritual advisor when you have a monumental case like this? I'm talking about with someone in whom you have confidence that they keep you balanced in deciding a case of significant proportion.

VRW: Well yes, I do recall a conversation. I was not seeking advice, but I recall a conversation with a long-time friend who I have a very high regard for, and a person who is a highly responsible citizen who has occupied positions of great responsibility. We met in my office. I was seeking to persuade him to become a member of the merit selection panel for the magistrate judges. He is not a lawyer and some members of the panel must be non-lawyers. The Proposition 8 case was fairly new at the time but I recall his advice: "You better find some way to get out of this case." I didn't seek any spiritual guidance, however.

JC: As you can see, Judge, I'm trying to get into your head.

VRW: As you know, there's only room for one.

JC: I imagine that those who are your detractors, who considered you "a tyrant in black robes," might be astonished to hear you say, that you feel that under the right conditions you could have tried this case for the Proposition 8 proponents. They would be astonished, don't you think?

VRW: Why should they? I was a lawyer.

JC: They would probably think that you were, for lack of a better word, a movement judge: you already had your mind made up based on your personal life decisions, and that therefore you were going through the motions in deciding the case. And yet, you're telling me you could have litigated the other side of the case.

VRW: I saw something the other day that referred to me as a leftist judge.

JC: I guess they forgot that you were first nominated by Ronald Reagan.

VRW: They forgot about Ronald Reagan. They forgot about a lot of things. I think lawyers can represent positions that they may or may not agree with. And do so faithfully to their obligations as advocates. My goodness, Joel, you surely have represented clients in situations . . .

JC: All innocent. [laughter.]

VRW: You were lucky then. So it is just part of the process.

JC: When I asked you before whether you got angry at all by the comments by some of the witnesses on behalf of Proposition 8, I seem to remember that there was some testimony that Reverend Tam had said that he encouraged voters to support Proposition 8 because homosexuals are 12 times more likely to molest children. There was other testimony that same-sex pairings are "immoral" and should not be encouraged. And other materials like that. How could it be that that didn't anger you?

VRW: What do you mean, how could that be?

JC: How could it be that you wouldn't get angry by somebody who is saying that kind of thing in your courtroom?

VRW: You don't get angry because you think an individual is all wet, and wrong—that he doesn't have his or her facts straight.

I don't know that you get angry every time you hear an offensive remark. In a sense, isn't an equally likely reaction to be one of sadness that someone would have this kind of an attitude? If you were to hear some bigoted outburst in the courtroom by someone who perhaps genuinely believed whatever it was that he was spouting, that can be just as much something that evokes sadness as anger. Or resignation; but anger is not the only reaction that one must have to comments of this kind.

JC: Were you saddened at the time?

VRW: I don't know that I had any reaction other than a feeling that this was an individual who was living in his own world that seemed to be disconnected from any sense of reality.

JC: Have you ever gotten angry on the bench except, for example if somebody commits perjury in front of you and it's clear?

VRW: Actually, I don't think I've gotten angry with perjury. Not that I approve of perjury by any stretch of the imagination. But the things that I got angry with on the bench were either at myself for doing something or saying something that in the cold light of day I would have preferred not to have said. Or when lawyers or others—primarily lawyers—were being obstructive and preventing the proceedings from going forward on an orderly basis, and making life difficult for everybody. That's the sort of thing that makes a judge angry.

JC: I take it then that you took nothing that these witnesses said on the stand or in the writings that became part of the record, as an offense against you or your partner or your lifestyle.

VRW: That may be hard for you to believe, but I don't think that I had that reaction. Well, I suppose I can understand that people, at least some people might think it's incredible that anybody could be cold-blooded enough not to be angry with some comments of this kind. Might not feel that his personal life is on trial in a case like this. Or feel that he has a particular stake in this case.

I can understand that people could think those things, and perhaps there is a bit of self-delusion in thinking that, "No I don't have those kinds of emotions or feelings." And I'm not saying for a moment that one's background, life's experience, do not in some fashion or other color your outlook as a judge and perhaps color what you do as a judge. None of us ever escapes our past, our backgrounds and our life's experiences. But the very job of being a judge is to attempt to divorce yourself from extraneous influences. Whether it's a result of your personal circumstances or the result of your life's experiences or the relationships that you have had in the past or have currently. Your job is to try to step back and as objectively as a human being can, assess the evidence before you, the facts, and apply the law in what you hope is a wise and caring fashion. That's the job. And the very antithesis of that function is to wrap yourself up in the emotions of the situation, to get angry, to feel that you have a personal stake in the case.

And going back to the role of a lawyer. A lawyer's role is not, in a sense, dissimilar from that. I'm sure you have seen lawyers who vouch for their clients, who seem to be so passionate about the position that they are taking on behalf of their client, that they don't do as good a job for their client as they could do if they maintained some distance and objectivity. So basically what a judge does is very similar to what a lawyer must do in attempting to maintain some distance from the case that he or she is handling. And while all that may be hard for some to believe that you can do that, and maybe you can't do it entirely, but that's certainly what you're supposed to do, what you try to do.

JC: And much as you say what the role of judge should be, I think we can probably agree that if Ronald Reagan had known and maybe George Herbert Walker Bush had known what we know now about you and your life, that they would never have appointed you to the bench.

VRW: Well, I don't know about that. First of all, Ronald Reagan's best friend in Hollywood was someone reputed to be gay.

JC: Right.

VRW: You smile. OK. I don't know exactly what their relationship was but they were pals. So I don't think he had any personal antipathy toward gay people. And after all he was a Hollywood actor so he was not unexposed to such individuals. And George Herbert Walker Bush is a very nice man—a gentleman who I've seen on very limited, but a few social circumstances and he couldn't possibly be more gracious. It is said that he nominated someone to the United States Supreme Court who may share the particular sexual orientation that I have. I don't want to be quoted on that subject but in any event that's been said. But here's the point, Joel. At the time I went through the nomination and confirmation process I knew that this issue was lurking, primarily because of the "Gay Olympics" case. I did not want to be confronted with the question: "Are you gay?" or something along those lines, and I never was. I wasn't sure what I was going to say if I was asked that question. I didn't want to be asked the question, I didn't want to have to answer it, but I never was asked by anybody—in the Administration, the Department of Justice, the FBI, the Senate, the Judiciary Committee, or the press—nobody asked the question. The FBI, I know, was asking the question, or at least friends who were interviewed by them in connection with the confirmation say they were asked about my sexual orientation. I've never seen the file. I'm not interested enough to try to get it. So the issue lurked throughout that process. That was a time when things are really best described as "Don't ask, Don't tell."

It was just a subject you didn't touch, and nobody touched it. I would be surprised to think that people like Ronald Reagan and George H.W. Bush, Ed Meese and others were oblivious to the subject, but it was just something where—you didn't go there. And they didn't. [Senator] Pete Wilson who was a strong supporter of mine, whom I just saw this weekend, never asked the question or anything touching on it. So I don't know whether it would have made a difference. No, there may be no connection with the point you're trying to make. If I had been marching in parades or had been a gay activist at that time it might very well be true that I would not have received their support. But the mere fact that I might be gay, that seems not to have been an obstacle.

JC: One final question: You have said here, basically, that you entered the *Perry* case with an open mind. Correct?

VRW: Yes.

JC[1]:   That said, do you think in retrospect that you could have been influenced to some degree—on some subconscious, or even conscious, level—that had you ruled to sustain Proposition 8, you might have been perceived in the gay community, or even the broader community, as somewhat of a traitor—a man willing to deny in some sense who he is?

VRW: Remember—in the so-called "Gay Olympics" case I took a great deal of criticism from the gay community and liberals in San Francisco. Yes, there are differences: one, I was then acting as a lawyer representing a client; and two, I was not very open about my sexuality at the time although it was widely speculated that I was gay; I was a 45 year old never married man that the daily newspaper in town described as a "well dressed bachelor."

---

1. This last question and answer were given via e-mail after the interview was completed.

As a judge, I was harshly criticized in deciding that Oracle could merge with PeopleSoft which resulted in the loss of a lot of jobs in the Bay area, in deciding against the plaintiffs in the Japanese slave labor litigation and against the local company Apple in its copyright litigation over the graphical features of Microsoft's Windows operating system. While none of these cases may be comparable to the Prop 8 case, criticism comes with the job and I got lots of it over the years.

As a judge, one tries to be impartial. I don't deny that life experiences affect one's thinking or emotions. But as a judge you try very hard to assess the facts and law as impartially, as possible. Also, don't forget that the proponents of Prop 8 put on very little evidence. They called only one witness on the merits, and David Boies made mincemeat of him on cross-examination. This witness has since recanted the views he expressed at trial. None of the proponents testified in support of their initiative. It would have been very difficult to have decided the case for the proponents no matter who the judge was.

Yes, maybe it would have taken away some basis of criticism of the decision if it had been rendered by a judge well known for his heterosexuality—is there such a beast? But to have recused on the basis of my sexuality would imply that a gay judge can't be considered impartial in a case involving gay-related issues. That is not an impression I wanted to leave.

Chapter 13

Judge Jack B. Weinstein

*After World War II my wife was a social worker with an advanced degree
from Columbia School of Social Work. She set up the first of the clinics
at Jamaica Hospital for soldiers with various psychiatric syndromes. About
a dozen psychiatrists worked with her and those people every night. I was
aware that there were lots of wounds, psychic and physical. And a lot of
these folks needed to know that the system was concerned about them,
and would do what it could within law and reason to assist.*
—Judge Jack B. Weinstein, May 16, 2013

*Appointed to the District Court bench by President Lyndon B. Johnson in
1967, Jack B. Weinstein, 92 years of age at the time of his interview, still
handles a full caseload. A list of his judicial accomplishments would span
dozens of pages. He—quite literally—wrote the books on evidence (Weinstein's Evidence Manual) and New York civil procedure (Weinstein, Korn,
and Miller, CPLR Manual). His opinions are thoughtful, influential, and
pointed (perhaps even "activist"). The settlements he has brokered, particularly in the area of mass tort litigation, are legendary, if not controversial.*

*In addition to his settlement of the Agent Orange cases (discussed here),
he has presided over cases involving DES, asbestos, handguns, Zyprexa, and
tobacco, using his knowledge of and affinity for statistics in evaluating the
evidence and affecting a matrix to settle thousands of claims. Although well
known for mass tort, multidistrict litigations, Judge Weinstein has addressed
innumerable matters and issues. In a unique 65-page ruling, he determined
that a gaming operator should not be prosecuted under federal law because*

poker is a game of skill, not of chance, and therefore not covered under the federal statute. (The Second Circuit reversed.)

Judge Weinstein has been an ardent and outspoken critic of federal mandatory sentencing guidelines, most notably in child-pornography viewing and drug cases. Indeed, in a 400-page decision, Judge Weinstein declared the guidelines unconstitutional and refused to sentence a defendant who pleaded guilty to distributing child pornography when he was 19 years old to the minimum prison sentence of five years (the Second Circuit reversed and disclosed the defendant's name, which Judge Weinstein had refrained from doing).

His concern about the individuals who appear before him is evident—he has met with tort litigation plaintiffs to better understand the damage they suffered and visited a school facing questions about segregation, where he met with parents, thus giving them a forum to voice their concerns. In 2003, he volunteered to hear hundreds of habeas corpus petitions, many of which had been languishing in the Eastern District for years.

His humble beginnings have informed his opinions and judicial temperament. Born in Wichita, Kansas, in 1921, he was raised in Brooklyn. He attended Brooklyn College at night, graduating magna cum laude despite working 60 hours a week during that time. After serving in the navy, where he achieved the rank of lieutenant, he received his LL.B. from Columbia Law School in 1948. Immediately thereafter, he clerked for the Honorable Stanley Fuld, Chief Judge of the New York Court of Appeals. During his brief stint in private practice, he was a member of the litigation team representing the plaintiffs in Brown v. Board of Education. *Judge Weinstein then served as County Attorney for Nassau County, New York, and joined the faculty of Columbia Law School, where he taught from 1956 through 1998. He began teaching at Brooklyn Law School in 1987, where he remains an Adjunct Professor.*

Judge Weinstein sits in Brooklyn, New York.

Agent Orange

What is the role of a judge in addressing this case: he perceives, rightly or wrongly, that the law and remedies available for the specific matter before him will not adequately address the social harm presented by the circumstances that led to the lawsuit being initiated? Should—indeed, may—the judge, all in the name of accomplishing a greater good, use the extraordinary powers of his judgeship to exact a substantial settlement for injuries that only *arguably* lie at the feet of the defendants, particularly if the judge himself questions the causality of the injuries?

When injured and diseased members of the armed forces returned from combat in the Iraq War, those *volunteer* victims of combat and the nation at large blamed the carnage on the enemy that the soldiers encountered, along with the administration itself, for having wrongly led Americans to believe that Saddam Hussein had secreted Weapons of Mass Destruction (WMDs) in Iraq and, beyond that, had masterminded Al Qaeda's horrific assaults of 9/11. The dead or injured U.S. soldiers were viewed only as victims.

Not so for the armed forces who returned maimed and diseased from the Vietnam War. Even while that troubling war was underway, an already fed-up nation blamed not only Presidents Johnson, Nixon, and their administrations but also, surprisingly, the U.S. armed forces themselves.

Even though the overwhelming majority of U.S. combatants in Vietnam and Cambodia had been drafted—thus, lacking choice but to serve—they themselves were often abandoned and treated with disrespect by Americans who stayed home, silently or even loudly protesting a war that the whole nation had seemed to turn against. For many who did live to return from Vietnam, their deep-seated emotional injuries denied them the ability to return to a meaningful civilian life. Countless others who likewise suffered the slings and arrows of their fellow Americans would only years later face horrifying diseases that seemed to have marinated within them and, at least ostensibly, to have been derived from the U.S. government's battle use of Agent Orange.

What was Agent Orange? Beginning in 1962, under President Kennedy, the U.S. Air Force began a defoliation program in Vietnam near Saigon employing herbicides designed to clear the thick jungle canopy from around roads, power lines, and other areas to lessen the potential of ambush by the Viet Cong. From 1964 to 1971, Agent Orange had become the most widely used herbicide. That finally ended in the face of the emerging controversy over health risks associated with its harmful, but prominent ingredient—dioxin.

Seven domestic U.S. companies accounted for the production of roughly 99 percent of the Agent Orange used. Putting aside the question of causation and other nuances, the presumptive diseases alleged to have stemmed from exposure to Agent Orange include neoplasms, liver cirrhosis, ischemic heart disease, chloracne, sarcoma, leukemia, influenza, diabetes, nephritis, bronchitis, emphysema, and birth defects. And it could never be certain which soldier's injury or disease was caused by which manufacturer's herbicide.

Notably, confronted with tort claims, the U.S. government would refuse outright to participate in any compensation for the losses of those who suffered, or stood to suffer in the future, claiming reliance on the Supreme Court's holding in *Feres v. U.S.* There, the Court had held that the U.S. government was not liable for injuries sustained by members of the armed forces while on active duty. Furthermore, the chemical manufacturers themselves defended on grounds, among others, that they too were absolved of tort liability given that they were military contractors whose product was approved by the U.S. government. And they relied on the agonizing questions of causality (i.e., lack of adequate proof that the horrific injuries that the servicemen had begun to suffer were actually caused by their wartime exposure to the dioxin contained in Agent Orange).

How would Judge Weinstein address such an unprecedented, massive class action lawsuit involving more than 15,000 plaintiff claims? The question was particularly difficult because causality was so irritatingly questionable. There was also the overarching social issue of societal "alienation" that presented itself in this massive series of cases that Judge Weinstein would inherit from District Judge George C. Pratt—who had been appointed to the Second Circuit midway through the litigation—and that Judge Weinstein had an altogether different view of the case than his predecessor.

Would Judge Weinstein adhere to Judge Pratt's view of the case? Or would he use his legendary legal legerdemain to extract a settlement from the corporate deep pockets, knowing that he faced a stone wall in forcing the government—clearly, the deeper pocket—to contribute? Would he seek to warn plaintiffs' counsel in extravagant terms that he might ultimately throw their case out given the obvious weaknesses in their proof of causation? Would he travel the country to earnestly be responsive to the "man on the street" victims? Or would he blithely sit back in chambers, hopeful that a settlement would come to him tied up neatly in a bow on the eve of trial? And what would he do to skirt potential naysayers on the U.S. Court of Appeals, who would surely realize, with a standard dose of skepticism, that what he was doing was all to gain a settlement to accomplish "rough justice" in the context of a terrible tragedy?

Beyond these more distinct problems, one must wonder whether factors in his makeup, too, may have been at play—such factors as Judge Weinstein's own service in the navy during World War II; his sons having been subject to the Vietnam War draft; his personal view of the Vietnam struggle and its impact on America; his sense of the role of a judge in "making law" when the law may not have already been in place; his view of whether there was a "communitarian" purpose in resolving such a case considering the four corners of the complaint, the needs of the individual plaintiffs, or even the class at large; and whether he was willing to defy established protocols to engage national public opinion to buttress his legal judgments and judicial "strategies." Yes, by the time Judge Weinstein heard these cases, the tides and currents had certainly changed.

In other words, his handling of this largest-in-history-until-that-point "mass tort" settlement, amounting to the then-astronomical sum of $180,000,000, may have constituted his own judicial experiment designed to be the paradigm, going forward, for mass resolutions of difficult, high-end tort catastrophes. If the latter was indeed his true purpose—even putting aside whether the particular settlement figure he chose had some quaint, talismanic significance—did he in fact succeed at that?

But most important, given the obvious "flexibility" Judge Weinstein imposed on himself, as it were, in achieving a settlement of *Agent Orange*'s proportions, one must consider what a legal philosopher (or politician) doctrinally opposed to "judicial activism" might think of this final paragraph contained in Judge Weinstein's "fairness" opinion:

In conclusion, it is well to remind ourselves of President Lincoln's admonition which is as relevant now, almost fifteen years after the end of the Vietnam war, as it was six score years ago. In his Second Inaugural Address he urged us "to bind up the nation's wounds, to care for him who shall have borne the battle and for his widow and his orphan—to do all which may achieve and cherish a just and lasting peace among ourselves." It is time for the *government* to join with plaintiffs and defendants in even greater efforts toward this noble goal, whether their hurt can be traced to Agent Orange or whether they are merely "casually unfortunate," C.L. Black, Jr., *The Human Imagination in the Great Society*, 5 (1983), is beside the point in the broader context of the nation's obligations to Vietnam veterans and their families. [Emphasis added.]

How did Judge Weinstein perceive himself in *Agent Orange*? Was he simply an extraordinarily diligent judge sitting on a case that was assigned to him in the ordinary course, employing his idiosyncratic judicial craftsmanship? Or was he—and was he doing something—altogether different?

The Dialogue

JC: As I understand it, the *Agent Orange* case was originally a multi-district panel case, assigned to Judge George Pratt sitting in the Eastern District of New York. When Judge Pratt was confirmed to the Second Circuit, its Chief Judge asked that he withdraw from the case because of the Circuit's heavy workload. How did it come to you?

JBW: I received a call from either the clerk or the chairman of the multi-district panel asking me to take it. I said yes—I was the Eastern District's Chief Judge at the time.

JC: Wouldn't that case ordinarily go back into the wheel for reassignment?

JBW: No, multi-district cases go by choice of the multi-district panel. When they're particularly burdensome, the panel chooses a judge either for geographic balance or because a judge has some particular expertise, or for a number of reasons they don't explicate. That's how I got it.

JC: Were you particularly interested in *Agent Orange* as a significant mass tort case?

JBW: I had a number of interests. One, I knew enough about it to know its uniqueness from a procedural viewpoint. I had had some cases involving schools which raised similar problems that I knew I would face in this case. So, as a proceduralist who had revised New York practice, had taught federal practice for many years at Columbia and written on practice, I was intrigued by the case.

Substantively, I was interested because I had been a veteran and had sailed in my ship ("boat," as we called it) in those same waters during World War II. I was also interested, having focused on the Vietnam War—I had three sons who were or would shortly be eligible to be drafted—and therefore I was interested in what was happening.

I was also interested—still am—in science and the scientific basis for the claims I knew would be relevant. I suspected that they would involve statistical analysis which interested me and which I had employed somewhat.

JC: Let's put aside for the moment your substantive interest in science and procedure. Let's focus on your military service during World War II, and that your sons were draft eligible. Could those have influenced you in a particular way in the case?

JBW: Yes.

JC: How?

JBW: To try to ensure that the veterans who might have been affected were treated as respectfully and considerately as was consonant with the law and the facts.

JC: You were appointed to the District Court in 1967. The Vietnam War, then, was becoming exponentially more unpopular. What was your view of the United States involvement in the War, then or later?

JBW: I thought it was a disaster—one of the stupidest things this country ever did. I had often been back and forth across the Pacific, and I knew what it would cost in men and material to project a war there. And I had an understanding of the jungles, the warfare and the colonial problems that would make it immensely more difficult to defeat the Viet Cong—backed by the Russians and Chinese—than it was even for England to defeat Washington.

JC: Put bluntly, could your view of the Vietnam incursion have influenced your objectivity in addressing the *Agent Orange* case?

JBW: No. My view of whether the war should have been started or accelerated had nothing to do with my view of the causal relationship of the herbicides to the illnesses that befell our soldiers.

In fact, since I myself had served in wartime, I was fully aware of the technological problems that a force as sophisticated as that employed in World War II in the Pacific, and that would be needed in Vietnam, would create. I understood the difficulties and sophisticated technological problems that were faced. So I had a very cold-blooded view of the technological and legal relationships. I had dealt with them and I had seen for myself at war how fouled up things became, and how large scale decisions were made.

JC: Were you bothered that the United States government would claim immunity to the lawsuit based on a Supreme Court decision, and wouldn't therefore pay a dime to this class?

JBW: Yes I was. The government should have pitched in the way it did in the Texas city disaster and in other cases. The way it did after 9/11. In fact, the government's response directly impacted on the individuals I appointed as special masters.

JC: Weren't you actually powerless as a judge to influence the government to waive its defense to tort liability?

JBW: Not true.

JC: Why not?

JBW: I did have influence through my opinions, through the masters I assigned, and through the way I handled the case. These were partly designed to get the Reagan Administration to pitch in. And I actually appointed a special master . . .

JC: Leonard Garment?

JBW: Yes, I thought Leonard had back door access to the White House. I've used that technique in other cases.

JC: Garment was totally unsuccessful in influencing the Reagan Administration, wasn't he?

JBW: They wouldn't give him the time of day.

JC: You've done that in other cases—successfully?

JBW: Yes.

JC: Something that judges besides Jack B. Weinstein do?

JBW: I don't know what they do. I know that when we have a political/sociological case sometimes one must go to political powers to affect the proper outcome. Because I've been in politics and was a county attorney, I have used my influence there to obtain what I see as a just result.

JC: Are you, thus, an activist judge?

JBW: Of course. So is every Supreme Court justice up there now who tries to change the course of the law.

JC: Did one of your special masters have a connection to Senator [Ted] Kennedy?

JBW: Ken Feinberg, who had been Counsel to the Senate Judiciary Committee, which Kennedy had headed.

JC: What were you hoping Feinberg would be able to accomplish with Senator Kennedy?

JBW: I had a Republican and a Democrat, and then I had an ordinary, if you could call him ordinary, foul-mouthed attorney. That attorney was going to use arm twisting. The other two would work the Republicans and Democrats hoping we would get some legislation. Ultimately, that worked.

JC: What exactly did the legislation accomplish?

JBW: Ultimately it allocated billions of dollars to those who claimed diseases that might have been caused by Agent Orange but couldn't prove it. We expended billions of dollars through that legislation by presuming causation without conducting—it's incredible to me—scientific studies to show it.

JC: You said that beside the masters that you appointed seeking to pigeonhole the Republicans and the Democrats, you used your opinions—was it to "embarrass" the government?

JBW: Not "embarrass." That's your word.

JC: What's your word?

JBW: I would say to "induce" the government to take an active role to meet the "fears"—because that's what they mainly were at the time—of these veterans, since it was the government that ordered the defoliation.

I wouldn't want you to misunderstand my position. I was a veteran. I helped kill Japanese. I would have killed more, and I would have been happy to kill Germans given the opportunity. And I had no compunction about using any tools available to do so. I thought it perfectly appropriate for those running the Vietnam War to spray these areas to protect our soldiers. Even though perhaps it would ultimately cause terrible diseases.

I had the same problem regarding the Brooklyn Navy Yard asbestos cases, when I tried 70 of them. It was clear to me that the Administration, right up to President Roosevelt, understood when building vessels at the Brooklyn Navy Yard—which I knew as a kid and when I served in the Reserves after the war—we all knew that the asbestos, with which those seventeen or eighteen-year-old kids waiting to be drafted were working, would ultimately cause deaths by terrible pain. To me, it was appropriate for Roosevelt to basically say "Let 'em die." He was sending over others just the same way. That's a necessity of war.

I knew each time my submarine went out in certain areas, that dying was a risk. So I have no compunction about such devices. When I was in World War II they exploded the atomic bomb not far from where my submarine sailed in the Japanese Sea. It didn't bother me particularly. Yes, all these people were killed—but it wasn't a question of feeling the government did something wrong. It was a command decision.

JC: But you thought the government was wrong in not stepping up to the plate to help repair the damage?

JBW: By not addressing the result of it, exactly.

JC: Did you use your legal opinions as a bully pulpit to get the government on board?

JBW: Sure.

JC: Would it have been appropriate to write an editorial in the New York Times or the Wall Street Journal, to complain that the government was not . . .

JBW: Me?

JC: Yes.

JBW: Absolutely not.

JC: But you were writing decisions hoping the press would pick them up, weren't you?

JBW: Yes—as we write many opinions for that purpose, knowing that the opinion may ultimately sway the public. I write them all the time now about mandatory minimum sentences.

JC: When the government invoked the defense accorded it by the Supreme Court—that for acts conducted during the course of war, the government isn't liable—the herbicide manufacturers wanted to raise the same defense. They wanted to say "Well, we were doing the government's bidding. The government is off the hook. Why shouldn't we be, too?" Wasn't that a fair argument?

JBW: Of course there was fairness in it, but not an argument that holds water in my opinion.

JC: Because the herbicide manufacturers simply didn't have a decision according it governmental immunity?

JBW: Correct.

JC: But you saw the manufacturers as deep pockets? You wanted a recovery for the class, and they were deep pockets?

JBW: They were the only pockets—the only ones that could be sued. The government wasn't the defendant. But I did keep the government in the case. I didn't allow it to escape, because I wanted the government there as an *amicus*, and also to be a conduit back to the government as to what was happening here. So the government was always in the case, even though it was clear to me from the outset that it wouldn't be liable unless it wanted to step up.

JC: That said, you saw a serious causality problem—that is, whether the herbicides actually caused the potential damage to the veterans?

JBW: Right from the outset I understood the statistical problem basic to the case. It was the same kind of problem we had in asbestos, tobacco, DES cases, Proxil—all of those big cases that I sat on. They tend to be statistical, and the plaintiffs never did the proper statistical studies. Some scientific folks at Columbia University cried that they never got adequate support, and they still don't. They have some statistical artifacts that have been misunderstood, but that's all they have. The case began with a social worker in Chicago who noticed people coming in, raising the problem. She then came to the conclusion, completely unscientifically, based upon the stories that she was interpreting, and then having her conclusion picked up by these veterans who accepted it as true.

JC: Despite your concern about the causality, you still pushed hard for an extremely large recovery against the manufacturers?

JBW: I was actually pushing for a trial. Yes, it's better to settle in such cases. But I was prepared to try the case assuming that the scientific proof would be developed by the two sides if it proceeded to trial, or through discovery.

JC: But given your broader view of the case, weren't you concerned that the plaintiffs might come up short and not prove causality?

JBW: Right. That's true of most cases that we have. We don't know how they'll come out.

JC: But, here, didn't you want the veterans to succeed?

JBW: No. I thought that they ought to be treated fairly and respectfully. But I was fully prepared to move the case to trial expecting that if it were well tried they would get no recovery. In any kind of settlement the judge and the parties say that there's not very much to the case but considering that, if we lose, the result would be so horrendous it's worth discounting the possible loss and reaching a settlement—as was done here.

JC: In your oral history at Columbia University you actually use the phrase "shakedown"—you wanted to "shake down" the manufacturers to some extent.

JBW: If I said that, I'm surprised. I was never in a shakedown mode.

JC: I don't mean that you used "shakedown" in an *ad hominem* way. You said you wanted to shake them down "a little bit" to get a meaningful recovery.

JBW: I thought that they had a responsibility, yes. It was clear from the outset that they were introducing a poisonous substance. It's effect wasn't clear—and that a proper manufacturing technique would have reduced it to a minimum. There were very wide variations in the percentage of dioxin in the herbicides produced by the various manufacturers—enormous differences. I wanted participation by those responsible for introducing this dioxin. Some of the dioxin could have been excluded completely. But some of it was being introduced into the atmosphere carelessly. It shouldn't have been. If there had been a verdict, some of the defendants would or could have faced enormous amounts of damages.

JC: Typically, a judge is concerned about the particular plaintiffs or plaintiff class in a lawsuit. Here, it seems, reading your opinions, articles, oral history, you wanted to address something far broader—the Vietnam veteran in general. Most Vietnam soldiers were drafted, with no choice but to serve. They came home to an America basically disdainful of them.

JBW: No. I wanted to see that they were treated with respect by the courts, the legislature and the executive. It's one of the reasons that I conducted hearings around the country, to listen to them and give them a forum. I understood, of course, that for many of them, without a trial, they would never understand the causation problems that undergirded the case. But given how they had been treated—some, so shamefully—I thought they were entitled to the respect of the court system in listening to and treating them in a responsible way.

JC: Was part of your goal in conducting that nationwide "road show" and holding public hearings, to give the veterans some kind of closure?

JBW: Oh yes, to make them feel that they were being well treated. I used much of the funds to set up social work organizations in each of the 50 states to help the families who also had been treated disrespectfully.

JC: Have you done that kind of thing in other class actions—giving a plaintiff class the opportunity to be heard, to have their day in court?

JBW: At a seminar conference at Columbia I introduced the possibility of using modern technology to bring all the members of a class into the proceeding in some meaningful way. And in the DES cases I actually sat down with the DES daughters and their lead attorney, and just listened to them for hours and hours about their problems and how they felt. That's something that the court system can do—it can give people the sense that government cares and will listen to their problems. And when I was Chief Judge here, I set up the Eastern District Litigation Fund, making money available for social workers and others to help people through the process.

JC: When you first came into the case, Judge Pratt had had a different view of it. He was about to grant partial summary judgment but hadn't yet signed his opinion. You inherit the case and say, "Guys, you're out of luck. Pratt didn't actually sign his opinion." When you inherit a case where the prior judge has done everything except the ministerial act of signing his order, don't you see some obligation to go along with what he did before you?

JBW: No. The case is mine. I'll decide it my way. I don't know what Judge Pratt would have decided. He didn't decide it. I decide my cases my way.

JC: We're almost 30 years since the resolution of the *Agent Orange* case brought by Americans, as opposed to Vietnamese (that was somewhat later). You've written much, lectured a lot. What would you do differently today?

JBW: Now? I don't know. Probably nothing different.

JC: At the end of your fairness opinion, you said this, Judge: *"In conclusion, it is well to remind ourselves of President Lincoln's admonition which is as relevant now almost 15 years after the end of the Vietnam war as it was six score years ago. In his Second Inaugural Address he urged us to 'bind up the nation's wounds, to care for him who shall have borne the battle and for his widow and his orphan—to do all that which may achieve and cherish a just and lasting peace among ourselves.' It is time for the government to join with plaintiffs and defendants in even greater efforts toward this noble goal, whether their hurt can be traced to Agent Orange or whether they are merely 'casually unfortunate' is beside the point in the broader context of the nation's obligations to Vietnam veterans and their families."*

Beautiful phraseology, Judge—but odd for a legal opinion. What were you trying to accomplish by saying that in a fairness opinion?

JBW: I wanted to justify what I was doing for the families who had been ignored. The children and the wives. You've got these soldiers who have returned broken, feeling betrayed.

There's one factor that may have had an impact that I didn't mention earlier. After World War II my wife was a social worker with an advanced degree from Columbia School of Social Work. She set up the first of the clinics at Jamaica Hospital for soldiers with various psychiatric syndromes. About a dozen psychiatrists worked with her and those people every night. I was aware that there were lots of wounds, psychic and physical. And a lot of these folks needed to know that the system was concerned about them, and would do what it could within law and reason to assist.

JC: From some of the things you say, and maybe some of your detractors might say, it sounds that perhaps you would have preferred to be a legislator—able to accomplish things that maybe you couldn't as a judge.

JBW: No, I wouldn't have wanted that. I served as counsel to state legislators, I advised national legislators and I was county attorney. I prefer the power of the judge. It's sometimes narrow in scope, but where it's operative it's substantial.

JC: But you were able to gain for the plaintiffs $180 million in this case.

JBW: I made them pay up immediately, and that came as a surprise to them.

JC: You're smiling, Judge. You seem very proud that you managed to push them to . . .

JBW: I was, because they thought that $180 million was a figure that could be overcome by paying it out over years—so that the current cost would be practically nil. But I wanted that money paid immediately, and that came to them as somewhat of a shock. Of all the things I did, that might have been the one criticized the most.

JC: From time to time Judge, you're been reversed by the Second Circuit. I'm quite sure that it doesn't bother you in the least. Did you get the impression that the Circuit has not been pleased, sometimes, with some of the ways in which you have handled mass tort cases?

JBW: Yes, they weren't happy about that case. The word came back: "Tell Jack he's not going to be able to do this again."

JC: Not able to do what?

JBW: The way he handled this mass tort case. That was one of the first of them. And they were not happy with my view that the underpinning of a lot of mass torts and other such cases depend upon demographic and other material and scientific proof. The Second Circuit has never been comfortable with statistical material, and I've had a number of run-ins with them on that basis. Where I've based my decision on what I consider to be rational statistical bases, most statisticians that have considered the matter have sided with me. The most recent one, of course, was with Judge [Nicholas] Garaufis this last week. They [on the Second Circuit] were really uncomfortable with his decision in . . .

JC: The Fire Department case.

JBW: Yes, with what he did statistically. You can read it in Judge [Jon] Newman's opinion. Newman is a great judge. And some of our great judges like Ruth Ginsburg, whom I admire and who was actually a student of mine, I don't think fully appreciate the statistical base that you have to use in order to get a just result for many people.

That's my view, but obviously not everyone's.

Epilogue

Where does this examination of judges bring us? We are taught early in life to believe that judges will be impartial and unbiased in how they address cases, fair to all who come before them and impervious to their personal philosophies. We want to believe they are not influenced or swayed by their "human limitations." As Justice Cardozo taught us many years ago, however, that belief can't possibly be so. Judges, at the end of the day, are human beings who cannot escape the "great tides and currents that engulf the rest of men." Some readily admit—to themselves and those who appear before them—the realities of who they are and what they believe. Some profess their "objectivity" when discussing their professional responsibilities, whereas others feel free to express their "subjectivity." Some avoid the issue, yet interpret the law so as to ever so slightly turn it on its side. Is one view better; should society prefer one style, one approach over the another? It is hard to say.

At bottom, judges are indeed human. When the pomp and circumstance of the judge's robes are removed at day's end, he can seek with all his might to confine his vision of a case through the prism of the antiseptic laboratory of the courtroom. But when, at nightfall, the judge walks out into the fresh breeze of reality, he is forced to confront the downtrodden, the conflicting political currents that surround him, the varied threats to society, the harsh realities of religious prejudice, and the inequities of any society.

Richard A. Posner—judge, jurist, professor, theorist, and prolific writer—illustrated the issue thusly:

> A judge must try to be aware of his priors, so that they do not exert an excessive influence on his decisions. The judge might have a soft spot for animals, and for environmental values generally; for the police; for paramedics; for asylum seekers; for people with serious mental

illnesses; and for marginal religious sects. He may have a range of antipathies as well, such as to the Internal Revenue Service or insurance companies (these were common judicial antipathies when I first became a judge, though I didn't share them and neither do my current colleagues), litigious people, hypersensitive people, and people consumed by *pleonexia*—Aristotle's word for wanting more than one's due. Through self-awareness and discipline a judge can learn not to allow his sympathies or antipathies to influence his judicial votes—unduly. But the qualification in "unduly" needs to be emphasized. Many judges would say that nothing outside "the law," in the narrow sense that confines the word to the texts of formal legal documents, influences *their* judicial votes at all. Some of them are speaking for public consumption, and know better. Those who are speaking sincerely are fooling themselves.[1]

In some instances, occupying the role of devil's advocate, the author confronted the judges who generously agreed to be interviewed for this project. It is a testament to each that they graciously accepted the questioner's sometimes probing, often personal, inquiries, notwithstanding the disequilibrium in our respective status in legal society. And I both commend and thank them for that.

Still, were their answers always completely ingenuous when their objectivity was on the line? Did the judges recognize subtle (or not so subtle) influences? And did they address them in these interviews, or were they guarded when speaking to me—an outsider writing a book to be read by other outsiders? Importantly, were they mindful of Cardozo's teachings and accept that they could never be completely and perfectly objective, unaffected by the world in which they live? Did they struggle with self-awareness, acknowledging—even if only to themselves—their sympathies and perspectives, yet conclude that despite such knowledge, or perhaps because of it, they were able to apply the law as statute and precedent required?

Judge Posner, in his Foreword, suggests that these judges are largely guarded or likely un-self-aware. Perhaps he is correct; perhaps not. The answer lies alone with the reader.

---

1. Richard A. Posner, Reflections on Judging, Harvard Univ. Press, 2013, p. 130.

Excerpt from *The Nature of the Judicial Process*

I have spoken of the forces of which judges avowedly avail to shape the form and content of their judgments. Even these forces are seldom fully in consciousness. They lie so near the surface, however, that their existence and influence are not likely to be disclaimed. But the subject is not exhausted with the recognition of their power. Deep below consciousness are other forces, the likes and the dislikes, the predilections and the prejudices, the complex of instincts and emotions and habits and convictions, which make the man, whether he be litigant or judge. I wish I might have found the time and opportunity to pursue this subject farther. I shall be able, as it is, to do little more than remind you of its existence.[1] There has been a certain lack of candor in much of the discussion of the theme, or rather perhaps in the refusal to discuss it, as if judges must lose respect and confidence by the reminder that they are subject to human limitations. I do not doubt the grandeur of the conception which lifts them into the realm of pure reason, above and beyond the sweep of perturbing and deflecting forces. None the less, if there is anything of reality in my analysis of the judicial process, they do not stand aloof on these chill and distant heights; and we shall not help the cause of truth by acting and speaking as if they do. The great tides and currents which engulf the rest of men, do not turn aside in their course, and pass the judges by. We like to figure to ourselves the processes of justice as coldly objective and impersonal. The law, conceived of as a real existence, dwelling apart and alone,

---

1. An interesting study of this subject will be found in a book published since these lectures were written, *The Foundations of Social Science* by James Mickel Williams, p. 209 *et seq.*

speaks, through the voices of priests and ministers, the words which they have no choice except to utter. That is an ideal of objective truth toward which every system of jurisprudence tends.

—Benjamin N. Cardozo, *The Nature of the Judicial Process*, Quid Pro Law Books, at pp. 107–108.

Case Citations

Judge Leonie Brinkema

U.S. v. Moussaoui, *see generally* 561 F.3d 263 (4th Cir. 2010).

Judge Denny Chin

U.S. v. Madoff, 09 CR 213 (DC), Transcript June 29, 2009.

Judge Martin Feldman

Hornbeck Offshore Services, LLC v. Kenneth Lee "Ken" Salazar, No. 10–1663, Order and Reasons [granting preliminary injunction to plaintiffs] dated June 22, 2010, and Order [denying motion to recuse] dated July 16, 2010 (E.D. La.).

Judge Nancy Gertner

Limone v. U.S., 497 F. Supp. 2d 143, *aff'd on other grounds*, 579 F.3d 79 (1st Cir. 2009).

Judge Alvin K. Hellerstein

In re WTC Disaster Site Litigation, 21 MC 100 (AKH), Transcripts March 12, 2010 and June 10, 2010, rev'd in part, aff'd in part, vac and rem inpart,

Cirino v. City of New York (in re World Trade Center Disaster Site Litig.) No. 11-4021, __ F.3d __ (2nd Cir. June 9, 2014).

Judge David Hittner

Resident Council of Allen Parkway Village v. U.S. Department of Housing and Urban Development, 980 F.2d 1043 (5th Cir. 1993)
    Allen Parkway Village Residents Council v. Housing Authority of the City of Houston, H-87–564, Judgment ent. August 16, 1993 (S.D. Tx.); [Vacate] Order ent. June 11, 1996.

Judge John E. Jones III

Kitzmiller v. Dover Area School District, 400 F. Supp. 2d 707 (M.D. Pa. 2005).

Judge Charles P. Kocoras

In re Brand Name Prescription Drugs Antitrust Litigation, 1999 WL 33889 (N.D. Ill. 1999) *aff'd on other grounds in a decision which aff'd in part, vacated in part and remanded* 186 F.3d 781 (7th Cir. 1999).

Chief Judge Alex Kozinski

U.S. v. Pinedo-Moreno, 591 F.3d 1212 (2010); 617 F.3d 1120 (9th Cir. 2010; Kozinski, C.J., dissenting).

Judge Jed S. Rakoff

U.S. v. Quinones, 196 F. Supp. 2d 416 (S.D.N.Y. 2002) and 205 F. Supp. 256 (S.D.N.Y. 2002) *rev'd* 313 F.3d 49 (2d Cir. 2002), *reh. denied*, 317 F.3d 86 (2d Cir., 2003).

Judge Emmet G. Sullivan

U.S. v. Stevens, 08–231, Transcript April 7, 2009.

Judge Vaughn R. Walker

Perry v. Schwarzenegger, 704 F. Supp. 2d 921 (N.D. Ca. 2010), *aff'd sub nom Perry v. Brown*, 671 F.3d 1052 (9th Cir. 2012) *aff'd sub nom*, Hollingsworth v. Perry, 570 U.S. ___, 133 S. Ct. 2652 (2013).

Judge Jack B. Weinstein

In re Agent Orange Product Liability Litigation, 597 F. Supp. 740 (E.D.N.Y. 1984).

Index